A GROUNDED THEORY OF LEADERSHIP AND FOLLOWERSHIP IN

MULTICULTURAL TEAMS IN SIL

———————————

A Dissertation

Presented to

the Faculty of the Cook School of Intercultural Studies

Biola University

———————————

In Partial Fulfillment

of the Requirements for the Degree

Doctor of Philosophy

———————————

By

EunSun Sunny Hong

May 2014

© 2016 EMS Press
All rights reserved. No part of this work may be reproduced or transmitted in any form or by any means, electronics or mechanical, including photocopying and recording, without the prior permission of the publisher. The only exceptions are brief quotations in printed reviews.

Published by EMS Press
5511 SE Hawthorne Blvd., Portland, OR 97215
www.emsweb.org

A Grounded Theory of Leadership and Followership in Multicultural Teams in SIL
By EunSun Sunny Hong

ISBN: 978-1-945607-01-1

ABSTRACT

A GROUNDED THEORY OF LEADERSHIP AND FOLLOWERSHIP IN
MULTICULTURAL TEAMS IN SIL

EunSun Sunny Hong

There is a growing need to understand what effective multicultural leadership and followership look like in a faith-based, nonprofit, international organization where communication is mostly conducted through electronic means. Very little research has been done on this subject. The purpose of this grounded theory study is to understand and describe what leaders and followers want leadership and followership to look like in this kind of setting.

Data for this study were gathered largely through interviews with ten leaders and sixty-five followers working in SIL International and its partner organizations. Study participants originated from twenty-one countries, and, at the time of the study, were based in ten countries. The core elements of desired qualities of leadership and followership emerged through the analysis of these semi-structured interviews.

This study proposes a substantive theory about the perception of leadership and followership: Both followers and leaders in SIL, where computer-aided communication is the most frequently used communication platform, perceive that effective leadership and effective followership derive from specific and identifiable relational qualities, task-oriented competencies, character-related qualities, spiritual qualities, cultural intelligence, and the way communication by computer is used and understood. Strengths and drawbacks of communication methods impact the relationship between leaders and followers.

TABLE OF CONTENTS

	PAGE
LIST OF TABLES	xxii
LIST OF FIGURES	xxiv
1. INTRODUCTION	1
SIL International	6
Problem Statement	8
Purpose Statement	9
Research Questions	9
Definitions	10
Ethical Considerations	11
Delimitations	12
Limitations	12
Significance of Study	13
2. LITERATURE REVIEW	15
Leadership Research	15
Research on Multicultural Leadership	16
Unique Characteristics and Abilities of a Multicultural Leader	20
Global mindset	21
Cultural interpretation	22

	PAGE
Multicultural communication skills	22
Flexibility	22
Ability to handle paradox and ethnorelativity	23
Cultural Intelligence (CQ)	25
Characteristics of CQ	26
A multicultural leader's CQ level	30
Culture Specific versus Universal Leadership Qualities	33
Summary of the Multicultural Leadership	34
Followership	35
History of Followership Theories Reflected in Leadership Theories	35
Followership Theory of Kelley	36
Followership Theory of Chaleff	37
Followership Theory of Kellerman	39
Summary of Followership	41
Summary of Different Cultural Expectations of Leadership and Followership	41
Multicultural Team	41
Characteristics of Multicultural Team	42
Dynamics of the multicultural team	42
Subgroups	44
In-group versus out-group	45
Faultlines	46
Fusion and hybrid culture	47

	PAGE

    Virtual Team 50

        Advantages of a virtual team 50

        Disadvantages of a virtual team 51

        Dynamics of a virtual team 53

        Virtual methods of communication 55

    Summary of the Multicultural Team 56

    Deficiencies in the Current Literature 57

3.   RESEARCH DESIGN AND PROCEDURES 58

    Methodological Approach 58

        The Rationale for Choosing Qualitative Research 58

        The Rationale for Choosing Constructivism, Advocacy, and Pragmatism .. 60

        The Position of my Research on the Five Different Philosophical Assumptions 61

        The Rationale for Choosing Grounded Theory 62

    Data Collection 63

        Selection of the Participants 64

        Method of Data Collection 65

            Interview 66

            Participant observation 70

            Archival and technical documents 70

    Data Analysis 71

        Coding 71

	PAGE

        Open coding 72

        Axial coding 72

        Selective coding 73

    Memo Writing 73

  Validation 74

    Methods of Validation 74

    Methods used for this Study 75

  Chapter 3 Summary 76

4.   RELATIONAL QUALITIES IN LEADERSHIP AND FOLLOWERSHIP 77

  Relational Leadership Qualities Desired by Leaders 78

    Communicate 79

    Care about for the Followers 80

    Promote Teamwork 81

  Desired Relational Leadership Qualities Expressed by Followers 82

    Communicate with the Followers 82

        Listen to the followers 82

            Listen 82

            Do not listen 84

        Communicate 85

            Regular communication 85

            Communicate prior to making a decision 86

            Miscommunication 87

	PAGE

        Organizational changes and communication 88

        Cultural issues in communication 88

            Communicate disagreement 90

    Care about Followers 92

    Be Relational 93

    Appreciate Followers 95

        Trust followers 95

        Value the followers 95

        Respect the followers 95

    Understand Followers 96

    Promote Teamwork 96

Desired Relational Followership Qualities by Leaders 96

    Communicate 97

    Respect 98

    Encourage 98

Desired Relational Followership Qualities Articulated by Followers 99

    Communicate 99

        Communicate with the leader 99

            Communicate disagreement 100

            Provide input 100

            Report regularly 101

            Report properly 101

PAGE

  Cultural aspects of communication 102

   Communicate with team members 103

 Care and Encourage 104

  Care 104

  Encourage 105

 Trust 106

 Unity 107

 Serve and Respect 108

 Understand People 108

Chapter 4 Summary 109

5. TASK-ORIENTED COMPETENCIES IN LEADERSHIP AND FOLLOWERSHIP 111

 Task-oriented Leadership Competencies Desired by Leaders 111

  Develop Followers 112

   Support followers 112

   Build up followers 113

   Know and use followers' gifts 115

  Have Vision 116

  Handle Conflict 117

  Be a Decision Maker 118

  Motivate the Followers 118

  Have Holistic Understanding about the Work 119

PAGE

Task-oriented Leadership Competencies Desired by Followers 119

    Have Vision and Provide Direction 119

    Develop Followers 121

    Do Not Micromanage 123

    Have Good Attitudes toward Work 124

    Delegate 124

    Have Administrative Skills 126

    Solve Problems 126

    Direct 127

    Make Decisions 127

Task-oriented Followership Competencies Desired by Leaders 128

    Take Initiative 128

    Be Responsible 129

    Follow a Leader 130

    Have a Leadership Mindset 131

Task-oriented Followership Competencies Desired by Followers 132

    Work Hard 132

    Follow a Leader 133

    Goal Oriented 135

    Work Together 135

    Understand Work 136

    Make Decisions 136

		PAGE

Chapter 5 Summary 137

6. CHARACTER-RELATED QUALITIES IN LEADERSHIP AND
   FOLLOWERSHIP 138

    Character-Related Leadership Qualities Desired by Leaders 138

        Humility 139

        Willing to Learn 139

        Transparency 140

        Have Integrity 140

    Character-Related Leadership Qualities Desired by Followers 141

        Personal Characteristics 141

            Wisdom 141

            Humility 141

            Honesty 142

            Patience 142

            Integrity 143

            Positive attitude 143

        Interpersonal Skills 143

            Fair 143

            Trustworthy 144

            Accountable 144

            Selfless 144

            Respectful 145

	PAGE
Work-Related Competencies	145
Leads by example	145
Flexible	145
Accepts criticism	145
Exercises authority properly	146
Leader's Background and Abilities	146
Experience	146
Linguistic ability	147
Character-Related Followership Qualities Desired by Leaders	148
Humility	148
Flexibility	148
Character-Related Followership Qualities Desired by Followers	149
Independence	149
Obedience	151
Integrity	152
Loyal and Being Faithful	152
Humility	153
Chapter 6 Summary	153
7. SPIRITUAL QUALITIES IN LEADERSHIP AND FOLLOWERSHIP	154
Leaders' Description of Spiritual Qualities in Leadership	156
Relationship with God	156
Understand God's Calling for the Organization	156

	PAGE

    Recognize God's Authority 156

Followers' Description of Spiritual Qualities in Leadership 157

    Relationship with God 157

        Attitude toward God 157

        Led by and listen to God 157

        Understand the Word 158

    Bear Spiritual Fruit 159

        In personal life 159

        In relationships with the followers 159

    Person of Prayer 160

Leaders' Description of Spiritual Qualities in Followership 160

    Bear Spiritual Fruit 161

        In relationships 161

        In personal life 162

    Relationship with God 162

Follower's Description of Spiritual Qualities in Followership 163

    Person of Prayer 163

        Pray for the leaders and the organization 163

        Practice corporate prayer time 164

    Relationship with God 164

        Recognize God's authority 164

        Honor God in relationships 165

	PAGE

    Bear Spiritual Fruit 165

        In relationships 165

        In work 165

    Chapter 7 Summary 166

8.   CULTURAL INTELLEGENCE IN LEADERSHIP AND FOLLOWERSHIP 168

    Leaders on CQ in Leadership 169

        Cognition 169

            Understand culture 169

            Understand cultural similarities 172

            Open-mindedness in understanding culture 172

        Behavior 173

            Communicate through a third party 173

            Communicate directly or indirectly 175

        Cultural Savvy 175

            Understand and respond to team dynamics 175

            Be a cultural mediator 176

            Promote cultural strengths 177

    Followers on CQ in Leadership 177

        Cognition 177

            Understand culture 177

            Be culturally sensitive 178

            Consider other cultures 179

	PAGE

  Behavior 179

  Cultural Savvy 180

    Leader's background and abilities 180

      Cultural similarity 181

      Exposure to different cultures 183

    Cultural learner 184

    Cultural adaptation 185

    Attitude toward culture 185

Leaders on CQ in Followership 185

  Cognition 186

    Understand culture 186

    Have cultural sensitivity. 187

  Behavior 188

  Cultural Savvy 189

    Danger of misusing culture 189

    Overcome cultural weaknesses 189

    Seek cultural maturity 190

    Cultural advantage and disadvantage 190

Followers on CQ in Followership 191

  Cognition 191

    Understand leader's culture 191

    Understanding colleague's culture 193

	PAGE
Understanding organizational culture	193
Behavior	193
Cultural Savvy	194
Have cultural ability	194
Attitude toward culture	195
Promote cultural strengths	195
Be a cultural mediator	195
Chapter 8 Summary	196

9. COMMUNICATION METHODS' EFFECT ON LEADERSHIP AND FOLLOWERSHIP 197

    Leader's Description of Communication Methods 201

        Email 202

            Strengths of email communication 204

                Documentation 204

                Monitoring time and organizing thoughts 205

                Straight talk 205

            Weaknesses of email communication 205

                More miscommunication and conflict 206

                Time related issue 207

                Depended on the recipient 208

                Language issue 208

                Not expressive 208

	PAGE
Technical challenge	209
Face-to-Face Communication	209
Use of face-to-face communication	209
Sensitive issues or conflict	210
Lengthy discussion	210
Strengths of face-to-face communication	211
Clear communication	211
Adds relational component	212
Shortens communication time	213
Weaknesses of face-to-face communication	213
Phone Call	213
Usage	214
Strengths and weaknesses of phone calls	214
SMS Communication	215
Strengths of SMS communication	215
Weaknesses of SMS communication	215
Skype	215
Facebook Communication	216
Finding Out the Best Way to Communicate	216
Followers' Description of Communication Methods	217
Email	217
Use of email communication	219

	PAGE
Send reports and information	219
Regular work communication	219
Simple things	220
Important issues	220
Strengths of email communication	220
Documentation	220
Freedom of expression	221
Organize thoughts	222
Convenience	222
Weaknesses of email communication	223
Relational issues	223
Time related issues	224
Unsuitability	225
Miscommunication	226
Language issues	228
Cultural issues	229
Face-to-Face	230
Use of face-to-face communication	230
Sensitive issues or conflict	230
Lengthy discussion	231
Important issues	231
Cultural reasons	232

	PAGE
Strengths of face-to-face communication	232
Clear communication	233
Body language and facial expression	233
More understanding	234
Relational	234
Language issues	235
Flexibility	235
Cultural	236
Weaknesses of face-to-face communication	236
No documentation	236
Language issues	237
Phone Call	237
Phone call use	237
Important issues	237
Time-related issues	237
Secondary option	238
Strengths of phone calls	238
Weaknesses of phone calls	238
SMS	238
Use of SMS communication	238
Strengths of SMS	239
Weaknesses of SMS	239

	PAGE

Skype 239

    Strengths of Skype 240

    Weaknesses of Skype..240

Facebook 241

    Use of Facebook communication 241

    Strengths of Facebook 242

        Informal social activity 242

        Promote team morale 242

        Encourage 243

    Weaknesses of Facebook 243

Pronto..243

    Strengths of Pronto 244

    Weaknesses of Pronto..244

Multiple Methods..245

Chapter 9 Summary 246

10. SUMMARY AND CONCLUSIONS 248

    A Theory of Leadership and Followership in a Multicultural Organization 248

    Relational Qualities..249

    Task-oriented Competencies..249

    Character-Related Qualities...249

    Spiritual Qualities 249

    Cultural Intelligence (CQ) 250

	PAGE

    Communication Methods 250

Answer to the Research Subquestions 251

    Question 1 - How Do Leaders Working in SIL and Its Partner Organizations Describe Qualities of Effective Leadership? 251

    Question 2 - How Do Followers Working in SIL and Its Partner Organizations Describe Qualities of Effective Leaders? 251

    Question 3 - How Do Leaders Working in SIL and Its Partner Organizations Describe Qualities of Effective Followers? 252

    Question 4 - How Do Followers Working in SIL and Its Partner Organizations Describe Qualities of Effective Followers? 252

    Question 5 - How Do Leaders and Followers in SIL and Its Partner Organizations Describe the Role of Communication Methods Affecting their Working Relationships? 253

Application of Findings 253

    Influence of Organizational Culture on Leadership and Followership 253

    Cultural Issues 254

        Cultural influence on leadership and followership 255

        Communication 255

        Same word with different definition 256

        Similar culture 256

        Majority vs. minority culture 256

        Using cultural strengths 257

    Paradox 257

        Independency and taking initiative versus trusting and following 257

        Work versus relationship 258

PAGE

  Communication 259

    Issues with email 259

  Remote Assignments 260

 Findings Compared to Other Theories 261

  Leadership Theory of Rosen, Digh, Singer, and Phillips 261

  Leadership Theory of Goldsmith, Greenberg, Robertson, and Hu-Chan ... 262

  Leadership Theory of GLOBE 264

  Followership Theory of Kelley 265

  Followership Theory of Chaleff 265

 Recommendations for Further Research 268

 Dissertation Conclusion 269

REFERENCES 270

APPENDIXES 279

 APPENDIX A LIST OF INTERVIEW PARTICIPANTS 280

 APPENDIX B SEMI-STRUCTURED INTERVIEW QUESTIONS 285

 APPENDIX C PEER REVIEW 287

 APPENDIX D THE TABLES OF THE LEADERSHIP AND FOLLOWERSHIP QUALITIES 296

LIST OF TABLES

		PAGE
1.	Comparison of Number of Missionaries by Sending Region in 1910 and 2010	5
2.	Summary of Relational Qualities in Leadership and Followership	79
3.	Summary of the Task-Oriented Competencies of Leadership and Followership	112
4.	Overall Character-Related Qualities of Leadership and Followership	139
5.	Summary of Spiritual Qualities in Leadership and Followership	155
6.	Summary Chart of the Cultural Intelligence Qualities of Leadership and Followership	170
7.	Summary Chart of Leaders on Cultural Intelligences in Leadership	171
8.	Summary Chart of Followers on Cultural Intelligence (CQ) in Leadership	178
9.	Summary Chart of Leaders on Cultural Intelligence in Followership	186
10.	Summary of Followers on Cultural Intelligence in Followership	191
11.	Summary of Communication Tools Used by the Leaders and the Followers	198
12.	Overall Chart of the Communication Tools Used by the Leaders	203
13.	Overall Chart of the Communication Tools Used by the Followers	218
14.	Comparison Between Literacies of Rosen, et al., and the Categories That Emerged with This Research	263
A1.	Demographic Information for Interview Participants	280
C1.	Demographic Information of the Reviewers.	288
D1.	Summary of Relational Leadership Qualities Desired by Leaders	296
D2.	Summary of Relational Leadership Qualities Desired by Followers	297

		PAGE
D3.	Summary of Relational Followership Qualities Desired by Leaders	298
D4.	Summary of Relational Followership Qualities Desired by Followers	299
D5.	Summary of Task-Oriented Leadership Competencies Desired by Leaders	300
D6.	Summary of Task-Oriented Leadership Competencies Desired by Followers	301
D7.	Summary of Task-Oriented Followership Competencies Desired by Leaders	302
D8.	Summary of Task-Oriented Followership Competencies Desired by Follower	303
D9.	Summary of Character-Related Leadership Qualities Desired by Followers	303
D10.	Summary of Character-Related Followership Qualities Desired by Followers	305

LIST OF FIGURES

		PAGE
1.	Nationalities of the interview participants	68
2.	Age groups of the interview participants	69
3.	Service years of the interview participants	69

ACKNOWLEDGEMENT

Looking back at why I decided to pursue my PhD, I must credit two people other than my Lord, Jesus Christ. One is Dr. Sheryl Silzer of Wycliffe, who encouraged me to write an MA thesis around the time I finished my MA in Intercultural Studies at Biola, and also provided me with many opportunities to teach classes and lead workshops together. The second is Dr. Steve Quakenbush of SIL, who encouraged me to enroll in a PhD program. I am also thankful to the Ken Pike Endowment Fund Committee and to SIL Asia Area, who supported my studies financially through scholarships.

I would like to thank my dissertation committee members, who worked hard to help me finish my academic journey. I especially thank Dr. Kimberly Snider, who journeyed alongside me with her thoughtful comments, encouragement, and prayers. I would like to extend my gratitude to all the Biola faculty members from whom I learned.

I cannot thank the interview participants who were willing to share their stories enough. All of the participants were very much cooperative and their enthusiasm gave me strength. Finally, I am indebted to my friends Edna Lush, Hanjay Kim, and Sharon Kim, who edited my dissertation tirelessly, and to my supporters and prayer partners, who sustained me throughout this journey.

I dedicate this dissertation to those leaders and followers working in multicultural teams to expand God's Kingdom. My prayer is that this study would be a helpful tool for their journey.

CHAPTER 1

INTRODUCTION

It was in the middle of a field entity conference. The day's agenda items were to elect a new entity director, to pass various motions to restructure the entity, and to decide on the entity conference location next year. There were three candidates, John, Peter, and James, on the ballot for the next director. John was the first to speak. He shared how he was going to serve the entity if he would become a director. He was very enthusiastic and positive, and clearly showed that he was willing to be a director to make the entity better. Peter came up and said that he did not know why he was nominated. He only wanted to be a member just the same as the rest of the people in the room. If he had a choice, he would not be a leader, but if nobody else wanted to do the job, he would be willing. James came up and hinted about his background of management skills, his networking with other entities, and his experiences in the previous years. However, he never clearly said that he wanted to be elected as a director.

After the session was over, members talked about the candidates during lunchtime. One person said that John was a visionary leader because he could clearly state the direction he wanted to take the entity. Another person was troubled because he believed John was being too arrogant by sharing in such a direct way how he felt he could lead the entity. Another person criticized the way Peter put himself down in public and said he did not understand why Peter was even running for a director when he felt that way about himself. Another person said that Peter showed he was a humble person by wanting to be equal to the rest of the members and that this kind of person would be best for the entity, because he would listen to everybody's opinion. Someone else said that he did not understand why James shared his background but failed to tell how he was going to lead the entity. Another person said that James properly shared his ability to lead the entity by only hinting at his background because it showed his humble heart.

Listening to all of these discussions, Mark, a new member, was very disappointed. He thought that senior members should know who might be the best person to be the next director. From the lunch conversation, he had hoped to gain some understanding about the entity leadership from the senior members so that he could know their opinions about the election. Listening to the opposing opinions left Mark confused. How could he figure out whom to vote for if the senior members did not give him better clues? He worried about how this entity would function if people's opinions were so very different from one another. Mark had looked forward to coming to the conference ever since he had been assigned to a remote place where the Internet connection was inconsistent. He felt very isolated from his organization due to the lack of face-to-face meetings with other members after the new-member orientation. His village living was manageable, and he had begun to enjoy meeting people there, but he felt very isolated and lonely because there were no other believers in the village. From time to time Mark had been disappointed when he received email from his supervisor because the contents were only about work. There was nothing personal to indicate his supervisor cared about him as a person. It was only when he had had a face-to-face meeting with his supervisor last month that he realized that his supervisor purposely wrote short emails because the email connection between them was so inconsistent that his supervisor felt he could only communicate essentials about work. In the face-to-face meeting he realized that his supervisor really did care about him. For this reason, he had looked forward to being with other members of his organization who would be of one heart, learning from senior members at the entity conference, processing issues in godly ways during the conference, and learning more about the organization. Seeing divided hearts, differing opinions in senior members, and no effort to come up with a consensus, he was very perplexed and wondered if he could ever trust the leadership in his organization regardless of who became the next director.

After lunch, the first item on the agenda was to make a decision on the location of the next years' conference. Three places were presented. It took thirty minutes to explain the pros and cons and the cost. Then it took more time to vote to select the place. To Mark, selecting a conference place was a very minor issue, and he felt leadership should have made the decision about a place. He was devastated to see the leadership of the entity could not even make such a minor decision on its own, and they wasted time at the entity conference by letting members do it. He started to doubt the validity of having an entity conference. To him it looked like the leaders did not know what to do, or how to lead an entity properly and so they delegated their work to the members. He lost interest in all the other programs at the conference and started to wonder if he should stay with this organization.

Obviously everyone in the story above acted out of their cultural values and expectations. This fictional account mirrors what happens in real situations in the SIL organization. Depending on their cultural background, people's expectations for leadership and followership will differ:

> Both leaders and followers have implicit and explicit images of what a leader ought to be and do. Leadership expectations occur for both leader and led. Leadership expectations are shaped by cultural backgrounds. In cross-cultural situations where leader expectations do not align with follower expectations, leadership dissonance may occur. (Crow, 2000, p. 185)

According to Jenkins (2007), by 2005 there were more Christians in the Global South than in the Global North, and the number is expected to increase rapidly. This is also true about the significant number of Christian cross-cultural workers from the Global South. According to the statistics provided by the Center for the Study of Global Christianity, in 1910 less than two percent of Christian cross-cultural workers were from the Global South, but in 2010 over thirty-one percent of Christian cross-cultural workers were from the Global South (Johnson & Ross, 2009) as shown in Table 1.

With growing numbers of Christian cross-cultural workers coming from the Global South, cultural issues among the members of the international Christian cross-cultural organizations become very complex. Previously, mission initiatives tended to move directionally from the Global North to the Global South. However, today there is no "to and from" in missions geographically. As Escobar (2003) expressed in the title of his book, *The New Global Mission: The Gospel From Everywhere to Everyone,* missions today is from everywhere to everyone. Previously, cultural issues arose mainly when crossing from the missionary's culture to the field's culture. Today's missionaries must not only cross from their home country's culture to the field culture, they must also interact with their colleagues' cultures. Lundy notes, "Great skill in cross-cultural communication of the Gospel is needed but what about intercultural skills with your

Table 1

Comparison of Number of Missionaries by Sending Region in 1910 and 2010

Sending Region	Missionaries sent in 1910		Missionaries sent in 2010	
	#	%	#	%
Africa	350	0.6%	20,700	5.2%
Asia	300	0.5%	47,100	11.8%
Europe	39,950	64.5%	132,800	33.2%
Latin America	400	0.6%	58,400	14.6%
New Zealand and Australia	200	0.3%	5,000	1.3%
North America	20,400	33%	135,000	33.8%
Oceania	400	0.6%	1,000	0.3%
Total	62,000		400,000	

Note. Based on Johnson & Ross, 2009, pp. 261-262

own missionary colleagues?" (1999, p. 148)

Dynamics among Christian cross-cultural workers have changed as multicultural teams from many different countries have formed. Leaders must be able to function effectively in multicultural settings, as well as help their multicultural followers function effectively. Leaders with effective cross-cultural communication skills appear to be the key to success in leading multicultural teams, but challenges are even greater in the twenty-first century because much of the communication is done via the Internet. Large geographical distances make face-to-face meetings of leaders and followers difficult, expensive, and time consuming.

SIL International

SIL International was founded in 1934 to serve ethnolinguistic minority communities with language development work. "SIL serves language communities worldwide, building their capacity for sustainable language development, by means of research, translation, training and materials development" (SIL International, 2014b, para. 1). In 2014, SIL had over 5,500 members from more than 60 countries working in nearly 100 countries (SIL International, 2014a). SIL partners with local language communities and nongovernment and government organizations to pursue benefits for the language communities. At the international level, SIL partners with the United Nations Economic and Social Council (ECOSOC) and the United Nations Educational, Scientific and Cultural Organization (UNESCO). Membership from over 60 countries along with the many different levels of partnership create complex multicultural issues for SIL.

SIL is a faith-based organization. Its members believe that all people are created in the image of God; all the languages and cultures in the world are the expression of God's richness; and everybody has the right to know God: "Thus, SIL service is founded on the principle that communities should be able to pursue their social, cultural, political, economic and spiritual goals without sacrificing their God-given ethnolinguistic identity" (SIL International, 2014b, para. 3).

SIL works in five areas worldwide: Africa, the Americas, Asia, Eurasia, and the Pacific area. This dissertation focuses mainly on SIL workers in various countries in Asia who do linguistic-related work.

According to the SIL Asia Area Human Resource department, there are 1,578 people, 1,252 supported staff, and 326 paid staff or volunteers, working with SIL in

Asian countries (Yuko Takata, director of Human Resource Department of SIL Asia Area, personal communication, November 20, 2011). Due to the geographic dispersion of team members, communication between leaders and followers is done through computer-aided virtual methods. Using a computer for communication presents both advantages and disadvantages. Additionally, the cultural differences between leaders and followers add to the complexity of building and maintaining relationships between leaders and team members. Leaders in SIL are either appointed or selected to fill this role.

Traditionally language workers lived in a village for their linguistic work and visited an SIL center a couple times a year. Because of their work, most of the language workers lived in a different place from their leaders. At the time of this research, patterns of working had begun to change. Expatriate workers worked more as consultants or facilitators to help with language projects, which were being done by the local people. That situation still called for expatriate workers to locate in a village or nearby city, where they did not live close to their supervisors in most cases. That environment fostered independence and individualism and these qualities became a part of the SIL organizational culture:

> Also we tend to be very individualistic… even though we come from different cultural backgrounds. Over all SIL members tend to be individualistic. Maybe because many American members but also it's because of our history. It's probably the personality types, historically we are more pioneering. (Follower C7)

Many language workers in SIL did not work as a team but had individual responsibilities. Many teams which served under one leader did not necessarily work together on the same project but individuals had their own projects: "SIL usually doesn't work as a team. Out in a village, you don't see other people for several months. We are not doing things together" (Follower D2).

One primary focus of SIL workers is the production of Bible translation. That focus cultivated a task-oriented organizational culture: "People who are more social sometimes have [a] hard time with SIL, because it's very much task oriented" (Follower D6).

SIL's organizational culture promoted an egalitarian atmosphere. One person explained the SIL organization culture as the following: "Pretty much driven by understanding democratic foundation, equal right[s] and equal opportunity to make a decision" (Leader C1). Another person noticed that egalitarian organizational culture did not differentiate people based on their positions: "In the organization, hierarchy is invisible. I don't see director in their forehead. I need to take a notice of that" (Follower E7). However, during the time of these interviews, SIL as an organization was trying to reinvent itself, and the communication style SIL leadership used with regard to these issues was perceived to be top-down. This communication style was foreign to the existing SIL organization culture.

Problem Statement

While the above information focuses attention to the growing need for effective multicultural leadership and followership in faith-based, nonprofit, virtual and international organizations, very little has been written on the topic. Top leadership within such international organizations seems to assume that geographically assigned leaders know how to lead people with diverse cultural backgrounds and multicultural followers know how to follow. However, it is unclear which factors contribute to making multicultural leaders and followers interact effectively in a virtual world, especially when expectations differ and sometimes even contradict.

Purpose Statement

The purpose of this grounded theory study is to understand and describe leaders' and followers' perception of desired leadership and followership (i.e., that fosters working relationships) in a multicultural organization where computer-aided communication is the most frequently used communication platform between leaders and followers.

Research Questions

This study's central research question was: How do leaders and followers in SIL and its partner organizations in Asia describe the qualities a person must possess to foster effective working relationships where computer-aided communication is used predominantly between leaders and followers? An effective working relationship means that both leaders and followers have clear understanding of their roles and tasks, pursue the same goals as parts of the organization, communicate openly, and can settle conflict when necessary. Subquestions included:

1. How do leaders working in a multicultural organization describe qualities of effective leaders?
2. How do followers working in a multicultural organization describe qualities of effective leaders?
3. How do leaders working in a multicultural organization describe qualities of effective followers?

4. How do followers working in a multicultural organization describe qualities of effective followers?

5. How do leaders and followers describe the role of communication methods affecting their working relationship?

Definitions

For the purpose of this study, the following definitions are used.

1. Computer-aided communication: This includes email, Skype, Facebook and other applications.

2. Entity conference: Mission and faith-based non-profit organizations sometimes designate their work within a country or region as a field entity. An entity conference is a scheduled meeting of its entity members to discuss relevant issues of their work. Branch was also used to indicate an entity. In this study, branch and entity are interchangeable.

3. Faith-based organization: A faith-based organization is an organization based on certain religious beliefs. In this research, a faith-based organization refers to an organization based on Christian beliefs.

4. Follower: Someone who reports to a supervisor who sets direction and oversees the work of the follower in this study. However, some followers have their own teams and so they are also leaders as well. In this study, 65 people who were serving under 10 different leaders were classified as followers.

5. Leader: Someone who supervises and sets direction for subordinates in this study. There were 10 leaders interviewed for this study. Those leaders also report to their own leaders, and so, in that sense, they are followers too.

6. Multicultural: The term *multicultural* in North American connotes an alternative life style. However, multicultural in this study refers to the diverse cultural and ethnic backgrounds of members (leaders and followers) of an organizational group.

7. Multicultural leader: Multicultural leader refers to a person who is in a leadership position over team members who are from diverse cultural and ethnic backgrounds.

8. Nonprofit organization: A nonprofit organization is one whose reason for being is not motivated by making a profit. Such an organization typically has academic, scientific, religious and/or humanitarian motivations.

9. SIL International: SIL was originally the abbreviation for Summer Institute of Linguistics. Now the organization is known as SIL International, which is a nonprofit organization involved in language development work around the world.

10. Virtual: Virtual, in the context of communication or meetings, refers to meetings or communication in which the interface is provided via computer rather than face-to-face contact.

Ethical Considerations

I explained the purpose and general information of the research to the participants and acquired permission from them for the interviews and recording of the interviews. I did not coerce the participants to give data; they could choose to withdraw at any time. To protect the participants in this research, their identity was kept confidential. I protected the anonymity and rights of the participants by not using their names, specific positions, country of origin when possible, place where they were serving, or language group with whom they were working. I did not use the data to harm, to criticize, or to threaten the work of any participant. Any data from the participants was not used to bring a division between the leaders and the followers. I followed the research guidelines of the Protection of Human Rights in Research Committee (PHRRC) as a researcher at Biola University.

Delimitations

The people chosen for this study are six American leaders and four Asian leaders who are based in India/Kenya, Indonesia, Nepal, the Philippines, and Thailand, and their immediate subordinates, who consist of 65 people from 21 countries, working for SIL International and its partner organizations. The focus of this study was limited to the experiences and cultures of the participants.

Limitations

As a member of SIL International I have certain advantages in understanding context and accessing people. However, because the interviewees and I are the members of the same organization, they may not have been completely open and candid in their communications.

Among the interview participants, 23 of 75 people were Americans, which might cause American values of multicultural leadership and followership to be dominantly reflected in the data.

Some Asian members might have avoided saying negative things about anyone or anything because saving face was important in their cultures; they might have shared things very indirectly without commenting on the real issues in accord with their usual style of communication. Whenever I noticed this style of communication, I tried to get stories or examples of the situation to have a clearer understanding.

Some subordinates were new to their job and had not have time to build up the relationship with the leader. Due to the fact that I used computer-aided interviews which were less personal than face-to-face interviews with 15% of the people, I was afraid that the new participants might not feel easy enough to share data. I made an extra effort by talking with them and by writing to them prior to the interviews to get to know them through the virtual methods available to me so that they were able to trust me during the computer-aided interview.

Significance of Study

This study seeks to provide theoretical, cultural, and practical insights about multicultural leadership and followership in a computer-aided communication environment for the benefit of individuals and organizations. By understanding how differences in cultural expectations held by members of a multicultural team affect the development of the team being researched, leaders and followers in similar circumstances will be able to gain insight, and be better equipped to promote, develop, and help their own multicultural teams to grow. A potential multicultural trainer or consultant who aspires to bring about cultural understanding between individuals from different cultures will find useful information for leading seminars, workshops, and speaking in conferences.

On the organizational level, leaders and followers of multicultural organizations will be able to use the findings of this research as a reference for dealing with multicultural leadership and followership issues.

The study also seeks to provide a theoretical framework that multicultural organizations can use for further research and as a tool to select and develop more multicultural leaders and followers. This research provides the academic world with the following information: (a) the complex expectations of leaders and followers in a multicultural and virtual environment, (b) an analysis of the perceptions of characteristics needed for effective multicultural leadership and followership, and (c) a suggestion for multicultural leadership and followership development.

CHAPTER 2

LITERATURE REVIEW

This chapter reviews the existing literature concerning multicultural leadership and followership. Much has been written about leadership in general, but the purpose of this section is to review only the literature on multicultural leadership and followership that relates to this study. First, I discuss multicultural leadership in a rapidly changing world. Second, I cover the followership theory developed historically. Third, I illustrate the different cultural expectations about leadership and followership. Fourth, I describe the problems with a multicultural team for whom the leader is interacting and supervising, including how the virtual environment impacts the relationship between a leader and followers.

Leadership Research

This section reviews the current research on multicultural leadership versus universal leadership qualities.

There has been active research on leadership for the last 100 years. It started with the *great man theory*, which focused on the traits and personality of the leader in the early 20th century. The great man theory states that people are born with inherited traits; that they are designed to rise as leaders; that leaders share a number of common personality traits and characteristics (Stogdill, 1974). This theory does not focus on the followers.

From the mid 20th century, situational leadership, contingency leadership, and transactional leadership theories arose which focused on the leader's behaviors and actions towards organizational situations and situational control, which result from learned rather than innate characteristics only. These theories focused attention to the relationship between leaders and followers by pointing out that the effectiveness of a leader can be measured by evaluating the relationship of the leader to the followers.

In the late 20th century, charismatic leadership, transformational leadership, and servant leadership theories arose. These gave more attention to the leader's relationship with followers, yet they still concentrated on leaders.

Research on Multicultural Leadership

Multicultural leadership has been researched extensively by different researchers since the 1990s. In *Global Literacies,* Rosen, Digh, Singer, and Phillips (2000) studied 1,000 CEOs from 28 countries and identified four global literacies: personal literacy, social literacy, business literacy, and cultural literacy. Personal literacy focuses on understanding and valuing oneself by having aggressive insight, confident humility, authentic flexibility, reflective decisiveness, and realistic optimism. Social literacy intends to engage and challenge others; it is comprised of pragmatic trust, urgent listening, constructive impatience, connective teaching, and collaborative individualism. Business literacy focuses and mobilizes an organization and the leaders have key roles as chaos navigator, business geographer, historical futurist, leadership liberator, and economic integrator. Cultural literacy values and leverages cultural differences and the leaders take the roles of proud ancestor, inquisitive internationalist, respectful modernizer, culture bridger, and global capitalist.

Rosen and Digh's (2001) research found common characteristics of global leaders and introduced the term of *global literate leader* to indicate a competent leader in a globalized business world:

> To be globally literate means seeing, thinking, acting, and mobilizing in culturally mindful ways. It's the sum of the attitudes, beliefs, knowledge, skills, and behaviors needed for success in today's multicultural, global economy. (p. 74)

Osland (2001) reviewed the studies done on the competencies and concluded that leaders should have six competencies: (a) business savvy—the ability to understand the world market and its competitive condition; and the ability to make money in global business; (b) continuous learning—willingness to be inquisitive; and at ease in rethinking hypotheses and assumptions; (c) managing uncertainty—cope with unknown issues and data, and at ease with changing conditions; (d) cognitive complexity—the ability to balance very opposing paradoxes and handle complex issues from various cultures and perspectives; (e) behavioral flexibility—handling different perspectives between globalization and localization, contradicting values, business and cultural imperatives; and handling multiple roles; and (f) cross-cultural skills—the ability to connect people from different backgrounds by motivating, inspiring, and managing diverse people; and capable of understanding and being sensitive to the cultural issues.

In the book *Global Leadership*, Goldsmith, Greenberg, Robertson, and Hu-Chan (2003) identified five emerging characteristics of global leaders: (a) thinking globally, (b) appreciating cultural diversity, (c) developing technological savvy, (d) building partnerships and alliances, and (e) sharing leadership. Cultural understanding gives a leader ability to motivate and inspire people in a culturally appropriate way. SIL could not avoid becoming a virtual organization since their operation is not limited to one location, and they constantly communicate by computer-aided communication methods. Therefore, leaders need to know enough about technology to understand, to use, and to lead through technology. More organizations depend on partner organizations and alliances for their business in the global market. Leaders should be able to negotiate and work with complex networks of relations and partners:

> In the future, there will be fewer single CEOs; instead, leadership will be widely shared in executive teams. New demands for collective responsibility and accountability for results will emerge, as will new competencies for sharing leadership. The sheer number of alliances and networks mean that more than one person will lead these structures. (Goldsmith et al., 2003, p. 4)

Beside the five emerging characteristics, Goldsmith et al. identified ten more characteristics of global leaders: (a) creating a shared vision, (b) developing people, (c) empowering people, (d) achieving personal mastery, (e) encouraging constructive dialogue, (f) demonstrating integrity, (g) leading change, (h) anticipating opportunities, (i) ensuring customer satisfaction, and (j) maintaining a competitive advantage.

The GLOBE (Global Leadership and Organizational Behavior Effectiveness) Research Project researched leadership prototypes across sixty-two cultures throughout the world in order to examine culture's influence on organizational effectiveness and leadership. The GLOBE research classified and described nine dimensions of cultural aspects in sixty-two countries: uncertainty avoidance, power distance, institutional collectivism, in-group collectivism, gender egalitarianism, assertiveness, future orientation, performance orientation, and humane orientation (Quigley, de Luque, & House, 2005, p. 353). GLOBE researchers then identified six leadership styles as follows:

1. Charismatic/Value-based leadership: reflects the ability to inspire, to motivate, and to expect high performance outcomes from others based on firmly held core values. It includes six subscales labeled visionary, inspirational, self-sacrificial, integrity, decisive, and performance oriented.
2. Team oriented leadership: reflects effective team building and implementation of a common purpose or goal among team members. It includes five subscales labeled team collaborative, team integrator, diplomatic, malevolent (reverse scored), and administratively competent.
3. Participative leadership: reflects the degree to which managers involve others in making and implementing decisions. It includes two subscales labeled autocratic (reverse scored) and participative.
4. Humane oriented leadership: reflect supportive and considerate leadership but also includes compassion and generosity. It includes two subscales labeled humane orientation and modesty.
5. Autonomous leadership: refers to independent and individualistic leadership. This is a newly defined leadership dimension that has not previously appeared in the literature. It includes a single subscale labeled autonomous.
6. Self-protective leadership: focuses on ensuring the safety and security of the individual. The leadership dimension includes five subscales labeled self-centered, status-conscious, conflict inducer, face saving, and procedural. (Broadbeck, Chhokar, & House, 2007, p.1037)

The GLOBE study indicates that different cultural clusters prefer different leadership styles. Among different leadership styles, charismatic and team-oriented leadership dimensions are fairly universally accepted.

Cohen (2007) pointed out five areas of skills and characteristics that are needed for a global leader to be successful: (a) global business acumen, (b) leadership characteristics, (c) worldview, (d) people leadership, and (e) business leadership. Global business acumen means the ability to understand the business environment, including entrepreneurial and financial skills, profit and customer awareness, domain of industry, and business knowledge. Leadership characteristics consist of self-assurance, energy and enthusiasm, focusing on learning, and showing empathy by being authentic regardless of different ethical standards. Worldview includes global environment awareness, cultural adaptation, and understanding of social, political and economic trends. People leadership requires communication skills, ability to motivate and inspire people. Business leadership includes ability to make decisions strategically, effective ways of allocating resources, efficient time management, effective problem-solving ability, ability to manage complexities, flexibility in different cultural environments, ability to adapt leadership style to different contexts, and a visionary mindset. Cohen also identified traits of successful global leaders as follows:

> Being open to new experiences; Being curious about the world; Being enthusiastic and energetic; Being willing to listen and learn; Being able to adapt rapidly to change; Being willing to ask the right questions; Being innovative and creative; Being self-assured; and being result-oriented. (2007, p. 19)

At least four terms are used in current literature to identify leaders of multicultural teams: (a) cross-cultural leader (Teagarden, 2007) which stresses crossing cultural issues, (b) transnational leader (Earley & Mosakowski, 2000; Fisher-Yoshida & Geller, 2009) which indicates crossing national boundaries, (c) global leader (Goldsmith et al., 2003; Rosen et al., 2000; Osland, 2001) which implies multinational operations, and (d) multicultural leader (Guerrero, 2007; Plueddemann, 2009) which refers to multiple cultures. To reflect the multicultural leadership and followership issues, the term multicultural leader was chosen for this study. However, the terms for leaders used above are interchangeable with multicultural leader in this research.

Unique Characteristics and Abilities of a Multicultural Leader

It is evident from the above research that there must be some specific qualities and characteristics a multicultural leader should have in addition to general leadership qualities. This section covers unique characteristics and abilities that relate to multicultural leadership.

Global mindset. Wankel introduces global mindset defined by different scholars as follows:

> Global mind-set is characterized by openness, an ability to recognize complex interconnections, a unique time and space perspective, emotional connection, capacity for managing uncertainty, ability to balance tensions, and savvy (Kedia & Mukherji, 1999) ... Global mind-set combines an openness to and awareness of diversity across cultures and markets with a propensity and ability to synthesize across this diversity (Govindarajan & Gupta, 2001) ... Global mind-set is a highly complex cognitive structure characterized by an openness to and articulation of multiple cultural and strategic realities on both global and local levels and the cognitive ability to mediate and integrate across this multiplicity (Levy, Beechler, Taylor, & Boyacigiller, 2007). (Wankel, 2008, p. 179)

Clapp-Smith (2009) claims a global mindset as the basis for a cultural paradigm in making judgments about a situation, the basis of producing culturally appropriate behavior, and a frame for a cognitive reference point. He says that the components of a global mindset are cultural self-awareness, cognitive complexity of cultural intelligence (CQ), a process of understanding one's capacity for understanding and displaying appropriate behavior in a multicultural setting.

A global mindset consists of openness to self, others, and context, which brings awareness of diverse cultural viewpoints, and which leads to correct judgment of situations in a fast changing globalized world to make an impact with culturally appropriate behavior. The global mindset is not a fixed set of skills but a process of understanding diverse situations and people. A global mindset helps a multicultural leader and a follower to understand the complexity of an environment as he or she works with people from various cultural backgrounds.

Cultural interpretation. Maznevski and Zander (2001) stated that a multicultural leader should act as a cultural interpreter to be successful in managing a multicultural-team:

> A cultural interpreter identifies situations in which two or more members have different frames of reference, preference, and assumptions guiding their contributions, but the differences go unrecognized and the assumed similarly leads to misunderstandings. Thus, a good interpreter intervenes explicitly by making the team members aware of underlying reasons leading to the communication problems before the team moves on its discussions. (p. 173)

Dalton, Ernst, Deal, and Leslie (2002) used a similar concept and suggested that a multicultural leader should play the role of an innovator by creating new and different ways of looking at problems, by going beyond normal ways of thinking in a particular culture, and by generating new ideas coming from different a worldview and value system so that culturally diverse view points are reflected.

Multicultural communication skills. The multicultural leader is required to gain a thorough understanding of the various cultures represented on his or her team, and then must acquire the skill to communicate effectively with the various multicultural team members. An effective method of communication in one culture may not be as effective in another culture. Cultural variations demand that leaders be sensitive and adapt to different contexts. Multicultural leaders should have a good understanding of the best ways to communicate based on the followers' cultures. Beyond the cultural differences, technical issues and time zone differences add complexity to communication for a team.

Flexibility. Many researchers state that flexibility or adaptability is valued as a necessary characteristic of a multicultural leader. The cultural variety of team members demands flexibility from a leader on both cognitive and behavioral levels. Earley and

Ang point out the importance of flexibility in relation to understanding one's own cultural identity. Due to the complexity of the cultural differences of team members, multicultural leaders should be able to "formulate their self-concept (and concept of others) in new complex configurations. Thus, flexibility and a capability to inductively reorganize one's self-concept are necessary" (2003, pp. 71-72).

Janssens and Cappellen state that flexibility is necessary to manage a virtual team from a distance, not only in dealing with different cultures but also in using various tools in communication: "So, flexibility is also reflected in the variety of communication tools that global managers need to rely on when interacting cross-culturally" (2008, pp. 359-360). Flexibility in multicultural leaders needs to include willingness to find out which tools work best for communicating with their teams located in different countries.

Ability to handle paradox and ethnorelativity. Zayani (2008) states the characteristics of paradox as follows: "Paradox exists when two opposing ideas or thoughts are present simultaneously and present the true picture. Paradox offers an opportunity for change, where new learning replaces old learning, thus facilitating growth and innovation" (p. 47). Multicultural leaders face paradox in their daily routine due to dealing with opposing ideas coming from contradicting worldviews. Hofstede and Hofstede's five dimensions of cultural-values—inequality and power distance, individualism-collectivism, uncertainty avoidance, masculinity-femininity, and long-term versus short-term orientation (G. H. Hofstede, 2001; G. H. Hofstede & Hofstede, 2005)—imply paradoxical cultural differences; and GLOBE's nine dimensions of national cultural sets, which were mentioned previously, compare different values in various cultures. Trompenaars' Value Dimensions —universalism vs. particularism, group vs.

individual, feelings and relationships, specific vs. diffuse, achieved vs. ascribed status, concept of time, and culture's orientation to nature (Hampden-Turner & Trompenaars, 2000; Trompenaars & Hampden-Turner, 1998) — deal with two sets of contrasting concepts. Therefore dealing with different cultures equates to dealing with paradoxes.

Fisher-Yoshida and Geller (2009) introduced five paradoxes a multicultural leader faces (a) the paradox of knowing self and honoring others; (b) the paradox of focus on I-centric versus We-centric; (c) the paradox of communication across differences; (d) the paradox of action in doing and reflecting; and (e) the paradox of response in the short term and the long term. Cultural differences bring paradoxical issues that are unavoidable for multicultural leaders facing opposing concepts. Coexistence of cultural diversity requires respect for different cultures and embracing different cultural frameworks and new perspectives. These paradoxes present a dilemma to a leader who may need to balance widely contrasting values while preserving any assets the paradoxes can bring about.

In addition to the cultural differences, there might be opposing demands coming from the headquarters, the host-country, and the local situation (Gannon, 2008; Mendenhall, 2001; Osland, 2001). In processing power for their role, there is a tension on overplaying or downplaying to acquire information or progress the work. The leaders need to understand the host-country nationals, but sometimes, not knowing them or taking advantage of them may bring more benefit to the organization. They may play the role of a stereotypical person from their home country, and they may look for local people who can function and work like people from their home country for the benefit of the work. They may give up some of their own cultural values but at the same time they may hold more tightly to their own culture inwardly.

There are also some personal paradoxes the multicultural leaders face as well. By adapting to the host-culture, or multi-cultures, leaders may feel less of their home culture diminish in them. The result is that they may function easily anywhere in the world, but belong nowhere. They are globally minded, but they are viewed by people around them as being idiosyncratic. (Osland, 2001, p. 143). Therefore, paradox may be an issue not only in their work but also in their personal life.

To be able to handle paradoxes, a multicultural leader should reach a state of ethno relativity and integrate people by comprehending multiple worldviews:

> Leaders who can function across cultures, who can create and sustain systems that draw on the strength of those differences, and who allow innovative approaches to emerge are essential in every human endeavor. This does not come just from building a set of skills but in acquiring a new mind map. Opportunities for acquiring a global perspective, for moving from ethnocentrism to ethnorelativism, and for developing the range of competences essential for global leadership must be provided even as we look for potential leaders outside the usual leadership frame. (Pusch, 2009, pp. 81-82)

Focusing on unity could result in less creativity with too much control. Focusing on diversity could create confusion. The key is to balance unity and diversity. Basically, a leader should be able to understand differences and then function as a glue to hold the team together while bringing creative synergy from diversity (Difstefano & Maznevski, 2000).

Cultural Intelligence (CQ)

Leading in the twenty-first-century world means maneuvering the twists and turns of a multidimensional world. The continually shifting landscape of global leadership can be disorienting; experience and intuition alone are not enough. But CQ offers a way through the maze that's not only effective but also invigorating and fulfilling (Livermore, 2010, p. 21). Therefore CQ becomes a very important issue, if not the most important, for multicultural leaders to be able to survive in their work. This section discusses the characteristics of CQ and why the multicultural leaders should have CQ.

Characteristics of CQ. Ang and Van Dyne define CQ as "an individual's capability to function and manage effectively in culturally diverse settings" (2008, p. 3). CQ provides capabilities for understanding successfully in a multicultural setting, knowledge of appropriate performance in a culturally diverse setting, and comprehension of cross-cultural interactions (Earley & Ang, 2003). CQ enables a person to make sense of new cultural situations (Tan, 2004).

According to Van Dyne, Ang, and Koh, (2008) there are four dimensions of CQ: (a) cognitive, (b) metacognitive, (c) motivational, and (d) behavioral. Cognitive CQ is an individual's knowledge of culture in terms of understanding of norms, and practices. It involves the mental operation of processing and accumulating cultural knowledge. Metacognitive CQ is a higher level cognitive process that controls cultural knowledge and knowhow and the cues for when to apply the cultural knowledge in a different cultural environment. Metacognition is "thinking about thinking" (Earley & Ang, 2003, p. 100) and has two dimensions: knowledge of cognition and regulation of cognition (Clapp-Smith, 2009). Motivational CQ shows one's capability to give attention and to provide energy toward learning about and functioning properly in a new culture with confidence (Earley, Ang, & Tan, 2006). According to Van Dyne, Ang, and Koh (2008), an individual with high motivational CQ has a tendency to be interested in a different culture, to give more attention and direct energy toward learning in a cross-cultural setting, and is more effective in a cross-cultural environment. Behavioral CQ is an individual's ability to demonstrate appropriate verbal and nonverbal behaviors with people from different cultures.

Self-efficacy, self-confidence and inherent motivation must precede motivational CQ (Van Dyne et al., 2008). Bandura (2002) states that self-efficacy is the central mechanism in belief and motivation of personhood that controls human functioning, especially in motivating themselves:

> Self-efficacy beliefs regulate human functioning through cognitive, motivational, affective, and decisional processes. They affect whether individuals think in self-enhancing or self-debilitating ways; how well they motivate themselves and persevere in the face of difficulties; the quality of their emotional life, and the choices they make at important decisional points which set the course of life paths. (pp. 270-271)

Culture influences the formation of self-efficacy. Self-efficacy is the basis of putting personal capabilities to either individual or collective use based upon cultural type. In a collectivistic society, collective efficacy is collective perception about how they behave and accomplish certain tasks as a group. Higher levels of collective efficacy bring higher levels of performance (Jung & Avolio, 1996):

> People's shared beliefs in their collective efficacy influence the type of futures they seek to achieve through collective effort; how well they use their resources; how much effort they put into their group endeavors; their staying power when collective efforts fail to produce quick results or meet forcible opposition; and their vulnerability to the discouragement that can beset those taking on tough social problems. (Bandura, 2002, p. 271)

Self-efficacy is engaged in and manifested in a cross-cultural situation as a motivational component of CQ. Self-efficacy enhances cultural adaptation (Bandura, 2002). People who have high motivational CQ have higher levels of self-confidence and take interest in new situations and show confidence in their cross-cultural effectiveness. They focus attention and energy to learn about multicultural issues (Ang, Van Dyne, & Koh, 2008). Self-efficacy plays an important role in CQ because self-efficacy is the main factor that makes for successful cross-cultural adaptation and interaction (Earley & Gardner, 2005; Livermore, 2009).

Livermore (2010) uses different terms to explain the same four dimensions of CQ as the authors above: CQ strategy means metacognitive CQ; CQ knowledge means cognitive CQ; CQ drive means motivational CQ; and CQ action means behavioral CQ. Then he provides suggestions for how to develop the four dimensions of CQs. To develop CQ strategy more he writes, "Become more aware. Plan your cross-cultural interactions" (p. 176). To increase CQ knowledge, "See culture's role in yourself and others. Review the basic cultural systems. Learn the core cultural values. Understand different languages" (p. 176). To be more culturally intelligent on the CQ drive, "Be honest with yourself. Examine your confidence level. Eat and socialize. Count the perks. Work for the triple bottom line" (p. 176). To increase the level of CQ action, "Adapt your communication. Negotiate differently. Know when to flex and when not to flex" (p. 176). Livermore points out that understanding oneself is the beginning of understanding others; intentional learning and exposure to other cultures and languages are critical issues to enhance CQ; and acquired cultural knowledge should be practiced as much as possible.

Thomas and Inkson (2009) bring out three components in their approach to CQ: knowledge, mindfulness, and skill. Using Livermore's terminology, knowledge equates to CQ knowledge, mindfulness comprises CQ drive and CQ strategy, and skill means CQ action. Knowledge deals with understanding the fundamental principles of cross-cultural interactions and issues. Skill implies development of cross-cultural behavior skills. Mindfulness is paying attention to observations of cross-cultural phenomena, recognizing cross-cultural issues, and being reflective on the issues.

The concept of mindfulness originally came from Zen Buddhism and has been used in CQ to indicate intentional alertness to different cultural aspects:

> Mindfulness is such a common idea that most of us do not appreciate how powerful it can be. It is basically paying attention to text. It means discarding out rigid mental programming. It does not mean abandoning who we are but rather using attention to become aware of differences and to think differently. It includes the recognition that despite cultural differences there will also be many similarities between us and people from other groups, and that the cultural differences that do exist do not matter all the time. In cross-cultural interactions, mindfulness means simultaneously paying attention to the external situation, monitoring our own thoughts and feelings, and regulating the knowledge and skills we use. (Thomas & Inkson, 2009, p. 54)

Being mindful of cultural situations helps in understanding cultural differences and situations, and in removing one's own cultural biases. The concept of *cruise control* is often used to explain mindfulness by different CQ writers. When we live in our culture, we have our cultural cruise control on without even knowing it, assuming many things according to our cultural values. If one steps into a different culture, the individual needs to turn off the cultural cruise control in order to slow down, pay close attention to the details, and interact with people to understand them in their cultural context (Livermore, 2009, p. 147; Thomas & Inkson, 2009, p. 46).

Ang et al. bring another aspect of CQ to light:

> Cultural intelligence is not specific to a particular culture. The emphasis is not on mastering all of the specific information and behavior needed for individual cultures. Instead, CQ focuses on developing an overall repertoire of understanding, skills, and behaviors for making sense of the barrage of cultures we encounter daily. (Ang et al. as cited in Livermore, 2010, p. 20)

Bucher (2008) suggests nine skills that increase CQ: (a) understanding one's cultural identity, (b) checking cultural lenses, (c) developing global consciousness, (d) shifting perspectives to understand others, (e) involving and practicing intercultural communication, (f) managing cross-cultural conflict, (g) working with multicultural teams, (h) dealing with bias, and (i) understanding the dynamics of power in different cultures.

A multicultural leader's CQ level. CQ provides crucial information for a multicultural leader to be successful in a multicultural setting, and many organizations in the 21st century recognize its importance:

> IBM firmly believes that cross-cultural competence is the glue that enables cohesiveness and collective performance…. Lufthansa, the German airline, believes that culturally intelligent individuals constitute a precious organizational asset during times of crisis. At Barclays, culturally intelligent individuals will be able to help the organization gain local ownership and commitment in the United Kingdom and beyond…. The Wall Street Journal has predicted that in the twenty-first century, managers and organizations will have to handle greater cultural diversity. (Earley et al., 2006, p. 9)

CQ has a direct impact on the cognitive model a leader develops in a multicultural environment, and improves a leader's understanding of the potential benefits that a diverse team brings. Advanced levels of CQ empower leaders to develop different level of approaches to leadership and team processes (Earley et al., 2006):

> Culturally intelligent managers aren't just learning the ways that people act and behave in a new place. They are also creating a new mental framework for understanding what they experience and see. That is why cultural strategic thinking is also what psychologists call higher-order thinking; it refers to how we learn, not just what we learn. (Tan, 2004, p. 20)

Therefore, a multicultural leader should build up his or her collection of cultural understanding, skills, and behaviors, so that this CQ can become a viable tool as he or she leads a multicultural team.

Culturally intelligent leaders are able to recognize members' cultural differences and transform them to synergy for the benefit of the organization. A leader should promote mutual respect for different cultures, distribute power equally among the different cultural groups for equal participation, promote the team's ability to produce, and use new information, perspectives, and solutions. A leader should enhance overall team metacognition to optimize the team performance. A leader should encourage team members to seek creative solutions using new cultural precepts or mixed cultural precepts (Dean, 2007, p. 87).

There are two very different approaches recommended by CQ writers for how a multicultural leader should use CQ. One suggests having a minimum of understanding of the culture but building up the relationship with the locals to handle local team issues. The other suggests that a multicultural leader should have a sound understanding of the cultural issues by having high CQ and exercise it.

According to the research done by Janssens and Cappellen, multicultural managers who handle multiple cultures simultaneously or within short periods of time behave in three different ways: "(1) they take a personal rather than a cultural approach; (2) they focus on cultural artifacts rather than on underlying values and assumptions; and (3) they rely on local informants rather than gaining the cultural knowledge themselves" (2008, p. 363). Without knowing much about the cultures a leader deals with, he or she rely on people from the culture by establishing good relationships, and rely on local people to make known the proper behaviors. The rationale behind this approach is that it is not possible for a leader to learn all the cultures with which he or she deals.

Janssens and Cappellen advise a multicultural leader to have a fusion approach in managing multicultural teams, so that the team members can behave in whatever way is is proper according to their own cultures:

> Focusing on global teams, these authors argue that creative and realistic solutions are produced if cultural differences can coexist and be combined such that the distinct qualities of each culture are respected and reserved. In this line of thought, culturally intelligent global managers ensure that foreign colleagues can maintain their cultural ways of working, searching for synergistic solutions when working across cultural boundaries (Adler & Bartholomew, 1992). (Janssens & Cappellen, 2008, pp. 368-369)

In this case, a multicultural leader needs to cultivate a safe environment in which to be different. Especially in a collectivistic society, which promotes conformity, it is hard to understand that it is okay to be different. The leader's job is to nurture the coexistence of different cultural practices and understanding between team members.

Mannor suggests that a multicultural leader must have a strong CQ that will lead him or her to accomplish a lot more than relying only on local people for information:

> To begin with, higher levels of top executive CQ make it easier to build quality relationships with foreign partners despite partner differences. Although extensions into culturally unfamiliar territories are risky for any organization, such risks are mitigated to a large degree by the CQ of the executive. (2008, p. 99)

In summary, multicultural leaders must have an adequate level of CQ, including a multicultural mindset to understand complex geopolitical and cultural issues; have multicultural leadership skills that can build effective multicultural teams; and can be change agents to develop people and the organization (Tichy, 1992).

Culture Specific versus Universal Leadership Qualities

Determining characteristics and abilities needed for effective multicultural leadership is a complicated process because some qualities are culture-specific, and others are universal: sometimes both are intertwined in the multicultural setting. Hartog et al. (1999) identified multicultural leadership traits under the categories of universal and cultural aspects. Universally acceptable traits are: decisive, informed, honest, dynamic, administratively skilled, coordinator, just, team builder, effective bargainer, dependable, win-win problem solver, plans ahead, intelligent, and excellence oriented. Universally unacceptable traits are: ruthless, egocentric, asocial, non-explicit, irritable, non-cooperative, loner and dictatorial. Culturally contingent traits are: enthusiastic, self-sacrificial, risk-taking, sincere, ambitious, sensitive, self-effacing, compassionate, unique, and willful.

Some scholars have stated that effective leadership is usually culture-specific. Earley, Ang, and Tan summed it up this way, "Although leadership may transcend cultural boundaries, what constitutes effective leadership is nonetheless culture specific….Wholesome leadership qualities or practices may be universal; other leadership qualities, styles, and principles are situational or culture specific" (2006, p. 175). According to research by G. J. Hofstede (2009), "an excellent leader should be (a) optimistic and dependable, (b) approachable and have a sense of direction, and (c) focused and a developer of his or her people" (p. 96). American employees added "(d) professional at the personal level and passionate about the job and (e) a team player in implementing the organization's vision" (p. 96). Asian employees wanted "(f) a caring, authoritarian parent figure and (g) a proactive guide" (p. 96). G. J. Hofstede's research also clearly shows there are universal leadership qualities and culture-specific qualities.

Research done by Thomas and Inkson (2009) emphasizes the difficulty of the task facing a multicultural leader. He or she is called upon to build up people on the team who demand that their leader somehow demonstrate the specific qualities they expect in their own culture, while remaining upbeat and maintaining all other personal qualities of a good leader. Therefore, the nature of multicultural leadership is different from that of monocultural leadership, and the cultures with which a leader works will determine what good leadership is.

Summary of the Multicultural Leadership

CQ, the ability to function effectively in a multicultural environment, is the prime component of the abilities and characteristics of multicultural leadership, in addition to general leadership qualities. The multicultural leader is capable of managing uncertainty, coping with unknown issues and data, handling multiple roles, maneuvering complex issues from various cultures and perspectives, appreciating cultural diversity, processing different perspectives between globalization and localization, balancing very opposing paradoxes, and balancing unity and diversity.

There are universally accepted leadership qualities and culture-specific leadership qualities. Different cultures have different expectations for a leader, and different cultures prefer different leadership styles. Some scholars have stated that effective leadership is usually culture-specific, and this makes multicultural leadership complicated.

Followership

Throughout the history of leadership theory, research on followership has been minimal, even though successful leadership depends on follower support. Leaders cannot exist without followers because most of work is done by followers (Fairfield, 2007; Maroosis, 2008). This section describes the history of followership theories reflected in leadership theories, and the followership theories of Kelley, Chaleff, and Kellerman.

History of Followership Theories Reflected in Leadership Theories

Situational leadership theory was the first theory to shed light on a leader's ability to get a commitment from followers to complete a task based upon the relationship that leaders had with their followers. Contingency leadership theory dealt with interactions between leaders and followers within an organizational system (Fiedler, 1967).

The path-goal model pointed out that a leader's success was determined by the ability to motivate followers to complete a task and the importance of satisfaction of the followers was addressed in the process (House, 1971).

Transactional leadership theory focused on the transactions that the leaders engaged in with followers to get them to pursue goals by providing rewards (Bass, 1985).

Transformational leadership theory stressed the importance of motivating followers through inspiration, engagement, support, collective identity, and the development of followers' leadership capacity (Bass, 1985; Ilies, Judge, & Wagner, 2006).

Leader-Member Exchange theory deals with the leader, the follower, and the dyadic relationship based on four different stages as the leader and follower progress with their relationship as partners rather than in a mere interdependent relationship between the leader and follower (Graen & Uhl-Bien, 1995).

Servant leadership theory stated that "the great leader is seen as servant first" (Greenleaf, 1977, p. 7) and paved the way for the importance of empowerment of followers, trust between leaders and followers, appropriate usage of power, ethical issues between leaders and followers, and building a sense of community.

Followership Theory of Kelley

Even though followership was addressed as a part of leadership, Kelley (1992) receives the credit for the first major work on followership. Kelley stated that "leadership is the reward for good following" (p. 28) because the leader is someone who attracts and retains followers for the success of the leader and the organization. Kelley acknowledged that the relationship between the followership and leadership is dialectic, interchangeable, interdependent, and synergistic rather than separate.

Kelley used a matrix with two dimensions (active engagement and critical thinking as axes) to define followership typologies, and came up with five different followership typologies: exemplary (high in independent thinking score and high in active engagement score), alienated (high in independent thinking score and low in active engagement score), conformist (low in independent thinking score and high in active engagement score), pragmatist (middle in independent thinking score and middle in active engagement score), and passive (low in independent thinking score and low in active engagement score).

Followership Theory of Chaleff

Like Kelley, Chaleff (2009) stressed the mutual dependency between leaders and followers by saying "The mark of a great follower is the growth of leaders" (p. 29). He stated that the leaders and followers circle around the common purpose rather than the followers orbiting around the leader. Chaleff uses two dimensions (support and challenge) to produce four categories of followers:

> The two critical dimensions of courageous followership are the degree of support a follower gives a leader and the degree to which the follower is willing to challenge the leader's behavior or policies if these are engendering the organization's purpose or undermining its values. (p. 39)

Partners are those who are high on support and high on challenge, who are purpose driven, are mission oriented, and hold people accountable. Implementers are those who are high on support and low on challenge, who are dependable, supportive, and compliant. Individualists are those who are low on support and high on challenge, who are confrontational, independent thinkers, and sometimes rebellious. Resource people are those who are low on support and low on challenge, who are available but uncommitted, and execute minimum requirements.

In his book, Chaleff (2009) articulated that courageous followers are cooperative and collaborative, having qualities essential to all human progress, integrating their ego to the communal responsibilities, guiding the leader to avoid pitfalls, and bridging the gulf between the followers and the leaders. Therefore, they are full participants, committed to shared values and a common purpose, are willing to stand out to accomplish the vision of the organization, and are inspired to give 110 percent. Even though these kinds of followers have a different type of power compared to their leaders, they effectively participate in the work.

Chaleff identified the type of courage that the courageous followers should have. First, the courage to assume responsibility: Courageous followers discover or create ways to achieve their potential and optimize their value to the organization instead of holding a paternalistic concept of the leader or organization, and do not expect the leader or organization to provide their needs. Second, courage to serve: Courageous followers are not fearful of the hard work to serve a leader, and stands up for their leader for difficult time of decision making. "The courageous follower is willing to both comfort and confront the leader, to assume additional responsibilities to relieve the leader, or to initiate dialogue to help the leader examine her own contribution to the overload" (2009, p. 63). Third, the courage to challenge: Courageous followers stand up for what is right and keep the common purpose and their integrity to examine leaders and organization when necessary. They help the leaders to see reality and to minimize self-deception by giving feedback. Fourth, the courage to participate in transformation: They champion transformation for themselves and for the organization. Fifth, the courage to take moral action: They will stand up and take moral action even if they need to resign for higher set of values. "Moral action is taken with the intention of bringing the actions of the leadership and organization into line with fundamental values that govern decent organizational behavior while preserving the capacity of the organization to fulfill its purpose" (p. 149).

Chaleff claimed that courageous followers not only respect the existing culture but also influence it: "Courageous followers don't allow their own values to be subsumed by the prevailing culture" (2009, p. 17). Removing cultural pressure gives freedom to make conscious moral choices and prevent people from following leaders or cultural norms blindly.

However, there are paradoxes a courageous follower must handle: being an implementer and challenger of the leader's ideas; being a mentee and at the same time being a teacher to a leader; being led by a leader but leading a leader from behind, and being a group member while at the same time being an individual to question and challenge the group and its leadership.

Chaleff (2009) described the danger of having a parent-child relationship between a leader and a follower. In this type of relationship, the follower is dependent and not able to relate to the leader equally. Chaleff advocates courageous followers who have an equal platform of relationship with a leader. He also warned of the danger of a leader's opinion and interpretation becoming dominant and said the role of the follower should be that of gatekeeper.

Followership Theory of Kellerman

Kellerman (2008) stressed the different understanding of the followers in the context of a changing world influenced by Internet, flatter organization, cultural and technological change, size of the organization, different environment either crisis or stable, the point in time when work occurs, position of the follower, and the concept of their leader being benevolent or malevolent. Her work is more descriptive in the explanation of five typologies based on the level of engagement: isolate, bystander, participant, activist, and diehard. Isolates are completely detached from leaders and from work. They know little, do little, are uninterested, uninformed, and unmotivated, feel powerless, and are not concerned. Bystanders make a deliberate decision to be observers, to withdraw from their leaders and group dynamics, and to not participate. They provide tacit support only to maintain the status quo. Participants are engaged up to a certain degree by either supporting the leaders and the group, or being against them. They do participate in a limited way to have some impact. Activists are strongly engaged, eager, and energetic for their leaders. They work hard to support their leader or sabotage them. Diehards are deeply committed, and willing to risk all even to the point of death for the cause. They are either deeply devoted to their leaders and provide all the support they can, or they eliminate the leaders at all cost.

No matter which terms are used – exemplary, courageous, disciple (Adair, 2008), or diehard –effective followers are empowered individuals who are highly developed, active, committed, thinking critically, willing to challenge the leaders and others to the point that they can tell the emperor he has no clothes (Chaleff, 2009; Kellerman, 2008; Kelley, 1992).

Recent research on the roles of followership deviate from the previous concept of followers portrayed as sheep or yes-people. The roles of effective followers are as teachers for other followers and the leaders, helping leaders make the right decision, and being an agent of change (Dixon, 2008; Kellerman, 2008; Maroosis, 2008). Leaders cannot lead without followers and "…the followers are more important to leaders than leaders are to followers" (Kellerman, 2008, p. 242). Their choice to follow can be the most important factor in whether leaders fulfill the purpose of an organization (Fairfield, 2007).

Summary of Followership

Three scholars' works were reviewed in the followership section: Kelley, Chaleff and Kellerman. Kelley was the very first person who did significant work on followership. He used two dimensions (active engagement and critical thinking) and came up with five different followership typologies: exemplary, alienated, conformist, pragmatist, and passive. Kelley acknowledged that the relationship between followership and leadership is dialectic, interchangeable, interdependent, and synergistic rather than separate. Chaleff used two dimensions (support and challenge) to define four categories of followers: implementer, partner, resource person, and individualist. He stated that the leaders and the followers gather around a common purpose rather than the followers gathering around the leader. Kellerman (2008) described five followership typologies based on the level of engagement: isolate, bystander, participant, activist, and diehard.

Summary of Different Cultural Expectations of Leadership and Followership

Cultures define what makes for good leadership and followership. In the multicultural environment, everybody has certain expectations of a good leader and follower, and they are not necessarily the same.

Multicultural Team

The multicultural team brings a leader many different challenges to handle. The characteristics of the multicultural team and characteristics of a virtual team are reviewed in this section.

Characteristics of Multicultural Team

This section reports dynamics of the multicultural team, the concept of subgroups, in-group versus out-group, faultlines, and fusion and hybrid culture.

Dynamics of the multicultural team. One of the challenges a multicultural team has are the different expectations team members bring: "Culture is ethnocentric by nature. It presents itself as a set of absolute beliefs. It does not normally equip us for living in a polycentric world full of relativities" (Simons, Vasquez, & Harris, 1993, p. 19).

Schmidt, Conaway, Easton, and Wardrope (2007) categorized sixteen different cultural preferences: individual-group oriented, flat hierarchy-vertical hierarchy, acquired status-given status, functional-personal, physical distant-physically close, low context-high context, reserved-effusive, written-spoken, monochromic-polychromic, speed-patience, short term-long term, future-past, fixed truth-relative truth, analytical-intuitive, theoretical-empirical, and choice-destiny (pp. 219-232). Similar to Schmidt et al., Goman came up with fourteen concepts that bring cultural differences: confrontation vs. consensus, the group vs. the individual, concept of time, concept of space, decision making, contracts and agreements, personal relationships in business, manifestations of power and status, loyalty, problem solving, locus of control, deference to authority, formality vs. informality, and negotiation styles (1994, pp. 92-94). The variety of different qualities identified by these theorists demonstrate that cultural uniformity is impossible in multicultural teams.

Cultural understanding is useful in designing appropriate management and leadership practice. The greater the cultural differences among team members, the more complex the management practices will be (Schmidt et al., 2007): "In this context, management guru Peter Drucker cautioned, 'Tomorrow's business challenges are less technical than they are cultural. Culture must be managed just like any other business phenomenon'" (as quoted in Rosen et al., 2000, p. 32).

For effective team management, a multicultural leader should understand the dynamics of a multicultural team in comparison to a monocultural team. According to DiStefano and Maznevski (2000), there is a danger in ignoring cultural differences and focusing only on similarities. If differences are ignored and not dealt with, only the dominant culture's voice or the voice of authority will be heard and minority cultures will be suppressed. A dominant culture in a multicultural setting constitutes cultural imperialism over other cultures (Newbigin, 1989).

Earley and Gardner report that "Homogeneous team members generally report stronger affinity for their team than heterogeneous team members (Ibarra, 1992). Attitude similarity and demographic homogeneity have generally been shown to be positively related to group cohesiveness" (2005, p. 18). Therefore, it is easier for monocultural groups to build up a strong culture. A strong organizational culture creates a common identity, unity, and vision and reduces uncertainty (Bolman & Deal, 2003):

> By strong cultures, they meant cultures that were fairly homogeneous, that showed a good deal of consensus throughout the entire organization. These strong cultures seemed to maintain this homogeneity more easily when the members were drawn from similar (formerly middle-class, male, white) backgrounds. Strong cultures, in other words, tended to exhibit demographic, ethnic, and gender uniformity. (Neher, 1997, pp. 143-144)

On the other hand, multicultural groups face more conflicts and poorer performance due to different perspectives, which result in miscommunication and misunderstandings (Earley & Gardner, 2005, p. 22). However, once multicultural teams are maintained over time, they then can bring satisfactory experiences, produce higher quality ideas, see things from a broad range of the perspectives, and offer alternative solutions:

> In the case of multinational teams, members come from varying cultures, and cultural diversity provide a base for differing perspectives and insights, which, in turn, are important for idea generation, error detection, and group's avoidance of groupthink or other common decision traps. (DeSanctis & Jiang, 2005, p. 101)

DiStefano and Maznevski (2000) categorized multicultural teams into three different models: the destroyers, the equalizers, and the creators. The destroyers' model consists of members who attack other members' differences and misunderstand each other. The equalizers keep the status quo and do not use the differences to bring innovation or performance advantages. The creators accept differences; promote creative synergy; and results exceeding their own expectations. DiStefano and Maznevski suggest that, to make the multicultural teams into creators, first, map out differences; second, find a way to communicate in spite of differences for team members to build a bridge among them; and third, integrate the team ideas by resolving disagreements and creating new perspectives.

Subgroups. Subgroups are the different affinity groups within a multicultural team whose members share commonality and homogeneity, feel belongingness, and have group identity:

> Group identity is defined as a "perceived oneness" such that team members experience the team's success and failure as their own (Mael & Ashforth, 1992). Identity is the "social glue" that holds the individual members of a team together (Van Vugt & Hart, 2004). (DeSanctis & Jiang, 2005, p. 106)

The commonalities of subgroups in the multicultural team impact the functions and behavior of the team. Subgroups can advocate their position effectively in a multicultural team and the collective opinions of subgroups bring different aspects to be incorporated into the final decision of the organization (Janssens & Brett, 2006). Gibson and Grubb state the dynamics of a subgroup:

> When members of a subgroup share numerous demographic characteristics (e.g. nation, gender, age, function), a "strong" and dysfunctionally diverse subgroup emerges. However, Gibson and Vermeulen (2003) demonstrated empirically that when subgroups are moderately strong. i.e. when members of the subgroup share some characteristics (e.g. nationality), but are different with respect to on other characteristics (e.g. gender or profession), and have those characteristics in common with members of other subgroups, then bridges are created across subgroups, and the team can still maintain an inclusive atmosphere. (Gibson & Grubb, 2005, p. 74)

However, there are dangers in subgroups. If the subgroup is strong, members identify with the subgroup only. This creates in-group and out-group dynamics, which will result the team division (Lau & Murnighan, 1998). Therefore, it is important for a multicultural leader to understand the dynamics of subgroups in his or her multicultural team.

In-group versus out-group. A collectivistic society consists of members with dyadic personalities, which cause those members to identify themselves with a group rather than thinking of themselves as individuals. Therefore, a collectivistic society has a strong concept of in-group verses out-group. An in-group provides identity, belongingness, pride, loyalty, security, and superiority for its group members. The in-group provides positive interdependence in pursuit of common goals and care for its members. It is natural for in-group members to promote the collective in-group interests.

In a multicultural team environment, some members might treat other team members from different countries or backgrounds as out-group members. For example, language could be a factor to divide in-group from out-group members:

> If the team members speak the same native language, and the other half of the team speak an array of other native languages, then these differences would likely result in an in-group/out-group separation, even if everyone in the team has agreed to use a common language for business. (Gibson & Grubb, 2005, p. 72)

This is another challenge to managing a multicultural team. One way to increase unity within a multicultural team is to promote "in-groupness" by fostering oneness in common goals or different categories of group identity so that people feel belongingness. Factors that increase the division of out-groups like nationality, language, or status, should be minimized with a common identity substituted in the teams. This issue is discussed more in the following faultline section. Gibson and Grubb call "cross-national inclusive behavior" (2005, p. 76) as that which provides different ways of bringing out-group members into the in-group. For example, cross-national inclusive behavior is including a person considered as an out-group member in a prestigious social network or on an important planning committee.

Faultlines. Lau & Murnighan (1998) defined faultlines as: "hypothetical dividing lines that may split a group into subgroups based on one or more attributes" (p. 328). For example, Group A consists of two white male engineers in their forties and two Asian female secretaries in their twenties. Group B consists of one white female engineer in her twenties, one white female secretary in her forties, one Asian male engineer in his forties, and one Asian male secretary in his twenties. The attributes of both groups are the same: ethnicity, gender, and age. However, Group A has potential strong subgroups compared to Group B because the faultline gets stronger as more attributes are correlated, resulting in two homogeneous subgroups. Group B's faultline is weak because attributes are not aligned, and as a result, the members of Group B will identify with the whole group rather than its possible subgroups: "Alignment refers to the extent to which groups formed on the basis of one characteristic (e.g., gender) will have a high level of similarity to other attributes" (Shaw, 2004, p. 67).

Groups with strong faultlines may have two or more homogeneous subgroups: "When faultlines are strong, the focus of the individual team members is likely to be directed more toward similarities within the subgroup of which they are part rather than toward dissimilarities between subgroups" (Molleman, 2005, p. 187). They may have difficulty in communication as a whole without unity. When subgroups are equal in size and power, conflict can be severe (Trezzini, 2008). They could be prejudiced and form negative stereotypes of the other subgroups. Groups with weak faultlines may have minimal subgroups because the group is completely homogeneous or completely heterogeneous. The result of the research done by Thatcher, Jean, & Zanutto (2001) concluded that faultline strength reversely related to performance and morale; subgroups can provide immediate support to its members; and there is less conflict between subgroups if there is no need of interaction among different subgroups.

Fusion and hybrid culture. Janssens and Brett (2006) used the metaphor of fusion cooking to illustrate dynamics of multicultural teams. In fusion cooking, "food is prepared using techniques and ingredients of two or more ethnic or regional cuisines" (Fusion, n.d., definition 2d) to produce new dishes. Therefore, fusion cooking implies co-existence of ingredients never put together before, a new technique of cooking, and creation of a new and unique taste. In trials, some dishes bring success but some failures depending upon ingredients and cooking technique. Therefore "...fusion cooking is sometimes called confusion cooking" (Janssens & Brett, 2006, p. 126).

Similar to fusion cooking, multicultural teams represent the coexistence of differences, which could require respect, tolerance, and acceptance of cultural differences, which should result in the rejection of ethnocentrism. There needs to be an endeavor to bring strength to heterogeneous teams: "Coexistence of cultural differences can be achieved through identifying compatibility of cultural precepts, which can be realized by replacing one cultural precept by another, introducing a new cultural precept, or mixing cultural precepts" (Janssens & Brett, 2006, p. 137).

Second, just like fusion cooking needs new techniques, the fusion approach to multicultural teams needs new ways of approaching or adapting existing methods:

> The fusion model of team collaboration aims to be culturally intelligent through encouraging the meaningful participation of team members who are culturally diverse when their knowledge, expertise, or social contacts become relevant to the team's task. To facilitate creative initiatives, this model encourages information extraction and decision making that rely on dynamic responsibility (shifting subgroups) and focus on multiple criteria. (Janssens & Brett, 2006, p. 144)

Third, a new and unique dish is created: "Just as it takes a wide variety of ingredients and cooking techniques to make a truly remarkable dish, it takes preserving team members' cultural diversity to produce a truly remarkable global solution" (Janssens & Brett, 2006, p. 127). While producing a new solution, power between different subgroups must be neutralized. Otherwise creative energy coming from meaningful participation among team members might be hindered. There are times that the fusion model fails: "A team fusing too many cultural precepts at the same time may create chaos and confusion among members. The team may lose a sense of direction and lack coordination" (Janssens & Brett, 2006, p. 149).

Some scholars use the same concept of fusion culture as hybrid culture. Hybrid culture mixes elements from different cultures and creates a new unique culture (Earley & Gibson, 2002; Earley & Mosakowski, 2000), which accepts a variety of perspectives, values, and norms. When multiple cultures coexist, over time a unique culture is developed to set mutual expectations and rules. A hybrid culture exists when a group develops shared schema on values and provides a group identity. A hybrid culture is developed with the characteristics in the multicultural organization. Having a positive hybrid culture is a symbol of integrating different cultures to synergistic culture. The members of a team have a set of rules, understandings, and norms so that they know how to interact with other team members (Shokef & Erez, 2006): "A successful MNT [multi-national team] can be characterized as having an integrated and synergistic culture or what is sometimes referred to as a hybrid culture (Adler, 2001; Earley & Mosakowski, 2000)" (Earley & Gardner, 2005).

According to Earley and Gardner, there are four elements in a hybrid culture: (a) goals, (b) rules for social interaction, (c) task-related monitoring, and (d) reporting. The goals are aligned with company structures, systems, and strategy to contribute to the success of business. Roles are the roles of leaders and staff members. Rules are about how to manage cross-national business and how to process group facilitation. Task-related monitoring and reporting indicate communication and the decision-making process (Earley & Gardner, 2005, p. 5).

Virtual Team

A virtual team is connected and maintains its relationship through technology. Ginnac defines a virtual team as "a group of knowledge workers who are geographically dispersed... They are working together toward a common purpose and goal and using electronic communication as their primary medium" (2004, p. 21). Talents, availability in a remote location, technology available to link different parts of the world, and reduced cost of travel are the contributing factors. Stanko & Gibson (2009) uses a term "e-collaboration technology" to refer to the tool used to communicate and to share information between organizations and individuals. Technology influences how the virtual organization is shaped and functions:

> An appropriate approach is to recognize a virtual organization as a process of virtual organizing. This changes the concept from a stagnant organizational form to a dynamic method of organizational management. Virtual organizing is, in part, the establishing and maintaining of a web of relationships between agents. (Gaudes & Brabston, 2001, p. 532)

Advantages of a virtual team. There are many advantages to a virtual team. Team members are inspired to be connected with people from different cultures. Virtual teams can bring innovation and synergy (Gibson & Cohen 2003, pp. 407-408) that come from different perspectives: "By integrating the diverse strengths of the various people on a team, solutions and strategies can be developed that produce greater results than the simple addition of each contribution alone" (Maznevski, 1994, pp. 537-538). It takes longer and goes through a harder process to form an effective virtual team, but once people build trust and perform as a team, they can come up with creative ideas in understanding different situations around them. Virtual teams make it possible to access expertise in a distant place, which was not accessible previously (Fisher-Yoshida &

Geller, 2009, p. 3). A virtual team is less aware of, and less concerned with, social status than when face-to-face. Therefore, low-status group members feel freer in group discussions using technology than they will in face-to-face communication. A virtual team receives less supervision than a traditional team, which promotes autonomy in their work due to the distance (Tyran, Tyran, & Shepherd, 2003, p. 184).

One of the drawbacks of the virtual team is not having adequate time in team communication, especially having limited face-to-face meetings. However, a virtual team can turn a problem to an opportunity:

> When meeting times are limited, people tend to prepare more effectively and stay focused throughout the meeting. When nonverbal cues are limited, people focus on the spoken or written word and remain much more task focused. Because of this, virtual teams often have lower levels of personal conflict than face-to-face teams. The use of structured communication tools such as conference calls, emails, and web meetings tends to decrease the dominance of extroverts and native language speakers, giving each member more of a chance to participate in a way he or she feels comfortable with. (Mendenhall, Osland, Bird, & Oddou, 2008, p. 108)

Cultural noise could be anything that hinders clear understanding in communication, such as gestures, physical distance, facial expression, tone of voice, arrangement of sitting, and many more. Communication through technology can block "noise" (Gaudes & Brabston, 2001, p. 533) that is there in a face-to-face meeting, which sometimes distorts the message and relationships. With less noise, team members' anxiety level is reduced and people can focus on the issues better (Dubrovsky, Kiesler, & Stethna, 1991).

Disadvantages of a virtual team. However, a virtual team has disadvantages, too. Team members have less personal contact with less social information; communicate less than face-to-face; and have less shared team identity due to lack of shared physical workplaces. Due to the limited opportunity of face-to-face meetings, building relationships and trust between different locations is difficult (Dalton et al., 2002, p. 61; Mendenhall et al., 2008, p. 107; Ridings & Gefen, 2001). Hallowell pointed out the deficiency of a human moment in the virtual team environment. He explains the human moment as:

> An authentic psychological encounter that can happen only when two people share the same physical space. …The human moment provides the zest and color in the painting of our daily lives; it restores us, strengthens us, and makes us whole. (1999, p. 58)

Without a human moment, it is difficult to build trust, and misunderstanding and barriers can creep in, which lead to loss of connectedness, cohesiveness, and unity, which results in more suspicious people in relationships and less commitment to the work. There are more potential communication mishaps (Dalton et al., 2002, p. 134: Hampden-Turner & Trompenaars, 2000, p. 184), and more conflict by not understanding people (Gibson & Cohen, 2003) in different locations. There is a tendency for a newcomer to not feel a part of a team due to lack of interaction with other virtual team members. During the virtual meeting, outspoken people could dominate the meeting without giving chances to the other people (Cheverton, 2006, p. 164).

A virtual team has difficulty developing a group identity, and loses opportunities to share unintended information in the way a face-to-face team does: "When social context cues are weak, people's feelings of anonymity tend to produce relatively self-centered and unregulated behavior. Group members become relatively less concerned about making a group appearance (Cottrell, Wack, Stekerak, & Rittle, 1968)" (Dubrovsky et al., 1991, p. 123).

Knowledge has two dimensions: tacit and explicit (Cramton & Orvis, 2003). Explicit knowledge can be transferred easily in writing on a chart. Tacit knowledge comes from experience over time, is contextually embedded, nontransferable, and even harder to transfer over technology. Tacit knowledge requires mutual trust and face-to-face is the best way to build mutual trust. Sharing tacit knowledge is hard (Cramton & Orvis 2003, pp. 203-205; Mendenhall et al., 2008, p. 107) for virtual teams.

Dependency on technology might hinder work significantly during the down times of the Internet (Gibson & Cohen 2003, p. 419). Overcoming time zones becomes an issue to conduct a meeting: "If a global virtual team spans more than six time zones, synchronous communication may be problematic" (Riopelle et al., 2003, p. 262). Virtual team leaders have the difficult job of not only needing to know and use various communication tools—hardware, but also of needing to be able to communicate the content in a culturally relevant way—software. The virtual team members also need to overcome the hardware and software issues in communication with the other virtual team members and with their leader.

Dynamics of a virtual team. Hinds and Weisband researched the relationship between diversity and team unity among virtual teams:

> In our study of product development teams, we found that the greater the distance, the greater the demographic dissimilarity among team members: virtual teams had more ethnic diversity and more diversity in educational background. Teams with high levels of diversity bring different perspectives, and thus start out with a narrower base of shared understanding than teams similar on many demographic dimensions, such as ethnicity, culture, and gender. (Hinds & Weisband, 2003, p. 28)

Therefore, they recommended starting the virtual team with team members with similar backgrounds for easier formation and group identity. The issue is how to maximize virtual team formation and development by integrating cultural differences to bring about the maximum potential performance of the team. Team unity/integration is the key factor with the virtual team:

> Groups with high integration perform better than groups with low integration on complex decision-making tasks…groups with high diversity and high integration perform better than groups with low diversity, but groups with high diversity and low integration perform worse than groups with low diversity. (Maznevski, 1994, p. 537)

McDonough and Cedrone (2000) recommend that to have successful virtual teams, it is important (a) to motivate members because members usually have divided attention between the local needs and global projects; (b) to create a safe environment to be at ease to brainstorm and to present untested ideas; and (c) to effectively manage communication by using appropriate communication tools. Creating electronic work places, reducing turn over, easy access to information and support, building strong team identity, visiting different work location, and frequent face-to-face meetings are recommended.

Managing a virtual team brings more misunderstanding, more issues, and more problems because of distance in addition to language and cultural differences. Virtual teams impact the relationship between the leader and the follower. According to Lord, virtual environments make the organization flatter and the followers make more decisions because their working environment is self-managing, very flexible, and independent (2008, p. 256). More times followers initiate their responsibilities, which require nontraditional and flexible style of reporting relationships to the leader. Being independent requires more leadership on the follower side, which decreases the distinction between leader and the follower. Leaders have less power and followers have more (Kellerman, 2008, p. 34) in the virtual environment. Also how an email has been sent (to whom, copied, blind copied, and omitted) creates different dynamics in communication. The fact that email communication can be monitored, recorded, and searched brings a different reality in the relationship between leaders and followers while the communication in the non-virtual team environment is rarely recorded (Collinson, 2008).

Virtual methods of communication. Computer technology brings to the virtual team an unlimited number of recipients, and an almost instantaneous message delivery. Reception is guaranteed at a time that is convenient to the recipient.

Gaudes & Brabston (2001) categorized virtual methods of communication into four categories: (a) highly transactional but low relational, (b) highly transactional and highly relational, (c) low transactional and low relational, and (d) low transactional but high relational. Outsourcing, fax, and the group decision support system are also highly transactional but low relational. Alliances, voice mail, email, audio/video teleconferencing, screen sharing, white boarding, integrated technologies like Lotus Notes, intranets, extranets, and the Internet are high transactional and relational. Electronic bulletin boards and mailing lists are low transactional and low relational. Teleworking is low transactional but high relational (p. 535).

One of the most frequently used methods in communication among cross-cultural workers is email. Email makes it possible to overcome time and space constraints. Its speed, reliability, and distribution capability makes it an effective vehicle to communicate, to exchange resources, to share information, to coordinate a task, to encourage, to care (Scheuerman, 2007), and to make people be part of a team. Email is inexpensive; reduces traveling or phone call expenses; removes paper usage and stamps; provides written documents for sorting and retrieval; and can be forwarded or deleted easily. According to Medland, email helps to accomplish a task; provides people a sense of autonomy and competence; increases a sense of belongingness; provides effective and respectful engagement; provides a way to understand how people interpret messages and process them (2007, p. 178).

The "virtual floor" (Schmidt et al. 2007) is one tool to improve communication among team members by providing a virtual space. Virtual floor or shared electronic workspace is provided to replace their traditional work place and to build team identity (Hinds & Weisband 2003, p. 31). According to Ziegler, IBM and various hotel chains have provided virtual dining rooms in which to have virtual lunch. The room has a video screen to provide telepresence between remote locations (Ziegler, 1995, p. B1). Adequate numbers of face-to-face meetings or of videoconferencing need to be arranged to help overcome some of the weaknesses of the virtual team.

Summary of the Multicultural Team

Subgroups with a homogeneous culture may be formed in a multicultural team, and the subgroup could treat their members as in-group and the rest of the team as out-group. Different cultural practices can create a new fusion/hybrid culture within a multicultural team. Virtual teams can bring innovation and synergy from different perspectives, but building relationships and trust between different locations is difficult.

Deficiencies in the Current Literature

Current literature on multicultural leadership and followership addresses the needs of multicultural leaders in business and provides background information in related areas. However, the current literature on the multicultural leadership lacks information about multicultural leadership in a ministry setting. There has been no work done to identify qualities a person needs to have as a leader to foster effective and successful biblical multiculturalism in the Christian cross-cultural organizations. Secondly, research has not been done on how multicultural organizations endeavor to bring cross-cultural training up-to-date to meet the needs of the current membership with the issue of building up more multicultural leaders and followers in a cross-cultural ministry. Thirdly, there has been a lack of research on followership in multicultural organizations. Current followership research was done in a Western cultural setting.

CHAPTER 3

RESEARCH DESIGN AND PROCEDURES

Forming a theory requires the right methods and procedures in addition to a thorough study of an object or people. In this chapter, I cover four different strategies that relate to the research as design and procedures used in this study. First, I give an overview of the methodological approach I used. Second, I explain the data collection strategy by providing information about the selection of the research participants and the method for data collection that includes interview, observation and the use of documents. Third, data analysis procedures are described by discussing coding and memo-writing to show the process of generating a grounded theory from the data gathered. Fourth, my data validation strategies are stated.

Methodological Approach

This section provides an overview of the methodological approach and explains the rationale and advantages for choosing qualitative research, my position on the worldview, philosophical assumptions, and grounded theory.

The Rationale for Choosing Qualitative Research

There are three different approaches commonly used in social science research: qualitative, quantitative, and mixed. The quantitative method is used to prove how some factors or variables determine an outcome when a theory is tested and when the research is objective and impersonal (Creswell, 2009, p. 99). Auerbach and Silverstein state qualitative research "involves analyzing and interpreting texts and interviews in order to discover meaningful patterns descriptive of a particular phenomenon" (2003, p. 3). Auerbach and Silverstein describe quantitative research as hypothesis testing versus qualitative research as hypothesis generating:

> Hypothesis testing research investigates a phenomenon in terms of a relationship between an independent and dependent variable, both of which are measureable numerically. This relationship is called a hypothesis. The aim of the research is to test whether the hypothesized relationship is actually true, using statistical methods. The grounded theory method allows the researcher to begin a research study without having to test a hypothesis. Instead, it allows her to develop hypothesis by listening to what the research participants say. Because the method involves developing hypotheses after the data are collected, it is called hypothesis-generating research rather than hypothesis-testing research. (2003, pp. 5, 7)

Mixed method research uses the strengths of both the qualitative and quantitative methods for the benefit of the study.

Qualitative research starts with curiosity or passion that leads the researcher to formulate a central question. Data is collected by using a variety of means including open-ended questions with participants in their natural setting. Data is gathered from many different perspectives and emic views. It is analyzed inductively to generate theories, and the researcher interprets and reflects on the data to come up with a holistic view of the situation. The purpose of qualitative research is to examine a problem or understand complex issues using a flexible style that allows the voice of the participants to be heard. Corbin and Strauss say that this type of research gets "at the inner experience of participants, to determine how meanings are formed through and in culture, and to discover rather than test variables" (2008, p. 12). Qualitative research makes it possible "to step beyond the known and enter the world of participants, to see the world from their perspective and in doing so make discoveries that will contribute to the development of empirical knowledge" (Corbin & Strauss, 2008, p. 16).

For my study on multicultural leadership and followership, I used qualitative research methods to discover participants' perceptions of an effective leader and follower in a multicultural organization. The data was collected in the participants' natural work setting using open-ended questions to get their emic view. After collection of the data, participant's concepts were inductively analyzed to generate a theory grounded on the data. The outcome of this research represents the voices of the participants.

The Rationale for Choosing Constructivism, Advocacy, and Pragmatism

Creswell (2007) categorized four paradigms, or worldviews, that a researcher presents: postpositivism, constructivism, advocacy, and pragmatism. Postpositivism "has the elements of being reductionistic, logical, an emphasis on empirical data collection, cause-and-effect oriented, and deterministic based on a priori theories" (p. 20). Constructivism seeks to understand people's lives and assign meaning. An advocacy worldview aims to accomplish a certain agenda to help the lives of the participants. Pragmatism focuses on solutions to problems by looking for "what works."

In this study I tried to understand the complexity of the views the participants held on multicultural leadership and followership issues in their natural work setting and interpret the data for development of a theory. This study reports the voices of the participants and looks for what works to provide the practical implications of multicultural leadership and followership issues in a multicultural organization.

Therefore, foundations of this study are the worldviews of constructivist, advocacy, and pragmatism.

The Position of my Research on the Five Different Philosophical Assumptions

According to Creswell (2007), all researchers have assumptions regarding ontology, epistemology, axiology, rhetoric, and methodology. Ontological assumptions deal with the nature of reality. The central question is "What is the nature of reality?"

Most qualitative researchers embrace relative truth or many realities from the findings of their study. They acknowledge that both the researcher and participants experience different realities with issues and those multiple realities should be recognized. Researchers quote words of the participants to provide different perspectives.

Epistemological assumptions are about the relationship between the researcher and the participants. The key question is "what is the relationship between the researcher and the participants?" The purpose of the epistemological approach is to get the emic data by understanding the participants' view. Therefore prolonged engagement in the field is important for a researcher to become an insider.

Axiological assumptions deal with the role of a researcher's values. The key question is "what biases do a researcher bring to this study?" It is unavoidable for a researcher not to bring personal values and judgments. Therefore, a researcher should admit the values he or she brings which influence the outcome of the data. Value systems could come from a researcher's religion, gender, race, education, life experience, and so on.

Rhetorical assumptions deal with the language of research. The key question is "how does the research use language to report research findings?" Qualitative research uses a personal and engaging style of write-up, and uses first-person pronouns. Methodological assumptions relate to the process of research. The key question is "what method is used?" Researchers use inductive logic, describe details of the situation, modify questions to collect more relevant data, and analyze data to form a theory.

In terms of ontological assumptions, I recognized multiple subjective realities of the participants on the issue of multicultural leadership and followership quoting the words of participants. Because I am an insider in the organization I studied, epistemological issues may have been easier for me since I can identify closely with the participants in many areas of their lives. My caution for myself with regard to epistemological assumptions was not to assume that I know how the participants think about the issues.

In terms of axiological assumptions, each of the participants and I have Christian values but may hold different cultural values. I did my best to keep my cultural values from influencing the responses of the participants and the interpretation of the data.

In terms of rhetorical assumptions, I did not use words like "internal, external validity, able to be generalized, objectivity" but rather I used "credibility, transferability, dependability, able to be confirmed" (Creswell, 2007, p. 18) to stay objective in reporting the findings. In terms of methodological assumptions, I used inductive logic and reported the details of the voices of the participants.

The Rationale for Choosing Grounded Theory

Grounded theory was originally developed by Barney Glaser and Anselm Strauss (Strauss & Corbin, 1990, p. 24) and has been further developed and used by social science scholars like Kathy Charmaz and Juliet Corbin to build theories about a phenomena. Charmaz defines grounded theory as follows:

> Grounded theory methods consist of systematic, yet flexible guidelines for collecting and analyzing qualitative data to construct theories "grounded" in the data themselves. The guidelines offer a set of general principles and heuristic devices rather than formulaic rules. Thus, data from the foundation of our theory and our analysis of these data generates the concepts we construct. (2006, p. 2)

Grounded theory is used for developing a theory through a systematic approach to certain phenomenon found in a participants' story. Grounded theory allows the selection of participants for the study from among those who have experienced a certain phenomenon you want to research. Grounded theorists gather data using a variety of methods such as interviews and observations. The data are coded initially line-by-line and then later are processed with focused-coding by making connections to the related data; data are sorted according to proper categories; memos are written to compare data and to research further; memos are sorted to identify the relationships among them; if necessary, more data can be collected to fill gaps in the data collected previously; and finally a substantive theory is constructed from the data. For this study I used the procedures of grounded theory to construct a theory from the perspectives of the participants in this study about their perception of what desirable leaders and followers looked like in a multicultural organization.

Data Collection

Getting rich data— "detailed, focused, thick, and full" (Charmaz, 2006, p. 14) is one of the key issues in research using a grounded theory: "The quality—and credibility—of your study starts with data. The depth and scope of the data make a difference" (p. 18). In this section I explain the data collection strategy for my study, provide the rationale for my selection of participants, and describe my data collection methods.

Selection of the Participants

It is critical to choose the right participants in order to have quality research because a grounded theory comes from data collected. Theoretical sampling is a method used to lead the researcher to the target participants:

> Once you have developed your theory on a single sample, you can collaborate it further using a procedure called theoretical sampling, which entails choosing research participants who have information related to your research concerns. In this way, your theory, rather than the requirement of randomness, determines which research participants will constitute your samples. (Auerbach & Silverstein, 2003, p. 19)

Participants in this study are supervisors in SIL International and its partner organizations based in Asia who have filled their current roles for over three years, who supervise more than seven people, and whose subordinates represent at least three different nationalities different from that of the leader. The four partner organizations that participated in this study are Door International, Wycliffe Asia Pacific, Wycliffe Thailand, and YBI (Yayasan Betania Indonesia). The reason for choosing leaders in Asia rather than leaders from around the world is to establish a common ground in the working environment. The rationale for requiring three years of experience in the current position is to build up enough of a relationship between leaders and followers for their comments to be accurate. The reason for having seven subordinates from three different nationalities is to have enough cultural diversity to compare perceptions of effective leadership and followership.

The leaders for this study consist of six Americans, one Hong Kong Chinese, one Indian, one Indonesian, and one Singaporean, who are based in India/Kenya, Indonesia, Nepal, Philippines, and Thailand. Two married couples shared their leadership responsibilities; therefore, this study researched eight teams. These 10 leaders and their 65 immediate subordinates from 21 countries who are based in 10 countries were interviewed for this study. They worked in four SIL teams, and four teams of SIL partner organizations. This is a good sample because it provided the research with valuable data about differences in cultural expectations from various nationalities. The prime reason for selecting the participants was their willingness, availability, accessibility, diverse cultural backgrounds, and meeting the criteria set for this research.

I researched the organization to which I belong and for which I had already been given approval to access people and other resources for the collection of data. Because I interviewed colleagues, I needed less time to establish rapport with the interview participants. However, I was very much aware of the possible dangers of studying people from my own organization and was careful how I formed questions for my interviews: "Although studying one's own 'backyard' is often convenient and eliminates many obstacles to collecting data, researchers can jeopardize their jobs if they report unfavorable data or if participants disclose private information that might negatively influence the organization or workplace" (Creswell, 2007, p. 122).

Method of Data Collection

The methods of the data collection used in this study were semi-structured interviews, participant observation, and examination of archival documents.

Interview. The interview is most often used for data collection in a grounded study because "interviews play a central role in the data collection in a grounded theory study" (Creswell, 2007, p. 131). Rubin and Rubin (2005) state that the goal of an interview is a solid, deep understanding of what is being studied, rather than breadth. Depth is achieved by going after context; dealing with the complexity of multiple, overlapping, and sometimes conflict themes; and paying attention to the specifics of meanings, situations, and history. (p. 35) Therefore, interview was the primary data collection strategy for this study.

I conducted face-to-face interviews with 65 people at their offices, and one couple whom I interviewed at their home. Twelve married couples were working on the same team. I interviewed nine of the couples together as a couple, and three couples separately by their choice. Most of the interviews were unemotional; however, in several instances, when the interviewees shared emotional issues, the interview was colored by laughter or tears. This occurred in both face-to-face interviews as well as in computer-aided interviews.

I interviewed eleven people using computer-aided communication. This represented fifteen per cent of the interviews. All the computer-aided interviews were done with video except for with two people who had poor Internet connections. In one instance, the Internet connection was lost more than 15 times due to poor quality, but the interviewee was persistent to call back many times to finish the interview. I removed one person from the list of interviewees whose interview was done through a computer-aided method because the recording was not audible due to poor Internet connection.

I interviewed six people with the aid of translators. I interviewed nine Koreans in Korean and then translated the interviews into English and had the translations verified. When I interviewed two people together at their request who were working on the same project, one person agreed with what the other person stated most of the time but did not add much information. I omitted his data and did not count the person as part of the study.

When the leaders in this research shared reflections on how they experienced leadership and followership when they were followers, that data were treated as the follower's opinion. In the same way, when the followers in this research expressed their reflections about the leadership and followership as leaders dealing with their own teams, their data was categorized as leaders' data.

See Appendix A for the gender, age, service years, country of origin, communication method (face-to-face or computer-aided), role (leader or follower), location of services, and the status of using an interpreter for the interview participants. Figures 1, 2, and 3 depict the nationalities, age groups, and service years of the interview participants.

The questions used to collect interview data:

1. How do you describe the desired qualities of effective leaders in SIL and its partner organizations?
2. How do you describe the desired qualities of effective followers in SIL and its partner organizations?
3. How do you approach your leader when you disagree with him or her? (to the followers)

4. How do you address issues with your followers if you have to tell them they are not doing good work and need improvement? (to the leaders)

5. What are the joys and challenges of being a leader? (to the leaders)

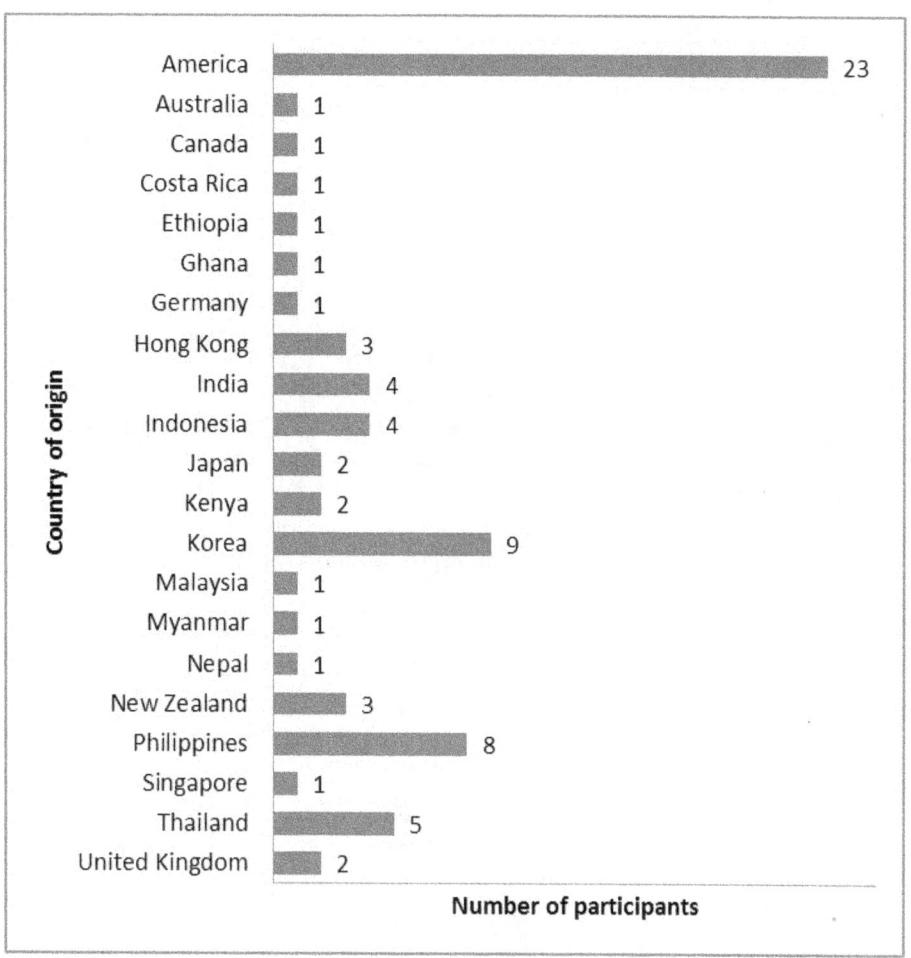

Figure 1. Nationalities of the interview participants.

The purpose of the first two questions was to collect information about what was considered desirable leadership and followership, and next three questions were intended to draw out understanding of how leadership and followership were carried out in SIL and its partner organizations.

I conducted one-hour one-on-one interviews with 10 leaders and 65 followers based in 10 different countries during December of 2011 and April of 2012. The participants, located in Papua in Indonesia, Davao and Manila in the Philippines, Chiang

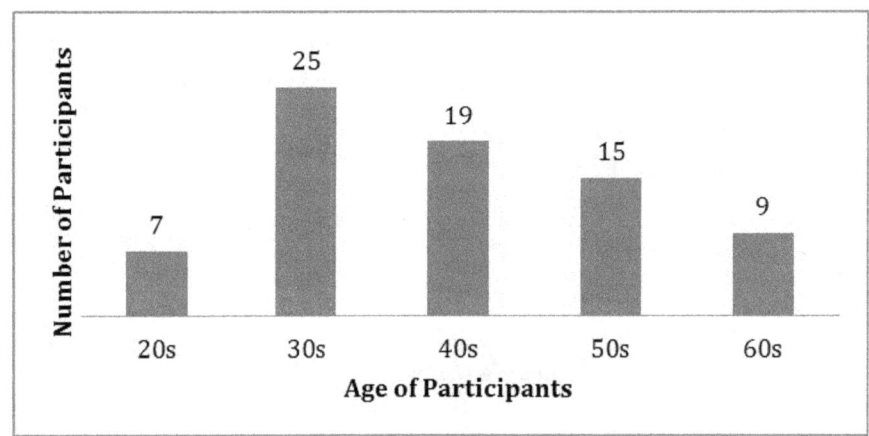

Figure 2. Age groups of the interview participants.

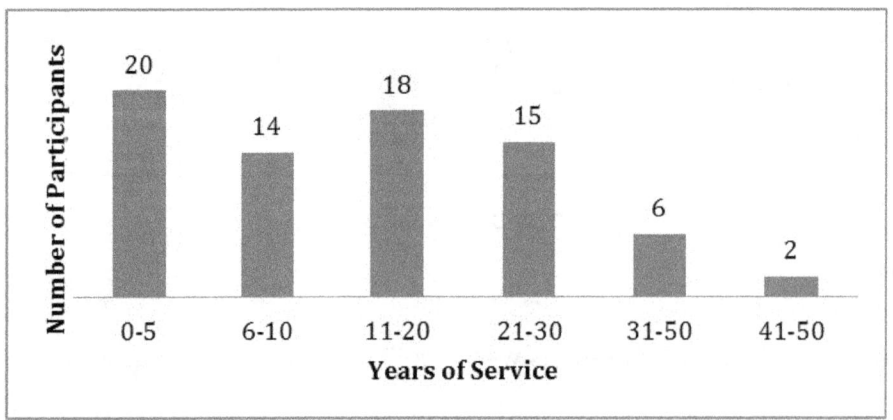

Figure 3. Service years of the interview participants.

Mai in Thailand, Katmandu in Nepal, and Nairobi in Kenya were interviewed face-to-face. I used Skype to approximate a face-to-face meeting for the rest of the people who were located in America, Canada, Hong Kong, Malaysia, and New Zealand. With permission from the interviewees, all interviews were recorded. After the interviews, I communicated through email to clarify the collected data and to pose additional questions. See Appendix A for the list of the interview participants and Appendix B for the semi-structured interview questions.

Participant observation. Another method of data collection used for this study was participant observation. When I conducted face-to-face interviews with the leaders, I observed the relationship between the leaders and the followers as much as possible. The observation sites were with people located in Davao and Manila in the Philippines, Papua in Indonesia, Katmandu in Nepal, Chiang Mai in Thailand, and Nairobi in Kenya. Some members were in remote areas and so observation of their interaction with leaders was impossible. The participant observation that I initiated for this study was purposeful and intentional.

Archival and technical documents. To understand the work in which people are involved, I examined technical documents, consisting of "reports of research studies, and theoretical or philosophical papers characteristic of professional and disciplinary writing. These served as background materials against I compared findings from actual data gathered in grounded theory studies" (Strauss & Corbin, 1990, p. 48).

Strauss and Corbin state the use of the nontechnical documents as follows:

> The nontechnical literature is comprised of letters, biographies, diaries, reports, videotapes, newspapers, and a variety of other materials....They can be used as primary data, especially in historical or biographical studies.... For example, much

can be learned about an organization, its structure, and how it functions (that may not immediately be visible in observations or interviews) by studying its reports, correspondence, and memos. (1990, p. 55)

Data Analysis

Data analysis is the process of analyzing data collected through interviews and other sources. It involves using codes to mark key points taken from the text, grouping the coded points into key concepts, and then forming categories which can become the basis for developing a grounded theory. Corbin and Strauss say that "analysis is the act of giving meaning to data" (2008, p. 64). In this section I discuss coding and memo-writing which are essential elements of the data analysis process.

Rubin and Rubin define data analysis as:

[Data analysis] is the process of moving from raw interviews to evidence-based interpretations that are the foundation for published reports. Analysis entails classifying, comparing, weighing, and combining material from the interviews to extract the meaning and implications, to reveal patterns, or to stitch together descriptions of events into a coherent narrative. (2005, p. 201)

Coding

After data is collected, it is broken down into digestible units for coding: word-for-word coding, line-by-line coding, and coding incident to incident (Charmaz, 2006, pp. 50-53). Charmaz states:

Coding is the pivotal link between collecting data and developing an emergent theory to explain these data. Through coding, you define what is happening in the data and begin to grapple with what it means. The codes take form together as elements of a nascent theory that explains these data and directs further data-gathering. (2006, p. 46)

Coding enables the researcher to discover and understand the meaning behind the recorded materials. Coding is an analytic framework for categorizing, defining, summarizing, interpreting, shaping ideas, making connections between ideas, and developing theoretical categories. Corbin and Strauss describe coding as the process of "taking raw data and raising it to a conceptual level" (2008, p. 66). Concepts, events, and any important notions can be coded. Repeated ideas or codes help us formulate themes, which can later lead to the development of a theory. Therefore, coding should reflect the purpose of the study. Through coding, any assumptions about language, preconceived ideas, and particular areas lacking data can be detected. A researcher should avoid putting an agenda on the coding, and using preconceived codes or categories. It is crucial to select the right term for each data unit. Different levels of coding—open coding, axial coding, and selective coding—are reviewed to understand the process of coding.

Open coding. The first step of data analysis is open coding, which serves to mark important concepts in the data. Open coding reflects the content of the data; it is grounded in the data, and is used initially to code the data without considering potential categories, structures, or relations to the other codes:

> Open coding requires a brainstorming approach to analysis because, in the beginning, analysts want to open up the data to all potentials and possibilities contained within them. Only after considering all possible meanings and examining the context carefully is the researcher ready to put interpretive conceptual labels on the data. (Corbin & Strauss, 2008, p. 160)

During the open coding, concepts are identified and developed, meaning behind the data is questioned, and different data units are compared to be processed further into axial coding.

Axial coding. Axial coding is the process of making connections among different codes in relation to categories and subcategories. This enables one to identify higher levels of concepts and the level of detail of the concepts in order to determine a practical way to arrange the data according to hierarchy:

Axial coding is the process of relating subcategories to a category. It is a complex process of inductive and deductive thinking involving several steps. These are accomplished, as with open coding, by making comparisons and asking questions. However, in axial coding the use of these procedures is more focused, and geared toward discovering and relating categories in terms of the paradigm model. (Strauss & Corbin, 1990, p. 114)

Axial coding identifies the relationships in the data and allows the major themes of the research to surface.

Selective coding. Selective coding is the process of organizing the overall data analysis to get the "story line" (Creswell, 2007, p. 67) and of choosing categories to develop a grounded theory:

The third step, selective coding, continues the axial coding at a higher level of abstraction. The aim of this step is to elaborate the core category around which the other developed categories can be grouped and by which they are integrated. (Flick, 2006, p.184)

Memo Writing

Memo writing is essentially the notes you record during the process of discovering insights, connections among data, and other pertinent information about the data during the analysis process:

Memos are the running logs of analytic thinking. They are the storehouses of ideas generated through interaction with the data. Generally memos start off quite simple (dealing with mainly one concept) and descriptive, and as the research progresses memos generally become more summary-like, abstract, and integrative (exploring relationships between two or more concepts). This means that later memos often contain the clues to integration, especially summary memos. (Corbin & Strauss, 2008, p. 108)

Faithful memo-writing by the researcher during the data gathering and analysis processes will provide information for developing concepts for pointing out the gaps in the data. That way a valuable record will be ready to use for writing a draft from the collected data. In memo-writing, the researcher's thoughts about the relationships among data, codes, and categories are captured and direction is given to the research.

In conclusion, during the data analysis process the researcher makes comparisons of the concepts and themes from the interviews and then allows the repeated themes and important concepts to lead him or her to theoretical conclusions. If done well, research questions will be reflected in the repeated themes; as important concepts emerge, they can be used to formulate a theory grounded in data.

Validation

Any study must establish its trustworthiness. The main concern of the validity of qualitative research is the relationship between what is studied and what is reported (Flick, 2006, p. 225). To examine the reliability of the research procedures and findings, Creswell says that "researchers need to look to themselves, to the participants, and to the readers" (2007, p. 201).

Methods of Validation

Prolonged engagement in the field enhances the credibility of a study. Prolonged engagement makes it possible to understand the culture and language of the field, to build trust, to avoid unintended mistakes, and to bypass misconstrued data: "Prolonged engagement also requires that the investigator be involved with a site sufficiently long to detect and take account of distortions that might otherwise creep into the data" (Lincoln & Guba, 1985, p. 302).

Triangulation involves the use of multiple types of data, methods, theories, and investigators to corroborate evidence and to see it from multiple angles. Different data gathering methods like interview, observation, and survey can be used to build the credibility of the research. The findings can be checked for credibility by demonstrating that the conclusions remain consistent when two or more theories are used to explain the data. Multiple investigators can check the data for its credibility and reliability.

Peer debriefing provides an external check and builds credibility (Creswell, 2007, p. 208). An experienced peer debriefer, by playing the "devil's advocate," (Lincoln & Guba, 1985, p. 308) can check the methods used, the interpretation of the data, ethical matters, and any other relevant issues.

Negative case analysis is another validation method. The purpose of the negative case analysis is "to refine a hypothesis until it accounts for all known cases without exception" (Lincoln & Guba, 1985, p. 309).

Member checking is the checking done by the participants in the research for the accuracy and interpretation of the data. According to Lincoln and Guba, the member checking is "the most crucial technique for establishing credibility" (1985, p. 314).

Rich and thick description offers details of the setting in the field. The findings should be transferable between different researchers (Creswell, 2007, p. 204).

An audit trail can enhance dependability and whether results from the study can be confirmed. The auditor should not have any connection to the study. The auditor can examine the process and the findings.

Methods used for this Study

Creswell recommends at least two validation strategies be employed in a study (2007, p. 209). This study used two methods: peer debriefing (Appendix C), and member checking. I asked eight peers to review accuracy of the interpretation of the data and any other relevant issues for the reviewers to assure trustworthiness of the research and to provide external checks. Member checking was used to validate the findings and the interpretation of the data. Whenever the meanings of the data are not clear, I went back to the interview participants for clarification. As I discover categories during the data analysis, I verified my findings with the members to make sure my understanding and analysis reflected and represented their ideas.

Chapter 3 Summary

This chapter covered methodological approach and explained the rationale and advantages for choosing qualitative research; the worldviews of constructivism, advocacy, and pragmatism; position of philosophical assumptions; and the rationale of choosing grounded theory. The main method of data collection was interview and the secondary methods were observation and technical documents. For example, when I visited Kenya, Thailand, Nepal, and Davao in the Philippines, I had opportunity to observe relationships between leaders and followers. Additionally I reviewed some SIL technical documents such as their rules to follow for Skype team meetings, and some studies of multicultural relations in SIL. This study used peer debriefing and member checking for validation.

CHAPTER 4

RELATIONAL QUALITIES IN LEADERSHIP AND FOLLOWERSHIP

The purpose of this qualitative study was to understand what qualities study participants deemed important so that effective leadership and followership in a multicultural organization could take place. The main method used to gather information was a series of interviews with eight teams of SIL and its partner organizations throughout Asia (Philippines, Indonesia, Thailand, Nepal, and India-Kenya). The substantive theory to emerge from the data was that both followers and leaders in multicultural organizations where computer-aided communication is the most frequently used communication platform perceive that effective leadership and effective followership derive from specific and identifiable relational qualities, task-oriented competencies, character-related qualities, spiritual qualities, cultural intelligence (CQ), and the way communication by computer is used and understood.

This central understanding is explained in Chapters 4 through 9 in this dissertation. Chapter 4 reports the findings dealing with relational qualities of leadership and followership; Chapter 5 describes task-oriented competencies of leadership and followership; Chapter 6 captures character-related qualities of leadership and followership; Chapter 7 describes spiritual qualities of leadership and followership; Chapter 8 explains the CQ components of leadership and followership; and Chapter 9 unpacks the impact of communication methods on the relationship between leaders and followers.

The leaders and the followers in this study articulated that communication and caring about the followers were the most important relational qualities in leadership. In addition to those qualities, while the leaders added building teamwork as a desired relational leadership, the followers added being relational, appreciating and understanding followers, and promoting teamwork. Therefore, the interview participants desired active communication; caring about, appreciating, and understanding the follower; and promoting teamwork abilities in leadership.

The desired qualities for followership were similar to those given for leadership. Both the leaders and followers articulated that the most important relational quality for followership was communication. While leaders considered respecting the leaders to be the second most important relational quality in followership, followers identified caring and encouraging leaders as the next important relational quality for followership. Of all the relational qualities articulated, communication was the single most important relational quality for both leadership and followership in SIL. Therefore, people in SIL and its partner organizations are looking for communication skills, caring, and promotion of unity as essential qualities in followership. Table 2 summarizes the findings of relational qualities in leadership and followership.

Relational Leadership Qualities Desired by Leaders

Seven concepts encompassing relational qualities for leaders emerged when I initially analyzed the data (See Appendix D, Table D1). After further analysis, three

Table 2

Summary of Relational Qualities in Leadership and Followership

	Leaders	Followers
Leadership	Communicate Care about followers Promote teamwork	Communicate with followers Care about followers Be relational Appreciate followers Understand followers Promote teamwork
Followership	Communicate Respect Encourage	Communicate Care and encourage Trust Unity Serve and respect Understand people

relational leadership qualities emerged from the data obtained from leaders in this study: communicating with the followers, caring about the followers, and promoting teamwork.

Communicate

Communication could be categorized as a task-oriented quality or as a relational quality because communication has both a relationship-building component and the element of communicating vision and direction. I categorized communication under relational qualities because the data appeared to be more relational than task oriented.

Leaders in this study wanted communication skills so they could build their relationship with their followers and communicate the directions of the organization. One leader expressed that, when the organization was in transition, good communication allowed the followers to understand the new directions and the reasons behind them so they would trust the leaders who were imposing change:

> Other challenges were to be able to articulate clearly to a team, policies that may be shifting in the organization, without either demeaning in a way or diminishing the leaders but being empathetic with the team's concerns. But also helping us all to realize that there are things that needed to change and we needed to find a way to work on it together. (Leader H1)

Another leader stated that one of the roles of the leader was to tell the followers what they needed to know. When followers did not know how to get resources, it was the leader who communicated with people in the organization, found the resources, and explained them to the followers. Structural changes in the organization, fast turnover in personnel, and remote assignments caused the leader to spend a large amount of time on finding resources and proper information:

> Communication is important to me. But it's really important in our current situation. What happened is, we had a branch that dissolved. The branch was dismantled and recreated and so our members, especially older members, are suffering from lack of structure. Even after three years, there's still confusion about who is responsible for what, who I turn to if I need help with a translation consultant or something. So communication is really important in order to keep things moving. And a big part of my job is just being a kind of a middleman for communication help. Lots of the services they need come from Asia Area. They don't even know who those people are. They find out the person, I need to ask someone in the US, some person I never heard about, in the US is supposed to answer this question. I am kind of a middleman to connect them. It just highlights the need for communication at least our current situation. If you are going to have a big virtual operation, you got to have good communication. In the old days, people just walk down from the other hall. (Leader D1)

Care about for the Followers

Leaders and the followers often spoke the word *care* as they articulated the relational qualities. I have chosen to use the word *care* to refer to the interest and concern leaders or followers would have for one another. Leaders in this study considered caring as an important quality for a leader. Two leaders used the term *pastoral care* to express the level of caring. If the followers could see that a leader cared enough about them, the result of leader's decision was accepted and a leader was respected even though the decision could hurt the follower's feelings:

> I have seen that he has a pastor's heart, he cares deeply for people. It's very, very obvious. And one could assume that that person, because of his compassion, wouldn't have any backbone to make a hard decision unless he was sure that it would not be hurtful to somebody else. That's not true, and I have seen him make very, very difficult decisions that have been hurtful, but they were the right decision. But somehow he's able to communicate compassion and care despite that. And so that showed me that it was possible to be a strong leader and still have people willing to follow and respect that person even if the decisions are not always what they want. (Leader B2)

Leaders whom I interviewed shared that visiting the followers at their location demonstrated a leader's care about them. The visit gave the leader an understanding of follower's daily life, struggles, and joys. Visiting the followers who were assigned in remote places encouraged the followers even more because the leader was concerned enough to take the time and undergo difficulties in order to visit them:

> It's kind of an emotional thing. In fact sometimes, people say, "You don't need to travel all the way out to see me. You can just email me. I am fine." But I think, deep down inside, I think, they really appreciate it. We have some people that are in fairly remote places, it's not quite like Papua, where they're way up. For example, one of the members, he is on an island, but he's in a city. But it's on an island. It's kind of hard to get to, and takes quite a while to get there. I went out to visit him last year for the first time. And I think he appreciated it, that I made effort to go there. But also it's helpful to me to actually see his environment. I actually went to his house and I saw what his life is like. And that helps me. If it's all done by email, even though he could send the pictures, but it's just nice to say, I have been there, I know that place. (Leader D1)

Promote Teamwork

According to interviewees, it was the leader who designed the "team promoting method" for his followers. For example, when a leader recognized that his followers preferred working closely together, he created an atmosphere of working together to promote teamwork. The followers' social needs were met and they grew together as a team by working together:

> They like to do things together. So you need to create environment. So when you do meetings, I always bring the whole team together and talk about [it], even though it's not their responsibility. So that they can get the total picture of what we are trying to achieve, and then they know that what their personal responsibility is. So by doing that, if the person is not around on the particular day, they should be able to fill the gap. So the team bonding, team meetings, teamwork has to come together. (Leader A1)

Desired Relational Leadership Qualities Expressed by Followers

Just as the leaders identified three relational qualities, followers I interviewed in this research noted twenty concepts of relational qualities in the initial coding that they wanted to see in leadership. Two concepts that only occurred once were dropped (See Appendix D, Table D2). With further analysis, six categories emerged: communication, caring about the followers, being relational, appreciating followers, understanding followers, and promoting teamwork.

Communicate with the Followers

As the leaders identified communication was the most important relational quality, the followers also noted that communicating with the followers was the most important element they desired in leaders in this study.

Listen to the followers. Followers desired their leaders to listen to them. Some leaders listened; others did not.

Listen. To be able to communicate with the followers, a leader should listen to the followers. If a leader listened to their opinions and understood their perspectives, followers accepted a leader's decision even if it was different than the one they recommended:

> It has to do with listening. It has to do with a leader desiring to really understand the perspectives of those people that are under that person. It doesn't mean that they only do what those people want. But they need to communicate very clearly that the opinions of the people under them are very important to them. And that they will take them into consideration. (Leader B2)

Listening to and spending time with a follower brought a sense of connectedness between a leader and a follower:

> I want a leader who listens to the followers well. Even though the leader is knowledgeable and just gives an answer to a follower. I saw a busy leader just say an answer, without hearing all that the follower had to say. Even though I respect a leader from a distance, when I meet with him, I don't feel warmth from the leader. He doesn't listen to me and doesn't connect to me. When I experience that, my heart is closed from him. Even though he has great ability, I wish he could connect with the follower, listen well, spend time with the follower, and feel his (follower's) hurts. (Follower F11)

A higher-level leader solicited input from followers of a lower-level leader, which allowed followers to share their input and then led to a good solution:

> Many years ago we had one leader who had a problem in relationship with members. Those days, like branch director assigned a regional director. I don't think we had an opportunity to say something face-to-face. But the higher director asked us, everyone, personally, not the group. If he assigns the same person, "How do we think? How do we feel? Do we accept, or what kind of attitude do we have? Do you want him to come back after furlough?" That's a very smart way to ask us. They are in the States. If a director says maybe you'd better stay there and find some other assignment. I think that leadership is very good, kind interviewed us. And then he would make a decision. (Follower F7)

Followers appreciated a leader who took time to listen to stories about their life and ministry in an informal setting that created a non-threatening environment:

> Then we used to see our leaders, maybe once a month, in a very informal setting, just because she invited us over to her place. We were having a dual date, so going out, her and her husband, me and my husband going out, for have something to eat and catch up on what we did. We did a lot of talking.

Normally… we spent 2-3 hours, eating and talking. And then we prayed together. (Follower H9)

It was especially critical for a leader to listen to the followers during transitions. If they were not given the opportunity to express their opinions about changes, the followers felt they were no longer a part of the organization:

I think in SIL more the relationship factor comes into play here because yeah, the way he relates to the membership, leads the membership, is quite key, listening to what the members have to say. I mean, this comes up because nowadays, there is so much transition. So that has been going on, now the director is trying to communicate to the members what's going on, listening to the members, what they think and feel, that's where we are at the moment. That's why it's especially important at this time. (Follower H3)

Do not listen. The followers shared many incidents when leaders did not listen. One follower identified three reasons why a leader did not listen to followers: (a) longevity of the leader on the field, (b) not being able to comprehend a follower's potential contribution, and (c) leader's predetermined directions:

I had hard time with my boss. It seemed like my boss thought that she knew the best because she's been on the field for twenty-three years so she made a decision by herself. She thought what she knew was the right way. She did not recognize what I could do and my experiences in the field. She stopped me talking to the local people many times. She didn't recognize other people's opinion and did not listen to the followers… She had her own measurement and wanted all followers to follow her way. She often ignored other people's opinions. (Follower F4)

Also a leader could be blinded by his own vision and not listen to the followers:

When we experienced leadership of the visionary type, it did not really have good followership. And that person was able to communicate that he heard people that he was listening to people. But it never, ever was reflected in any change in his own perspective; and we do not insist that a leader always has to change to our way of thinking, but over the course of a number of years, one would think that a leader would at least have his perspective changed once, perhaps, because of something he heard from those that he's trying to lead. But we never saw it. And so the evidence that the person was really listening and allowing what he was hearing to affect him was not there. (Leader B2)

When one leader had a preconceived notion about a certain aspect of a work, she would not listen to anything that disagreed with that preconceived notion. For instance, one follower's experience with a leader who had a strong opinion about protecting local people noticed that she did not listen to followers with different ideas about working with the local people:

> I wanted to work with the local people with a mindset of working together. I thought we could freely talk about the work but my boss stopped the conversation. My boss thought that the local people should be protected so that we should just do what they asked. But I thought "If we work together as a partner with the local people, we should communicate freely. If we just accept what they are asking, I don't think we are partners. We should share our thoughts freely and grow together as partners." That created conflict between her and me. From my observation, my boss only wanted to accept whatever the local people said. To me that was not treating the local people as a partner. (Follower F4)

Another follower observed this same leader did not listen to followers because she had her own ideas: "One leader, I observed, had too many of her own ideas and pushed what she thought. If a member didn't follow her, a warning came" (Follower F7).

When no action resulted after a leader repeatedly heard a follower's opinion, the follower stopped sharing his ideas and became angry because the follower thought that the leader did not listen to what he said:

> During the meeting I get encouragement and am given opportunities to share but nothing happen after that. Even if I give input, I guess it takes a process to make it work. However, when I saw no action was taken after providing input, and seeing that happening many times, I became angry. (Follower E12)

Communicate. While followers wanted leaders to actively listen to them, they also wanted to hear from the leaders. Communication needs to flow both ways.

Regular communication. Followers appreciated a leader who communicated with them easily and regularly so that they were updated on personal and organizational issues. The crucial times for communication were after a follower came back from furlough and when the organization was going though transition. In addition to these crucial times, leaders should be intentional about communicating on a regular basis:

> I appreciate that the director is communicating with the membership. For some of that's happening really right now. When X became director, he immediately communicated by email with different people, what are their positions. And we never had that and I found that so helpful. He's touching base with the membership and that's very, very nice. (Follower H3)

A follower expected to hear a leader's opinion after providing input to the leader. When the leader did not share his advice with the follower, the follower was frustrated:

> I think one leader I have in mind is not very direct, he has kind of a leadership style of listening a lot to a team discussion and but not very often to give his own perspectives on the issue, almost never would he be personally giving direction. If I asked for advice, he will listen to me, laying out the options, but won't give his advice, which option he thinks is the best. (Follower C6)

Communicate prior to making a decision. Followers expected a leader to communicate with them before making a decision that would impact their work. In SIL, followers usually had more information about their projects than the leader did. Input from them would enable a leader to make the right decision:

> I would assume the same things that the SIL leader would come to me, would not make a decision without having information that I have. For example, I wouldn't react to a leader make a decision who hasn't consulted me first on the issue just to make a decision. And it affected me and a leader didn't have all information... Maybe I should say the leader who would come to me first and ask for the information before the SIL leader would make a decision. I would appreciate that. That would feel much better than a decision being made without consulting me. (Follower B4)

Followers were hurt when a leader made an arbitrary decision about projects they were involved in without asking for their input:

> There was an incident when they merged two programs into one and gave that job to my co-worker. They never discussed with me but just announced the change.

So I expressed that I wanted to leave the work… Through that process, I was very surprised and hurt seeing how they made a decision without my involvement even though that decision impacted me a lot. (Follower D4)

In addition, it was hard for a follower when a leader changed his decision but neglected to communicate back to the follower:

Sometimes what I think was communicated was not actually intended to be communicated, He's making decisions and changing decisions based on conversations with different people, and sometimes those happen between what I talked to him about a particular decision I thought made back here. (pointing his finger on one point) I am still acting on down here, (pointing his finger at other point) and it's changed. I found out "Okay, when did that happen? All right, and trying to adjust according to that." It's difficult for me to say how much of that is just, well, things change, not everyone can be involved with every conversation. How much it is things indirectly communicated that this was what he was thinking at the moment and not an actual decision yet, it's understandable. It's just frustrating in the moment. (laughter) Sometimes highly so because I made a big decision based on it. (Follower C7)

Miscommunication. Miscommunication between a leader and a follower resulted in mistrust and broken relationships. In one incident, miscommunication started with misunderstanding about intention, and misunderstanding about the roles and the procedures of how and by whom the work was to be executed:

With [the leader] I think we had miscommunication, because he wanted things to be in a structure. He read my action as something that reflects that I'm not abiding by his rules, something like that. So there was an instance that we had a really big disagreement, because he assumed, because we've been dealing with different clients. He thought that I bypassed his rank, something like that. Because people would approach me first before they approached him. And he expected people have to approach him first before… So he read that in a different way. There was an instance that he was like really angry at me. And he tried to tell things that are not true, and that hurt me a lot. So we kind of had a disagreement. Because I told him that I clarified things and even if he had said "sorry" for saying things that he assumed that I did. But for me the damage has been done because in my culture we value our leader so we keep it to the point that we abide by the rules. So that for me you know, being accused of something that you didn't even do was really painful, and it kind of created gap between our relation as superior and a subordinate. I think trust was kind of destroyed when you accuse someone especially your subordinate with something that he didn't do. I think a good leader should clarify things first before you actually speak words that eventually would mess up a relationship. (Follower E3)

Organizational changes and communication. SIL started as a grassroots' organization and followers had ample opportunity to express their opinions about many aspects of the organization. However, due to the increasing size of the organization, decisions in recent years have tended to be coordinated from regional or global levels as indicated in Chapter 1. Followers noticed the change in communication style:

> The thing that I am noticing that's different from when I first joined is the communication. We don't know what's happening as much as we used to. I don't know that's because the organization has become too large. It's rather rare to have a meeting like we had today. We were hearing what's been happening in a lot of other parts of the country I am working for, let alone the world. And we hear about the people who are thinking about coming and joining. We haven't had that kind of meeting for a long time. It seems like we used to be very much grassroots organizations. I don't think I get the feeling that we are not that any longer. We have categories of leaders. Sometimes I hear even leaders say, you just have to get used to it because that's the way we are going to be. (Follower D6)

The new directive communication style made some followers frustrated or feel that their input was no longer appreciated and they expressed that they did not know where the organization was heading:

> For me the important part is communication and kind of knowing where these people are at. If the leadership know where the people are, because it seems right now, that there is a lot of this top down stuff going on that some of us don't agree with (laughter) and we are feeling the frustration like they don't know what's going on down here. (Follower F5)

Cultural issues in communication. Not only was the method of communication complicated but different cultures had different understandings about communication. An American follower realized that his British leader's way of respecting him was by not asking probing questions, but the American's culture was the opposite. Without questions from his leader, the follower automatically thought that his leader was not interested in his life or project:

> A British director from his cultural perspective kind of showed respect for us by not, in his thinking, asking probing questions. From our perspective he was disinterested. We came back from the first field visit to our language project when it first began. He didn't ask any questions about it. So for us that was very rude and cold. I assumed that it was expected of us to share it, if we wanted to. That was a little bit of a clash. ... It was kind of a cultural view on questioning. From my perspective, I show interest by asking lots of questions. He kind of showed respect for us by not asking questions. (Follower C6)

Some Asian followers expected leaders to know about followers' problems even though they did not tell them. They expected leaders to have a sixth sense, to understand things that were not spoken just like what would be true in their own culture: "Sometimes we don't talk because they [leaders] should know the problems. They should understand ... that we don't talk" (Follower A5).

Some Asian followers wanted to have a safe environment like a meeting to discuss difficult issues. They would not talk directly to a leader about those issues but preferred to be given a chance to share their opinions in a safe environment:

> If I have to ask something, I just don't really talk face-to-face. But sometimes if I can have a chance to in a meeting, I could. ... If we didn't have a meeting, I could not have a chance to explain. (Follower A5)

Asian followers were passive about initiating communication but wanted leaders to start communication by asking about their feelings:

Researcher
How did you communicate with your leaders that you were hurt?

Follower H7
We just learned, like commending ourselves to tell them. So one way is to also study or learn their culture. They are like this and that. [When leaders asked] "How are you?" "How do you feel?" Then it helps us to open, to tell what our feelings... To just let us initiate to tell that we were keep quiet instead of telling.

There are many times it happened, "Oh, I hurt you." It's important for us [leaders ask us] "Did I hurt you?" Because in that way, they can look for a solution. For us we never tell that you hurt me. But if they approach us to tell that "Oh, did I hurt you?" Then that's the time we can say. I think that two ways of, they need to ask us. And then we can open our hearts, something like that. We all learn about that. We are still learning (laughter).

Communicate disagreement. Communicating disagreement with a leader illuminated cultural differences about how a follower approached a leader. Most Westerners respectfully approached a leader directly about disagreement:

> I think I felt that I had a right to challenge my leader if I disagreed with the leader, but I did in a meeting. Yeah, I felt that I had a right in a meeting context when we were brainstorming or talking about ideas or setting direction or whatever. I felt perfectly comfortable to raise my hand and ask questions, to ask why, I mean questions like, "Why are we doing this?" or "Why did you do it that way?" or "Here's another idea. Have you thought of these?" I mean challenging questions sometimes. And I felt that I was totally comfortable doing that. (Leader E1)

However, Asian followers in general had many procedures they went through before bringing disagreement to a leader. Some Asian followers wanted to check with a group of people to validate their disagreement first before approaching a leader:

> My cultural way is not to go directly and confront your leader, if you have some disagreement. It will always, go around into group of people whom you could talk about and at least internalize "Is this a real problem or not?" Because there are times that people could easily react, because to them this is a problem. But you don't have to deal the problem alone. You have to have other brain and discuss it first, if this is a really a problem. You have to really discuss the result if you react to that particular thing as a problem. So you need a group of people that you can talk. Then finally you could communicate to your leader in such a way that is not offensive. (Follower B6)

One Asian follower expressed that she would not communicate disagreement to a leader initially. If an opportunity was given, then she would express her opinion indirectly first but if the leader did not understand, she was willing to say it directly:

Follower A8
> I disagreed with a leader a lot in my heart (laughter).

Researcher
: Have you approached your leader about that?

Follower A8
: No, never approached but just followed. But if given a chance to speak, I would open up my opinion but trying to make it really not so direct.

Researcher
: If that leader did not get your indirect communication, what would you do?

Follower A8
: If he didn't get the indirect way of approach, I would have no choice but to speak directly. It matters if they give me a chance to speak or not.

Another Asian follower said that he would communicate to a leader about disagreement indirectly first. If necessary, he would use a third person to communicate. That was the culturally appropriate way to communicate disagreement in his culture:

> Expressing disagreement is not easy for us. We have to express our disagreement indirectly. That means we could not put everything in language, that we could argue or whatever. But we will express some positive things to be able to help our leaders see what is needed and what is really the things we intended to suggest. But you cannot just put everything in language, and try to disagree or things, because you have some kind of disagreement in your heart. The other way that I think almost [all] people from my country used to do is to use a third person. To talk to somebody, and express everything in someone who is outside of your team and you know someone who could also express it for you to your leader. I think that is the very cultural way to express disagreement. (Follower B6)

However, when an Asian follower had a good relationship with her leader, she could share her disagreement with her leader directly:

> I will tell my leader right away that I don't agree about what she's saying, and I will offer what I think will work. It's been working well. Because I have worked with her for six years now, she's open to thinking. Not that I will get my way but I always express what I feel. "Oh, I think this might work better." If she thinks that's good idea. If not, she will say, "Maybe it will not. Remember, this happened. Remember the experience of somebody else...." So it's good dialogue. It's not like taken as offence. (Follower E2)

Power distance (G. H. Hofstede, 2001) was another issue in communicating disagreement. One follower expressed that she could talk freely to her supervisor about a disagreement but not to a director:

> I don't find it difficult to approach the supervisor, when it comes to something that I am not happy about or disagree with, unless it's like a person, maybe like my leader. We know each other and we can talk openly. They are able to do that. You know this is what's going on here. But say if it's really a director, I would have a hard time (laughter). I would have a hard time (laughter). (Follower H3)

In my understanding, this may have two components. It might be a big gap in power difference and also relational gap because this follower had good relationship with her leader but not necessarily with a director because she did not have enough time to build a relationship with her director.

Care about Followers

In addition to communication skills, caring was another leadership quality the followers wanted to see in a leader. This quality was the second most important quality that the leaders indicated. To illustrate caring relationships, the followers used the following words: mother, friend, sister, shepherd, father, and pastoral heart. Interviews revealed that the followers wanted a leader who not only cared about the work but also cared about family, emotional aspects, professional growth, and spiritual growth. One follower articulated that a leader should care about the followers equally:

> As Paul said to Timothy, there are honorable vessels in the house and there are also less honorable vessels in the house. But each of these vessels is important. So honorable vessels are useful for honorable purposes and less honorable vessels are also needed, because honorable vessels will not be used for a less honorable purpose. In the same way, in an organization, in the entity, there are different kinds of people with different capacities… the leader should pay attention to each individual and should give the notion… that all people are cared for equally. (Follower G2)

Different cultures defined a leader's care for a follower differently. One Asian follower expressed that a leader should be like a parent who would take care of the followers and the followers should listen to the leader:

Follower F9
> A good leader is someone like our parents, who can give the way out, help us to solve the problem, and care for us, just like a father to the team.

Researcher
> If a leader is like a father, are the team members like children?

Follower F9
> Yes, and also need to listen to the leader.

Another way to care about the followers was to acknowledge the followers for their accomplishments:

> I would say that a good leader can encourage the team, and that probably has to do with recognizing where they have been successes, recognizing where they have met goals and, you know like a team player, accomplish this and just to be able to say, "Yeah, that's great." To know them well enough to know what's going on and to be glad with them. To give thanks to them with if they've accomplished something.... I would say an ideal is maybe to know what's going on in people's lives, to be able to cheer together when they accomplish something. (Follower D3)

Be Relational

In SIL and its partner organizations, the relationship followers desired with a leader was that of a friend, an egalitarian approach in most cases. One of the reasons could be that the followers elected some to leadership positions, and after leaders finished their term they resumed a peer relationship:

> One neat thing about SIL, I am sure other... organizations are similar, is the fact that in some cases you can be a director one year, then next year be a regular person. That's pretty unique. Because I mean, in most cultures you go up the ladder, you don't normally ever come down from that. You are continually progressing to a higher position, but there are cases where you can be a top position or near the top position, and become a regular person after that role is

finished, which is pretty unique. But what the beauty is that it's the relationships that people can interact, relate to each other as colleagues as well as looking at someone as a leader. He can be a friend, someone also, they can be your leader. That's kind of a strange combination because you don't normally see. If you look at government or other type of things, senator, president, whatever, you are not the friend of that senator, president. They are at a much higher level. So in this situation it's a little bit unique, so that's kind of a neat thing. (Follower H4)

The followers liked a leader with whom they could enjoy fellowship and spend time. They wanted a leader as a friend after working hours:

If we fellowship as a group, and ... even outside office hours, we can bring to my leader and he jokes with us. He plays with us. He's not like proud. We can meet him. We can talk to him in a very easy manner. We are not like, "HE IS OUR BOSS. WE HAVE TO RESPECT HIM." (emphasis added due to raised voice) He doesn't demand respect in that way. He loves one another. And we can play with him. We can have fun with him. We can play volleyball together. And we feel like it's very easy to follow someone like that. (Follower G5)

Another follower wanted a leader who was approachable, available, and easy to relate to:

I can approach him. He is more approachable. You meet the leader every day, you can approach him. You can meet him, ask for any clarifications, you are able to express what you feel, about the work or the responsibilities, we can share [on a] day-to-day basis. (Follower G4)

One follower viewed her leader as being hierarchical and demanding a difference in status in the SIL setting. Her response to that leader was not positive: "I think he values the ranking system, like he is the boss and we are the subordinates, like you are under me" (Follower E3).

A mentoring relationship between a follower and a leader demonstrated a good relationship between them: "In my case she was able to first mentor me spiritually, and then she coached me on how to do things. She walked through me to various aspects of my assignments. She is a spiritual mentor to me" (Follower E3).

Appreciate Followers

In additional to being relational, the followers wanted their leaders to appreciate them. The leaders could show appreciation by trusting, valuing, and respecting the followers.

Trust followers. The trust the leader has for the follower can not only bring about a good relationship but can also have a positive effect on the follower's performance as well: "Her leadership style was effective for me. Even if she is not around, because of the trust she's given and the confidence she's given me, that alone encourages me to perform well even if she is not physically present" (Follower E3).

Personal mistrust of past leaders impacted the relationships a follower had with the current leader as well as with other leaders in the organization:

> Well, and because of that situation, the story that we told you before, our trust in the leadership went down. And we didn't, we no longer trusted them. We trusted God. We didn't trust them. …Can we really trust you guys? (laughter) Because we have an experience that we work differently, I don't know it's just difficult to regain, to grow trust again. Breakdown of trust with poor leaders. That's it. Influences further attitude towards other leaders or new leaders. (Leader B1)

Value the followers. A follower wanted their leader to value the follower's work even though that work might not require significant knowledge or experience to do it: "Someone [a leader] who considers all the work important. Someone who can consider the receptionist's work as important" (Follower F2).

Respect the followers. A follower appreciated the mutual respect shared between her leader and herself, which had resulted in an open relationship: "I think the current relationship that we have now is pretty ideal. Just he respects me and I respect him. We can sort of be open with each other" (Follower F3).

Understand Followers

A follower wanted a leader to be present with followers to know and understand them just like Jesus did with people:

> But this Christian leader is with people always. So he knows the pulse of people; they are suffering; they are in pain. So the leader is with us really, not a leader sitting in the office, leading us and dictating something. He is with us. You know that when Jesus came down, his name was Emmanuel; He was with people, that feeling, with the people. That is one thing that was really fascinating for me. Because he was humble, he was able to get along with people. (Follower G2)

A follower wanted their leader to understand the challenges, needs, and feelings followers experience in ministry life:

> One [leader] who is able to understand what you go through, especially when you are in ministry. There are special challenges you go through individually or as a family. The leader, if he can understand that, that could be a great thing. I think that will help the relationship go smooth. (Follower G4)

Promote Teamwork

The followers wanted a leader to promote teamwork and unity so that the work could be accomplished by the followers:

> I think the ideal leader would have a sense that there is a team, and that he is leading a team. And so he is not going to be the one do everything, and accomplish everything. But it will be the team. But I think that he or she should really have a clear sense of what the goal is, what they seek to accomplish, and the leader should be able to motivate, and help the teamwork together to achieve the goal. Part of that, like I said, to know the goal, and then to know how they are going to achieve the goal, and then to help each member of the team do their part well. Together accomplish the goal. (Follower D3)

Desired Relational Followership Qualities by Leaders

As the relational side of the leadership qualities were identified by the leaders and followers, desired relational qualities of followership were also articulated. Nine concepts emerged concerning relational qualities for followership by the leaders during the open coding. Axial coding condensed them into three relational followership qualities: communicate, respect, and encourage. (See Appendix D, Table D3)

Communicate

In this research, the concept of communication was repeatedly given as the most important relational quality for both leaders and followers. Leaders wanted the followers to freely communicate their ideas:

> I want a follower to feel comfortable talking with me and contributing ideas, and working together with me to make my department successful. Although I have to admit, sometimes I really like the idea that I can say something and they go do it (laughter). (Leader E1)

A leader wanted followers to respectfully communicate why they disagreed with stated policy and procedures. Unless the followers communicated their thoughts, a leader would not know what the followers were thinking:

> I would say a good follower, when he disagrees, should at least give his leader the courtesy of understanding why he disagrees, even if he feels compelled to follow despite his disagreement. The leader needs to really receive the benefit of understanding why there may be disagreement. Changing the question slightly, if I was the leader, and I could sense that there was disagreement on my team, with my leadership, but nobody would come and tell me about it, that would bother me. And I would not feel real comfortable with my team even if they obeyed everything if I knew that they were unhappy and nobody would say anything. That's why I said that a good follower will also communicate any disagreements with the stated policy and procedure, but do it in a respectful way. (Leader B2)

When Asian followers expressed their own opinions, even though those opinions were against a leader's opinion, a leader valued the relationship because the Asian followers would only be able to say those things if they had a trusting relationship with a leader:

> When my Filipino friend, or my Japanese, or my Singaporean friend looks at me, "I hear you, I appreciate what you are saying, but I don't agree with you,"—I love that. To me, that is a sign of followership that is appropriate, because there's a

respect for me. It's very clearly felt. Even though an appreciation of my ideas, but a freedom to say, "I don't see it that way." And then though it would not rupture our relationship...But I have come to love my cross-cultural relationships, follower-leader. And that's even when I have a "right" to tell them what to do, so to speak, if you know what I mean. Right is in a quotation mark, because I am a supervisor. And still I love it when they say, "I don't see it that way. Let's find another way to go about this." It's great (laughter). (Leader H1)

Leaders wanted the followers to feel free to communicate in ways appropriate to their culture. What was important for the leaders was that the followers expressed what they were thinking to a leader:

I would place a high value on communication that they are communicating with each other and with me or whoever the leader is. And again, that doesn't mean it has to be the American style of communication, where they share feelings and opinions. Even if someone's from a different culture, you don't feel comfortable speaking up directly. They go through another person, somehow communicating and letting everybody know where you stand, what your feelings are. I think just overall the team would work better. (Leader D1)

Respect

A follower needs to show respect to leaders. A follower may disagree with a leader but respect should be maintained when communicating disagreement:

When a follower has a disagreement with something that's been told him by a leader, to agitate in pockets with other people is not my idea of a good follower. That doesn't mean you can't be disappointed in an edict to that count but the way it is handled is everything. I read the [internal] blog of SIL president now. I get them every one that comes on the Wiki, I scan. And I have learned to almost disregard when I see a certain name and a long tirade because that person has characteristically been allowed a tone of disrespect for leadership. And I think that is very troublesome to the rest of the organization. There's others always speak in a well balanced way, that they don't always agree, but they speak in a way that reflects the respect to the leadership. And I think that the followers need to reflect a respect for the leadership. (Leader H1)

Encourage

Encouragement from a follower made a leader to go forward with his vision:

> Honestly, his email was encouraging me as well. So I appreciate him for encouraging. He appreciates the vision I have for this organization—accelerate Bible translation more. …. I still in my heart … see this organization … [doing] more [to] extend the visions on doing Bible translations … together with Wycliffe, reaching the vision of 2025. My expectation is when I shared that with people, people would welcome it, be excited to support it. (Leader F1)

The same leader expressed appreciation for followers who were supportive and helped the leader by making the leader's job easier. He illustrated follower's support role using Aaron and Hul who helped Moses when they fought against Amalek in Genesis 17:

> I would just say that I am glad that they didn't take the stone and put it upon Moses. But there are some people in the team, instead of playing the role, putting the stone under the leader, but putting the stone upon the leader. It means instead of helping, supporting, and making things easy for the leader, they make things hard and difficult for the leaders. But Aaron and Hul, they played their role and made it easy for Moses. Not only did he stand up, his hands up, not just supporting his hands but also putting the stone under him so he can sit. (Leader F1)

Desired Relational Followership Qualities Articulated by Followers

Just as the leaders noted relational qualities for the followers, followers also expressed that they wanted to see relational qualities in followership. Twenty-five concepts emerged during the open coding and were summarized under six themes during the axial coding. (See Appendix D, Table D4)

Communicate

The followers stated ability and willingness to communicate as the most important among the relational qualities for followership. The majority of communication problems that followers described were with leaders, and a few with colleagues.

Communicate with the leader. Some followers proactively communicated with the leader by asking critical questions, suggesting different ideas, or expressing disagreement. On the other hand, some followers were passive in communication with the leader by not expressing their opinions, or hesitating to approach their leaders. This section reported the range of communication from the most active communication to the most passive communication mode.

Communicate disagreement. Some followers felt it was their responsibility and right to point out when the leader was taking a wrong direction. Using Kelley's (1992) term, those followers were *exemplary followers*, or *partners* using Chaleff's (2009) term mentioned in Chapter 2:

> I think a good follower needs to be one who can evaluate a situation at his end and if necessary, to speak up and say "I think this is wrong. We need to change something here." And try to work with his leader in correcting whatever needs to be corrected. Not just blindly going ahead with whatever it is. I think that's important. (Follower F6)

Some followers believed that they should communicate directly with a leader in case of problems or disagreement so that the leader could be aware of the issue:

> We do have mechanisms if there are problems. There are ways to talk about it. And sometimes… people will chat among themselves but don't talk to the leader if they disagree or if there is a problem. How does a leader do something about it, if they don't hear about it? Perhaps a desirable quality for a follower is good communication with leaders. Perhaps that's more of a group quality that should be the opportunity for good communication. (Follower C8)

Provide input. Some followers in this research believed that it should be the follower's responsibility to give input to the leader, even though sometimes this could be viewed as a follower challenging a leader:

> I think it's appropriate for a good follower to approach the leaders and say, "There's something you should consider. This is something maybe you should do differently." Because leaders need good input from people that are following them. They need to know how the leadership's affecting the people. So when I said the followers need to trust their leaders, I don't simply mean they need to shut up and follow, if they don't agree. I certainly think that the following has an aspect of, there is an active component to it. And a follower can impact the

leaders in very profound ways, so do the leaders affect the followers. (Follower H5)

Followers should share what they know with the leaders so that the leader has proper information:

> An ideal follower in SIL context, I think are those people who wanted their leader to see what they have seen. There are things that they have seen down here (on the field), in which the leader could not see. So ideal followers are the ones who uncover all those things so that the leader could see what is really down there. That is necessary for them to address. So that the decision or the things they have to do will produce helpful results. So as a follower you really have to let your leader know what is down here, what you feel, what the community feels. You don't have to cover those, it means real transparency. (Follower B6)

One follower observed that, if followers had been with the organization for a long time, they wanted to express their ideas and felt validated when they were listened to: "I think it probably depends on amount of their experiences in person. If they have been here for a while, experience and knowledge, they have higher expectations for being listened to" (Follower C7).

Report regularly. Regular reporting to keep a leader updated about his project is the follower's responsibility. A leader with proper knowledge can make the right decisions about the follower's project:

> He [the leader] wants to know what's going on and would like to know how things are going with me. So I report to him regularly. Since I am used to reporting when it's necessary in SIL, the leader of this organization wants to hear from me before making a decision about my project. (Follower F10)

Report properly. One Asian follower said that followers wait for the right time to express their opinion:

> He or she [a follower] had an opinion and spoke up their opinion but waited until the right opportunity was given or waited until the floor was open. So they were discerning about timing, when they can express. They were very careful when to express. But sure, they had their opinion and let people know because that was part of their freedom or right, they considered. (Follower E7)

Another Asian follower observed that the followers in his organization expressed their opinion more than they should. He thought followers should limit their input to relevant opinions:

> From my experiences, this organization is very Americanized in decision making.... I think sometimes leaders are trying to listen to the opinions of the followers too much, unnecessarily, and the followers are trying to share too much of their own cases, which are not applicable to the group. I think if the opinions are reduced, it would be better. It'll be good to filter some of the opinions. People in my country do not share unless things have been thought through. I saw very extreme cases [in this organization], when a leader wanted to even listen to the unrelated things. I hope that followers would give opinions that are relevant. (Follower E12)

Cultural aspects of communication. Some Asian followers talked about difficulties in communicating with Western leaders. One follower stated that, even though she knew she should communicate with a leader, she felt uneasy talking to him:

> In SIL we should talk. If we don't talk, they don't understand us. That's what I understand. But in real situations, we are still afraid to talk. Generally not only for me in general, but people in my country, they feel inferior than the Western people, I think. Sometimes we face a problem that is not big but we thought it was very big and we feel inferior. That's not my situation. One of my friends' situation. We thought they are very wise; we are not wise, something like that. (Follower A5)

I assumed that the follower above might have talked about her own situation by saying that it was her friend's case. She might have expressed it in a way to save face.

Another follower pointed out that followers in his organization were supposed to initiate communication with a leader, while in his culture it was the leader who initiated communication. Unless followers from this culture learned to initiate communication with leaders, their voice would never be heard. These followers had to make cultural adjustments to be able to initiate the communication:

Due to American influence, they are very individualistic. While leaders in my country cared for people, it seemed like SIL leaders let the follower do their own thing instead of caring. If a follower doesn't communicate about a difficulty, a leader doesn't help. So a follower has to initiate the communication. Some followers from my country had hard time because they could not understand the different style of leadership. In my culture, the leaders initiate communication and ask the followers about how they are doing. In SIL, unless a follower initiates, he will not get much attention. I have to intentionally approaching the leader to initiate conversation because of the cultural differences. Without those efforts, I may have been left out for years. (Follower F10)

It was even harder for non-Westerners to communicate when they disagreed on issues with their leaders. One Western follower observed different communication styles of Western and Asian culture:

I know with SIL culture, because my limited understanding of Asian culture is more of, I sense that it's often times not appropriate for the follower to give an opinion to the leader. I don't know whether that's true or not. But that's my observation, my assumption. Whereas in Western culture, it's more acceptable that the follower will give an opinion, well, at least the perception that could be received. Whereas in Asian culture, the perception is that if the leader doesn't agree with that, it's not worth listening to. But that may not be true. That's just my own perception. So that's the Western side. It seems that hierarchical is more Asian [and the Western side is] much more egalitarian. So everyone is equal, whereas conceptually everyone is equal, whereas in Asian culture there's definitely a hierarchy. (Follower H4)

Communicate with team members. One follower emphasized the importance of communicating with team members so they could understand their co-workers, bridge cultural gaps, and be on the same page with the work:

What I am trying to say is, when you have different cultures working together, it's important to have times for you to process what has been happening. And you get together and you debrief, what is going well, what is not going well, then you have to change the situation so that we know how to improve. And assess everyone's gifts, and assess everyone's time, and just communicate together. Maybe even though we are from different countries and different cultures, we are finding that each of us is experiencing the same problems. And then we need to still come together and try to find the solution for those problems. But the important thing is when you find, no matter if something good is happening or something bad is happening, but to communicate and debrief together as a team. (Follower G7)

Care and Encourage

Followers articulated that caring and encouragement were another important relational quality for followership.

Care. Many more Asians than the Westerners in this research stated the importance of having a caring attitude. Actually only Asians expressed the importance of caring as a followership quality. One Asian follower described how he cared about a leader in work and in the leader's personal life:

Follower A
    [A follower should] help the leader when you notice a leader is tired. Help the leader even though the leader doesn't ask for help.

Researcher
    How can you help when the leader is tired?

Follower A
    Take care of the [leader's] family. Sometimes when a leader's traveling a lot, and very tired, and we can help their family. [If they] want to go to the market to buy something, then drive them, take them, buy something. The leader especially drove a car, but the car is very old, because they don't have time to take care of their car. But we can notice about the car and we can help. Sometimes a leader traveling alone, like a many traveling is safe or not, like an accident we can ask and help or go with the leader. In the free time like Saturday, we can persuade a leader to go fishing and just relax. (laughter) Every time we are busy and very serious, so maybe providing time to relax is good.

Another Asian follower emphasized the importance of caring about people first and focusing on work second. The following statements expressed the concept of caring and building a good relationship before focusing on producing good work:

> If we focus in work, we don't care about other people, not love you. Our work is not successful. Because we only focus work, and not care for other people. Because in harmony, we work together, we share ideas. Like something happens, we work together. (Follower A3)

Another Asian said caring needed to involve more than work. It had to involve knowing about the personal lives of the team members, sharing their lives, and spending time together outside of work:

> We help together, because if someone in my team is sick, but we care. If someone in our team is sick or has something in their heart, we care. We have friend with them, spend time, spend food and eat together and anything. We want to make team every time, not just work time. If outside of the work, make a team. Everyone is important in our team. (Follower A4)

Another Asian follower articulated that a family-like relationship would be desirable in a working relationship:

Follower A6
: Good relationship like a friend and a brother. When they have problem, we can help, pray for them.

Researcher
: What kind of problem do you help?

Follower A6
: In the team, we have a different duty. If the team has some problem, if I can help, and if possible, I do. If I cannot help, then like pray for them, like suggest some help. In the team, some people have problems with family. We help each other and share some things and we pray together for them. We help with the family problem if we can.

Encourage. The followers in this research shared that they could encourage one another by refraining from gossip and complaining and build each other up by working things out appropriately. When gossip is used to spread a rumor, it was viewed as very destructive:

> And along that line, again, it's just, Christian value is not to gossip. If you have a concern, you don't talk to your other follower, you know, just deal with it in a godly way. Don't gossip and cut down your leader. You try to understand. You work it out appropriately. Not with gossip or cutting him down. And so if there is a time when there was a misunderstanding, something is a problem, so you just try to work it out in biblical ways. You address it and seek reconciliation and forgiveness. (Follower D3)

A follower could encourage a leader by communicating that the follower was following well:

> Someone shared a picture of geese. When the head goose goes forward, he goes against the air pressure, so it's hard. But the geese following make noise saying, "You are not alone, we are with you." I was very much touched by that story. Followers need to encourage a leader by saying, "I am following." (Follower F4)

Trust

Trusting a leader was another relational quality followers wanted to see in followership. Interview participants are very independent, and that might hinder the followers in trusting a leader. One Western follower observed that Americans did not trust their leaders automatically but the leaders had to earn respect and trust while Asian followers automatically trusted and gave respect to the leaders:

> I think having trust, that's always seems to be always a challenge in SIL for followers to trust the leadership. I think sometimes I feel though, because SIL is largely American, I wonder sometimes if Americans distrust their leaders. Always questioning American politicians, things like that. ... I see from the Asian side much more willingness to follow and respect leaders. (Follower C8)

As reported earlier, many interview participants, especially Western interview participants did not want to be blind followers. However, not all of them agreed about this. One follower expressed that a trusting relationship between a leader and a follower meant that a follower trusted the leader without asking any questions: "An ideal follower is the one who trusts the leader to the point that there's no need to ask questions, or second guessing what he is doing, because he knows that he's doing the right thing" (Follower B8).

Another follower recognized that, if the new members trusted a leader, they were willing to follow a leader with an open-minded attitude toward a project:

The younger new people, they don't know what's there. If there's a change, they don't know what's there so [they say], "Sure. That sounds great." And if it's connecting with them, and they can see how they can fit into it, and if they trust to those who bring change, what is happening, at least in our group, there's a lot of openness to go with it. "Show me how to do it. Lead me, guide me to do it and I will make it happen." A lot of new members have really great attitudes. They want to go for it. They want to learn. They want to be led, as long as they trust and see that'll make a difference. (Follower C7)

Unity

One follower described unity in the following way: "We are, not I am. We are going together. We do this. Wycliffe do this, not the director, not personal, not I but we are" (Follower A4). Unity was understood as "us" (group) rather than "me" (individual) and the group was accomplishing the work.

Compared to the definition of unity above, the following definition was more based on a common goal:

> We work together cooperatively for a common good, and so that would mean following the leadership as agreed to being in SIL. I guess my personal thing is that, that means a lot to me, we would work together and especially with a Christian organization. I would expect as brothers and sisters in Christ we would work together in unity, for to do otherwise dishonors the Lord we serve. It gives a bad witness, and it creates all kinds of problems … so genuine cooperation, to work together. (Follower B5)

Unity was an important component in promoting teamwork. Understanding team members and their responsibilities was necessary in order to be to be a good team member: "To be a member of team players, he should understand his role and function, and be responsible" (Follower E5). Also it was deemed important for a team member to be dedicated to the purpose of the organization and care about team members: "He [follower] is a good team player, showing all the aspects of the good team player—commitment to organizational goals. Also a team player is concerned about the fellow team members and what they go through" (Follower G7).

Serve and Respect

Followers also verbalized the need to serve and respect. Having an attitude of serving was a great asset for a follower to have: "Someone [follower] who is willing to serve and to do what's needed when it's needed" (Follower C4).

One way of showing respect to a leader was to recognize the leader's authority. Recognition of leadership authority could be demonstrated by following what a leader had asked the followers to do: "[A good follower is the] one who respects the leadership and authority of a leader and [is] willing to do what they were asked even when they don't fully agree" (Follower C6).

Understand People

Understanding people was one of the key elements in building relationships. The followers whom I interviewed mentioned that the understanding of leaders and team members was important for building good relationships. Sometimes followers might have more knowledge than leaders in certain areas or might have had more experience in those areas. In that case, it was important for the follower to understand the leader's level of leadership and be gracious to the leader:

> Sometimes it requires wisdom to know about the leader's level of understanding and exposure. And sometimes we [followers] could be more exposed than the leader. So we expect them to solve the issues in the same manner, only to find that they don't. So giving them an opportunity and understanding, because they would just most likely solve within the context of their exposure, and understanding, and training. (Follower G6)

Understanding people's weaknesses and strengths was essential to having a good relationship: "The most important thing is to know people's weaknesses and strengths. If we don't know, we can't understand them" (Follower A5).

Spending time together, experiencing the same thing, and working for the common goal usually made a team come together. Especially when a team went through difficult times, it became a good opportunity to understand other team members deeply and to have a strong bonding experience:

> Team members are happy to follow and are willing to follow the purpose of the team, and accomplish the goal together. ... From my experiences, a good team shares difficulties while working. They come to understand people through working together. Teamwork comes through sharing time together. People get to know each other by watching people go through a difficult time without complaining. If a team complains and doesn't want to go through difficult times together, it's not a good team. Through those experiences, good morale is established. (Follower E12)

Chapter 4 Summary

There was very little difference between relational qualities for leadership and followership in SIL and its partner organizations in this study. For both leadership and followership, communication was the most important relational quality. However, some cultural differences were detected in communication.

The data from the interviews clearly showed that the Westerners were more direct and took initiative in communication. Western followers stated that they should be able to express their opinions freely, to ask questions, and to challenge leadership, while non-Western followers said that, even if they shared their opinions, they needed to be sensitive to timing; they could share opinions but should not insist upon having their way accepted; or they should limit sharing of their opinions. Some Asian followers had difficulty in initiating communication with a leader because they were not used to initiating conversation with a leader in their own culture, and some of them felt inferior to the Westerners. Non-Westerners had to learn to be direct and learn to take initiative in communication with leaders in this study.

Most of leaders in this study and some followers in this research learned to use a third party when they wanted to talk about a difficult subject without breaking relationships with Asians. Some Western leaders had very hard time understanding Asian followers when they communicated indirectly. At the same time some Asian followers did not understand why the Western leaders did not comprehend their intent.

Caring was the next important relational quality in both leadership and followership in SIL and its partner organizations in this study. Cultural differences were identified in the concept of care. Some followers expected a leader to care about them and have a friendship relationship with them while others wanted a leader to be like a parent and care about the followers as children. Unless expectations were understood, some followers felt like they were over- protected while others felt like leaders did not care enough. Asian followers mentioned the caring quality the most. Some expectations of caring by the Asian followers were parent-like or sibling-like care for the emotional and spiritual aspects of lives in addition to good working relationships. Even though relational qualities articulated were similar for both leadership and followership, the meanings behind the words were different based on expectations from different cultures.

Followers stated more relational qualities for both leadership and followership because the followers in this research outnumbered leaders (65 to 10). Followers added that leaders should be relational, appreciative, understanding to leadership, and have trust in, unity for, and understanding with followers.

CHAPTER 5

TASK-ORIENTED COMPETENCIES IN LEADERSHIP AND FOLLOWERSHIP

The previous chapter described the desired relational qualities of leadership and followership in SIL and its partner organizations. In addition to relational qualities, interviewees in this study identified task-oriented competencies as the next-important qualities in leadership and followership. The order of this chapter reflects the order of recurrence.

I categorized the data on task-oriented competencies into what the people I interviewed identified as important for both leadership and followership. Both leaders and followers in this study wanted a visionary yet supportive leader. Leaders preferred to have self-starters as followers, while followers wanted other followers to be hardworking. Table 3 summarizes the findings of SIL and its partner organizations' leadership and followership in regard to task orientation competencies.

Task-oriented Leadership Competencies Desired by Leaders

Fourteen concepts emerged during the initial analysis (open coding) of the task-oriented competencies desired by the leaders. After further analyzing the data (axial coding), I identified six themes: develop followers, have vision, handle conflict, be a decision maker, motivate, and have holistic understanding of the work. I dropped five concepts which occurred only once. (See Appendix D, Table D5.)

Table 3

Summary of the Task-Oriented Competencies of Leadership and Followership

	Leaders	Followers
Leadership	Develop followers Have a vision Handle conflict Be a decision maker Motivate Have holistic understanding of the work	Have vision and provide directions Develop followers Do not be a micro manager Attitudes toward work Delegate Have administrative skills Solve problems Direct Make decisions
Followership	Take initiative Be responsible Follow the leader Have a leadership mindset	Work hard Follow Be goal-oriented Work together Understand the work Make decisions

Develop Followers

Although developing followers could be considered both a task-oriented and a relational quality, it generally involved helping followers in their professional work. Therefore, I categorized it as task oriented. Ten leaders in this research identified this quality as the most important; actually, developing followers was the quality most often identified across all interviews. Developing followers encompassed supporting them, building up the followers, and knowing and using their giftings.

Support followers. Traditionally in SIL, someone who had administrative skills usually took a leadership role in supporting the language projects so that the language workers (followers) could focus strictly on their projects. One leader talked about his supportive role in language projects:

One of the reasons for doing it [taking a leadership role] in the first place was to help other people. Free other people up. For example, we were a part of a team in one location, and several people were already doing translation projects. But they had to take on additional responsibilities. They have to do the finances or the guesthouse, something like that. And I realized that when I did those things, I was freeing up their time to focus on translation. And so I could see right away the value in that. And so in a similar way, now I am in a role of bigger way. So I am helping, supporting them so they can do just their work. They came to do translation. I am trying to make sure all the other services are in place so that they can focus on that. There's a feeling of satisfaction that comes with that. Because of what I am doing, they can just translate and not worry about logistics. (Leader D1)

The importance of leader support was not limited to the language project but was present throughout the organization. One leader saw her main role as serving and equipping her followers to achieve the goals communicated by leaders:

I think, how I describe a good leader, would be someone who can show the vision out there and then make sure I have everything I need to achieve those goals. So in that sense the leader is serving me by resourcing me and helping me to be successful. If I am successful, then the goal is being achieved. So the leader just sort of keeps guiding us to that goal. (Leader E1)

Build up followers. Interviewees used the words *build up* many times regardless of their nationalities or the locations where they served. A leader who built up followers provided resources and opportunities for followers to grow into their positions or helped the followers to be successful. Participants assessed effective leadership on the basis of the growth followers experienced:

When I left, it went on. It never went backward; it went forward. Of course, I went every now and then there. Whatever help I could offer by visiting them, I did. But they took the challenge and they moved forward. And that gave me, even though initially I worried, after seeing the success of those people, year after year. Even now, even today when I go back to my home country, I see the success of their work. I could see that… I did a good job. Why is it that I did a good job? Not because of what I did, I did a good job because what I see, what these people were doing… But now I could say, "I left but they achieved." But I still could take pride [in] where they started, at least [in] where they got those [progress]. I was part of that. So it's not me, it's us. I could see that collective growth. People who follow that challenge, follow that passion and the vision, and continued. For me, that is effective leadership. (Leader G1)

Participants perceived successful leadership in terms of building up followers to become the next generation of leaders. Leaders in this study helped others to internalize a vision for passing on leadership to language communities themselves:

> It's exciting to see the nationals really take leadership, and be significantly involved, and working for their own language community. We get to hear stories about what's going on as a result of getting the Word in their language. We get to hear their enthusiasm. They will talk about their desire to have the Old Testament, for instance, and then it gives us an opportunity to see if there are ways that we can help them figure out funding or whatever, make something like that a possibility. We see ourselves ... primarily as resource people, providing a pathway to get the kind of help that they need, encouragers. (Leader B2)

There were different ways a leader could build up a follower depending on the follower's skill level. If the followers were entry level, the leader demonstrated by doing the work and teaching the follower how to do the work. If the follower had sufficient skills, then a leader inspired the followers to do a good job:

> In the past, I think servant leadership is a leader who actually does things, being an example to other people. So that, using less words and doing more action. ... Now I am learning that it's not a servant leadership at all. Of course you can do it by example and other people follow it. ... But in leadership, it's not always that. There are times you do it. That is the servant heart. You do it and others follow it. ... But that's not all. But a leader also has to know how to teach... That is also a gift and skill of a leader. And then you also have to give this, what you call, inspire them, motivator. A servant leader has to have all these three. (Leader G1)

The leaders should understand the abilities of the followers and gradually build them up so that the followers not only grew in the areas in which they were working, but also were stretched in their capacity. The leaders should have an action plan to build up followers:

> We had to address the individual assignment first, the responsibility first, until the person is able to handle [it] very well, without problem[s], constant reminders. Then I can see that he can pick up more responsibility and more work. I push their

capacity. And I always tell them their capacity can be stretched. "It doesn't mean that you only can have this capacity. You can do more than that." (Leader A1)

A leader should have an intentional plan to build up the followers. SIL requires a professional growth plan for all members. A leader could take an active role in helping the followers produce a good working professional growth plan and execute it:

> The leadership that we experienced helped to produce a professional growth plan for us in SIL. And that I think is something noteworthy, something that should be repeated again and again. So that part of SIL leadership is: how can they build them into our members in the new definition of our members; how can they build in plans to bring people into using the gifts that they have, train them to something greater. (Leader H2)

Know and use followers' gifts. To develop the followers, it was important for leaders to understand their gifts so that the leaders could help them use their gifts, and to provide tools for the followers to discover their strengths and giftings. Putting the right people with the right gifts and experiences into the right roles was one of the main components cited in producing satisfactory results and successful people:

> Also challenging in my job is how to help the team people, the players, to be successful in the ways which God has gifted them. We went through Strengths Finder and just looking at their Myers Briggs, this who I am. And we did Strengths Finder, and these are the strengths we have. And then I look at their skill set and their training and their experiences. … How can I use those different skill sets in a good, coordinated way so that we achieve our goals? So each person feels successful themselves. And they are not working outside of their own skill set and feeling frustrated. … There was a pastor once who talked about one Sunday, "Are we so often trying to do things that we are not good at and we spend so much energy, trying to do something that God never intended for us to do rather than just focusing on the things that he gifted for us to do?" And not only are we draining our energy because we are trying to do what we were never intended to do or created to do, but also, the people who were intended to do that aren't having the opportunity to do so because I am in there trying to do everything. And that was a lesson I had to learn. (Leader E1)

Sometimes the followers did not know their own gifts and did not use them as a result. A leader should be able to identify those unused gifts of the followers and encourage them to maximize them:

> So, identifying what the quality of the person is, identifying what are the gifts and skills of the person and how much he is using, how much he is not using. Sometimes they don't realize that. But you as a leader, you can look at the person and see how much quality he has, how much gift he has. Once you identify it, you know, this is actually a talented person, but he's not effective… The reason is he is hiding his talent. He doesn't want to use [it]. He is not confident. Or he is not, you know, it's like you don't realize something. He is not thinking about [it] at all. (Leader G1)

Have Vision

A leader should have a vision and help the followers to understand and own it. A leader should support the work of the followers to accomplish that vision. One leader I interviewed expressed it this way:

> I believe a leader ought to be a visionary and be able to express, communicate their vision. They need to have significant phases of that vision in their mind, and describable. And then I think they also need those that work with them, that have ability to, often somebody who is that visionary may not be the detail kind of person. So that type of a leader needs to have somebody working closely with him or to direct the process to keep things moving, to be so process-oriented that there's a good reading of how this is affecting people. (Leader H1)

Another leader voiced that a leader with a strong vision may have the tendency to become a dictator. He expressed that a leader should listen to followers because the followers were the major resources through which the leader could accomplish the vision. It was important for a leader to balance his vision with his ability to listen:

> But to find somebody that has a very clear vision for where they want to take their organization or the group that they are leading, who also has a very great followership, is very rare in our experience. You either have a dictator or you have somebody that is driven by the polls. But rare[ly] do you have somebody that is a visionary that still has people to follow. (Leader B2)

Another leader explained that, when a leader presents a vision and some followers internalize his vision and follow it, the leader can expect those people to influence others who had not previously understood or agreed with the leader's ideas:

> And I was convinced that—that something we needed to do. I recognized that I needed to support people who were willing to try in very tangible ways, rather than just saying this was a must-do. I found ways to come alongside, to give them support… So it was, how do you deal with it when people don't see things the way you think is the right way to go, and that is to find a way to assist them to make their discoveries about the importance of it. And that has been very satisfying, but slow. It won't go quickly (laughter). It did not go quickly. It has had sustained influence, I believe. (Leader H1)

Handle Conflict

Another important quality a leader has is to resolve, or to help resolve, any conflicts within a team:

> As a leader, it's part of my responsibility to make sure that there's conflict resolution, I mean solved. If there are two people on the team, [and] they are having problems with each other, it's my responsibility to do something to help with that. Or even if it's a conflict between me and someone else, I have a responsibility to make sure that is dealt with. (Leader D1)

Leaders in this study were aware of the need to resolve conflict carefully. One leader said he usually prayed before handling conflicts:

> Lots of prayer first and just [being] very, very careful with words, gentle and lots of quiet time. Just measure the words very carefully. I think it seems like God has blessed me with perhaps an ability to say difficult things and hard things in ways that are perhaps accepted. Doesn't make it easy; it's very hard. (Leader B2)

Even though a leader knew it was her responsibility to settle a conflict, personality-wise, she had a difficult time dealing with conflict:

> But also, she has said, "If you want to tell me something, you just tell me. Don't pussyfoot carefully around it. You just come and you tell me, straight." Well, it's hard for us to do that. We're not Filipinos, we're not Asian, but we just don't like to talk to people and TELL THEM THE PROBLEM (raised voice. Emphasis added; laughter). (Leader B1)

Be a Decision Maker

According to the interviews, one of the leader's roles in SIL is making decisions. In some cases, an SIL leader had to make a decision without enough information and time to consider all the sides of the problem. For that reason, some decisions affected people's lives and work negatively, and so were not popular decisions. No matter how the leader arrived at his decision, one interviewee said he should be responsible for the consequences:

> I would say in some situations, when it is needed, he needs to demonstrate his leadership by making decisive decisions in a timely and responsive way… he cannot always get advice from his office or his clients. There will be times that he's making decisions …and he is willing to bear the responsibility for it. (Leader C1)

Motivate the Followers

Another leadership quality identified by the leaders was motivation. When a leader successfully transferred his vision to his followers, he no longer had to fulfill his vision alone. The followers took that vision as theirs and implemented it:

> It's my baby. I am slowly, slowly getting into realizing it's not my baby. Because of what I see, the vision, or my passion, my dreams becoming their dreams…. You know, now it's their dream. If it's their dream and if it's their vision, they will automatically work because it's theirs. There's not much push or punch needed because now it belongs to them. (Leader G1)

One leader expressed that there were different ways to motivate the followers when they did not see things the same way a leader did. One way of motivating the followers was demonstrating a successfully implemented vision with good results. When followers saw that a leader's vision was achievable, they would follow:

> I will not try to force them to understand, but I will convict them, that they will see, not convict by words, but I will convict by doing. Every one of those who are not supportive, those who are not agreeing with the visions we have, they like to

stand and watch. Once we succeed, then they would say "Oh, that's right." (Leader F1)

Have Holistic Understanding about the Work

One leader expressed that a leader should understand the work from many different angles. His holistic understanding would enable him to implement good policy:

> That [holistic] means he is not just focusing on one point. Let's say, if it's a Wycliffe director, not just say, "I want to recruit." But he must think of recruiting and where to place the person; how to train the person up; how to talk about issues in family life; prepare the person for the actual field situation. (Leader A1)

Task-oriented Leadership Competencies Desired by Followers

I identified 26 concepts emerging from the data related to task-oriented leadership qualities. During the axial coding, those concepts merged into nine themes: have vision and provide directions, develop followers, do not micromanage, have good attitudes towards work, delegate, have administrative skills, solve problems, lead, and make decisions. One concept was dropped due to infrequent occurrence. See Appendix D, Table D6. While leaders considered developing followers the most important task-oriented competency, and having vision as the second most important for leadership, the followers' expectation was reversed.

Have Vision and Provide Direction

The followers in this study considered having vision and providing direction to be the most important task-oriented quality in leadership:

> Sometimes a good leader has a vision for what they want to see accomplished. I think in this organization, there have been good leaders who have clearly expressed or articulated a vision that motivates people to be a part of that, and helps people to see, here is where we are headed. If a leader can't say, here's where we are headed, then you can't achieve that goal. That's not articulated. (Follower D3)

Although followers wanted the leaders to provide direction and guidelines, they did not want leaders to control their projects:

> A leader should give guidelines, and check if the follower is doing well within the boundary... So a leader should check on the follower to see if there is anything he lacks to do his work well. A leader should have a personal interest in the follower and give directions, but if a leader gets involved too much, it becomes over-controlling. How to balance this is the issue. (Follower F10)

One follower was very frustrated when her leader changed the direction of her work many times because she did not understand the reasons behind the changes:

> The people group I work with, they are here in this country and also in the neighboring country. But 90 percent of them are in the neighboring country. They are originally from there. But geographically it's very close and before there were the two countries, it was just one big area. So that I live here, I've never lived in the neighboring country. I just visit there. A couple of years ago, the leaders were telling me, "You should go, move to the neighboring country." And I was very sad because I love the S people here and it broke my heart and I cried. I prayed, I prayed about it and cried but I was willing [and] open to it [moving to the country where the leader wanted me to move]. So some friends of mine were going down to the same area for Christmas. So I went with them. I found some sense of [what it was like] going down there, but it wasn't totally encouraging. And then later on, another time, the leaders were telling me, "You have to partner with the S church denomination down there. You can't work on a translation unless they want one. Even though the S people here want it, you can't do translation just for 10 percent of the people here. You have to go with the church denomination down there." So I tried to partner with them. So I went down there again.... We visited the church leaders and they didn't want a partner. So now they [leaders] are telling me, "Just focus on S here" (laughter). (Follower D5)

Additionally, a leader, who reflected on a situation that occurred when she was a follower, articulated that she was frustrated when the leader did not give her adequate directions and she later realized that the leader was giving her, instead, the freedom to do her work. However, knowing that earlier would have given her a better understanding of how to approach her tasks:

> I didn't know what he expected of me. And so I felt as though for a couple of years, I really was running in a fog, not sure how to get out of the woods. And

that was difficult for me. In the end, it turned out to be that I had pretty much, if I read him right, could have done what I wanted. He would be happy with it. I don't think he had plans for me or goals for me. And he would be endorsing me on what I did, if I could at least give some logical defense for it. So I had never had that experience yet, where I was given that much authority and freedom with very little direction. (Leader E1)

Sometimes a visionary leader did not provide clear directions. When the leader was not able to give proper directions, the followers were frustrated not knowing how to process the leader's vision:

> Coming to my newer supervisor, I probably had the most difficulty under her management style more than any other times. I had very difficulty in understanding and direction. She was a visionary person but knew very little about the actual process to get to where she needed to go, or what we had to do. (Follower E7)

Develop Followers

Like the leaders, followers in this study considered one of the major roles of a leader to be "building up followers:"

> One of the best definitions I have heard of leadership was from a director of Asia Area. He said, "A good leader clears away obstacles from potential heroes in the front line," seeing how he can enable those he is leading to be more successful. (Follower C6)

One follower appreciated a leader who gave followers many opportunities to try their ideas, even though they made mistakes. Trusting the followers and giving them second chances showed that a leader was determined to build them up:

> We have …the director [for one region] and many things he messes up. But a leader never comments on those things. He leaves him at that moment, encourages, he has many occasions, has to give other people opportunities to examine. When I work with him, he doesn't push me. He doesn't make me feel that I've done nothing. (Follower G6)

One national translator shared her story, saying that she did not know much about translation work when she started working in SIL. After ten years, she became a translator and that was a result of her leaders' intentionally building her up along the way. Through that process of her being a translator of her own language rather than having a foreigner being a language worker, the language community had ownership of their own language development and language project:

> They are our mentors. Before, we were still very much slow [to obtain] knowledge about the translation and we were not well-equipped on it. All ideas would just depend on them. All our part before was just to see the naturalness. As the years go by, through all the training and through their mentoring with us, so we learned a lot, little by little until we are able to say that we can do our own analysis and we can do our own exegesis and learn about it. The thing we appreciate about them is, they are always listening to whatever suggestions we are giving to them. Because they respect that we are the insiders and we learn [know] better our language than them. We know when is natural and when is right in our language. …We are doing our translations in every step of translation. We just come to them if there is a difficulty. Their part is just to check what we have done and give it back to us and to see their suggestions. The final decision is still to us, in terms of all the languages. Actually not to us, it's to the people in our community, especially choosing the terms and the structure. (Follower H7)

The followers wanted a leader who knew and used their strengths and gifts and enabled them to maximize their gifts:

> And also it is very important in my mind that he [a leader] knows the gift of God of his team members. If he knows the gift of God of his team members, he knows how to mobilize, how to facilitate the skills and knowledge to use in the team. It's very important. (Follower C4)

The followers specified that a leader handled issues such as government relations for visas and work-related issues, to support the followers:

> One [leader] provides broad guidelines or parameters for which to work in, but also dealing with government relations stuff, someone who does things they need to do so we can continue to have our visas in the country, in other words, interfaces with government leaders and with educational people. And also we have problems at the province level or municipal level. Then he can give us advice on how to approach the problem. So that, to me, that's what a leader is, at least within the SIL context. (Follower B8)

Do Not Micromanage

Historically in SIL, field workers (followers) led projects and their leader supported them in the language development and translation work. SIL's culture promoted independence and the followers usually knew what they wanted to do. Consequently, followers in this study wanted their leader to provide adequate direction but not to micro-manage:

> Some American members in the past complained about certain leaders because they didn't feel that they got enough directions. But on the other hand, micro-managing is also not—I don't appreciate that either. I don't know that they were asking for micro-managing. But I know some complained about certain administrators not giving them enough directions. (Follower D2)

Followers in this study were independent and preferred their leader to enable, not to hinder, them. The followers wanted the leader to give them autonomy and support:

> For me a leader needs to allow us to have a fairly high level of autonomy to work in our project… We need to be able to have the freedom to be able to do what we need to do…. Still we have a pretty good level of autonomy to be able to make decisions on the field without having someone at the top, micro-managing everything we are doing. (Follower B8)

A leader also demonstrated his support by supporting a choice that a follower made:

> A leader is also supportive; by supportive I mean, if I had to make a choice, the leader will support me and the choice. But recently I had to drop my involvement in a project which involved three languages because I was already involved in three other projects. I was bringing myself towards…and it was a hard decision, it took me a long time to come to that decision. But my leader here supported me in that, even though there was a little bit of pressure to continue. (Follower D6)

One follower shared her experience about her supervisor micro-managing her:

Follower E3
> He is very hands on. He wanted things to be his way, so it's like you are confined in a box. So you just have to live with the parameters he set, and you have to be systematic.

Researcher
    What do you mean by systematic?

Follower E3
    Like you have to organize things or do it how he structured it. Like for example, these are step by step. So it's more of, you are confined in a ... system ... you have to follow. You have to be in a certain system you have to follow in order for you to produce the same that you want to accomplish.

Have Good Attitudes toward Work

The followers wanted their leader to have commitment and passion, to take initiative, and to work hard. The followers expressed that their leaders are to be committed to the goal of SIL: "It would be vital for a leader to be committed and to understand organizational goals, vision, and objectives" (Follower G6). The followers wanted their leader to take initiative in work and to go before the followers:

> A leader generally initiates. When I think about a leader, I guess the conceptual metaphor that I think of is like people go on a hike or they are walking to somewhere as a group. And the leader at least theoretically goes first. Anyway the leader is also with the others. (Follower D8)

Delegate

Followers felt fulfilled and appreciated when there was proper delegation with adequate communication. When a leader did not delegate work, or there was vague delegation without communication, followers did not know how to accomplish the work: "He does come with some directives. I am not sure what he wants. He will just drop it.... He has these expectations, concrete things like that I have to pick up on and make it happen" (Leader E1).

A follower working in a national organization had a hard time with work when the work was not her responsibility and when adequate information was not given. Those things occurred many times with her. In this specific situation, the follower was not able to talk to her leader because she was working in a hierarchical culture where there were differences in status, and her status did not permit her to talk to her boss directly:

> Sometimes work is imposed on me without proper information. Even though it is not my work, it's dumped on me (tears). I was not able to talk to my boss about it. There is no way to handle this issue without someone getting hurt. I need to go through a third party. At this time, I don't initiate conversation, not to hurt anybody. If I am older than my boss, I could talk to him. (Follower F2)

One Western follower was working under an Asian leader and observed that this leader did not communicate clearly about delegation. She felt that she had to guess what the leader wanted because the leader took a fatherly role, as if he was in a family. When the leader operated like that, the follower who was from a different culture was confused and was not able to work properly:

> With the situation we talked about before…the leader there was like a father over the family in one sense. And the family was supposed to figure out what his needs were. And so we're trying to figure out, "What are we supposed to be doing?" And if we kind of, wanted to, it was kind of like, "Well, I can do this," or "It's covered." And yet it seemed like we were supposed to be doing something. (laughter) So we were very confused. (Follower F5)

One Western follower working in an Asian country observed that, even though things were delegated, the followers still needed their leader's approval. This enabled people in that country to sometimes use their lack of communication with their boss as an excuse to not work on a project:

> Even if you delegate this responsibility you still can't really act without a stamp of approval by the head. So that makes it hard. At the same time, sometimes, it's a good excuse. You can say, "Oh, my boss does not permit [it]." It's a good excuse for me. I can use that excuse, because many use it all the time. It's kind of a socially acceptable way of excusing yourself from something. (Follower D2)

The issue of delegation was brought up by followers about their Asian leaders:

Four different American followers had difficulty with three different Asian leaders. One

American follower observed that his Asian leader sometimes delegated improperly. One Asian had difficulty with improper delegation in her own country, as described above. It seemed that some Asian leaders did not delegate work clearly.

Have Administrative Skills

The followers in this research specified the administrative skills they desired their leaders to have. One of them was prioritizing because there were many demands:

> There are so many things; we can get involved in the good things. Sometimes we can't be distracted from the goal. Some community come to us, "Can you help us?" It's easy to get sidetracked to those things. Sometimes you have to ask, "Why are you here? What is our organization about? What should we be doing?" So that's a challenge. (Follower C8)

Solve Problems

Problem-solving and mediating were other qualities that the followers wanted their leader to have. There were many different ways of solving conflicts that were noted. One of the ways of solving conflict among followers was projecting common vision:

> I think it's also important for a good leader in SIL to be able to promote harmony within the organization because a lot of people in SIL, translators in particular, are independent people. They tend to do what they like, and that can create a lot of conflicts. So a good leader means to be able to intermediate those conflicts and bring about harmony. Even among people who disagree with each other. And if a leader is quite good, people who would disagree with each other come to work together and agree, because they are focused on the common vision that a leader has presented to them. (Follower H5)

When there was a problem internally in the organization, a leader's role was perceived by followers to be that of mediation, promoting understanding between the people who were involved:

> It was definitely good to have somebody who knows how to bring different people, and different personalities, different opinions, to get someone to be a mediator. So I think in that situation, that's really necessary and it was also good,

somebody not from, in the team, but like my supervisors, and they are not necessarily the director. So somebody in-between, not again in the highest level, that's too inspiring. So for our team, it was just very good to have supervisors [to handle conflicts in a team]. (Follower H3)

The followers appreciated a leader who did not ignore difficult issues but handled them sensitively:

> It's difficult to deal with when there are negative things happening. It's good to have someone who is willing to deal with [them] and who does not just try to ignore it and let the problem continue. But at the same time, he can do it in a sensitive way. (Follower D2)

Direct

One of the followers voiced that a leader should be able to give good direction and lead people toward that direction:

> Someone who gives good direction, sets clear goals that need to be achieved, and motivates people to attain those goals. Sports is very big in my country. I may be thinking of managers and coaches in sports. They lead, but also in business as well. That would be a good leader. (Follower C8)

Another follower added that a leader should keep the followers moving toward the goal.

> I would separate the decision making from actual leading. So the leader really is the one who knows where the group is headed even though the others don't. And one of the important roles of the leaders is to keep the group moving together. (Follower D8)

Make Decisions

Responses indicated that a leader should make sound decisions even though some decisions were hard to make because the decision affected people's work and life: "Making decisions, the leaders who are not afraid of making decisions. Sometimes it's hard, sometimes it's not even popular to some, being decisive and making decisions" (Follower G3). Followers in this study wanted their leader to make a decision after getting their input: "Someone who makes decisive decisions. They get input and advice from other people. They are not making decisions on their own" (Follower H4).

Task-oriented Followership Competencies Desired by Leaders

Just as the leaders articulated task-oriented competencies for leadership, they also expressed task-oriented competencies for followership. Eight concepts emerged from open coding regarding task-oriented competencies that leaders desired to see in followership. One concept was dropped on account of having only one occurrence. After axial coding, four themes emerged: take initiative, be responsible, follow a leader, and have a leadership mindset (See Appendix D, Table D7).

Take Initiative

The most important task-oriented quality leaders in this research desired in their followership was taking initiative. Traditionally, SIL members generally took initiative and were independent in their work because language projects were done by a married couple, or by two single people, and they took on the leadership role in a language project. That kind of working atmosphere pervaded the organizational culture:

> Translators are leaders in their realm. They are independent, making decisions for their project mostly by themselves because they will be the ones to carry it out. They have the responsibility to do what they said they would do. They must be self-motivated, or better yet, spirit-motivated. They control their time and energies. They must be leaders, or they will not get work directed and accomplished. (Leader B1)

Followers in SIL usually knew what they wanted to do with their projects and the leaders did not force them to follow a certain way of doing their work:

> Generally speaking, a lot of the people that I work with are independent, especially Westerners. They have strong ideas about what they want to do and how they want to do it. Historically, it's been that way in SIL. So I approach them

> with, I try not to force them, as much as possible, I would not force them to change their ways. I try to give them some leeway to, as long as they're not making really bad choices, [and] they're not breaking any rules. Give them some slack. (Leader D1)

Taking initiative was related to internalization of vision. The followers who internalized organizational vision as personal vision took initiative without a leader pushing them:

> And then also, we like people to take initiative. When a person with vision, they get the vision and now they know that. Instead of, I will always come and push it, you know, this is my vision now. In other words, organizational vision becomes their vision. If it becomes their vision, the next step is how they carry on that. (Leader G1)

One leader referred to the passage about Aaron and Hul, which I used previously in Chapter 4, as an example of followers encouraging a leader, as an example of taking initiative in helping Moses when the Israelites fought against Amalek. It was not Moses who asked Aaron and Hul, but the followers who initiated the actions of bringing stones for Moses to sit on and helping to hold up Moses' arms (Ex. 17: 8-16):

> The second position is the middle-liner. And to me Aaron and Hul are the people on the middle-liner. They played the role as the team member in the middle-liner. That doesn't mean that they are not important. They are as important as Joshua and those people that go by him. And the key word for this middle liner is initiative. And the rule is making easy time support the leader. Because Aaron and Hul seem like they are sitting and watching. Actually they see something significant, that once Moses' hands are down, Israel loses, but once Moses' hands are up, Israel won. And they took initiative. Moses never told them, "Can you guys help me?" No, he was just doing his work. Praying and lifting up his hands, and these two men watching him, they come and hold his hands. Not only that, but they took the stone and put, the Bible says that they took the stone and put it under Moses. (Leader F1)

Be Responsible

A leader wanted the followers "to be responsible [a leader doesn't have to keep pushing you back or pushing you forward], the person has to be independent themselves"

(Leader A1). Another leader was very frustrated when some followers were not responsible:

> I really don't know how to provide leadership in that kind of a situation... and they don't learn to take their own responsibility. They don't learn how to be their own people. They don't learn to stand on their own two feet. (Leader B2)

Follow a Leader

Paradoxically, because SIL staff tended to be independent and take initiative, it seemed like some followers had difficulty following their leader. Leaders wanted their followers to see the bigger picture beyond their own project and to follow gladly:

> An ideal follower is someone who follows you gladly. I would say, you know, it's not by force, somebody follows you. An ideal follower is following because he likes the way you do things, or he likes the relation, likes the things you do, likes to do things you do. That's what I mean by doing it gladly and willingly. If they are doing it by force, I don't think they are followers, right? The follower is somebody who is deciding, that they have decided, to follow. (Leader G1)

One aspect of the leader's job is casting a vision while the followers *catch* (internalize) the vision and follow. Leaders were frustrated when followers did not see the big picture and did not follow:

> I felt years before that group was ready to move into a new location. I saw a lot of advantages to having people in a new location: largely, making our presence known for the sake of distributing Scripture, being influenced by other groups, and influencing other groups. We even invited people to come up to the previous location from other missions to talk to us. And I was deeply disappointed that our members from the previous location, for their own reasons, could not see the benefits of being in the new location as overriding the benefits of staying in the previous location. (Leader H2)

Some followers were very focused on their project and treated any other work that came to them as extra work or as a hindrance to their real work. When the extra work gave the followers different opportunities, the leaders wanted the followers to understand those opportunities and follow the leaders:

But there are times when it seems like an idea, it's at the right time of development, and you might have disappointment if the group of people that I am working with do not see the opportunity at the time. I tend to be an inclusive person. So I want more joining. We are going to have a prayer group. I don't want to just to be in our small group. I want to get others involved, other missions, and that type of thing. But I think some of our teams are working so hard, that's an interruption, that's a problem where they are socially exhausted. Although I am no extravert, I see importance as to this. And so if others do not catch that and sustain it, that's a disappointment that I have. (Leader H2)

Have a Leadership Mindset

People who had been leaders understood the difficulties of leading a team. Having these kinds of followers on a team made the leader's job easier. The leaders wanted their followers to have a leadership mindset in understanding them:

This is an observation that people who have never been in a leadership position themselves don't always appreciate, or don't necessarily understand the challenges that we face. Recently I was speaking to a group of people. Most of them were not in a leadership position. There was one person there who has had—he's not really in a leadership position now, but he has been in the past. Just from that, different comments people made, it was very obvious to me this guy understood the challenges that I faced. … He understood that, because he has been in the position before. He knows that [with] the changes going on, we have to be flexible, but other people had a harder time with that. So I guess what I am saying is, I appreciate it and it makes my job easier when they have been on the other side of the fence. They understand leadership. (Leader D1)

If a follower had a leadership mindset, he could exercise leadership with his co-workers and to his leader by supporting them:

I read the leadership books over the years. One thing that had an impact on me … is John Maxwell's *360 Degree Leadership.* That's the concept that I try to keep in mind. He talks about how we tend to think leadership is downward: you are leading the people under you. But he points out there are aspects. You can really provide leadership for people above you and people beside you in different ways. So for example, in the way I relate to my boss and the way I do my job. There's a sense in which I'm providing leadership for him, by helping him, by making his job easier. I am not telling you what to do. I make his life easier by the way I do my job. And there's lateral leadership. … And so what I am saying is I am trying to provide leadership in all different directions, helping these other regional team leaders in certain ways, trying to help our area leaders, and make their jobs easier, and the people underneath. It's different types of leadership and different types of involvement, but it all falls in general under the umbrella of leadership. That what John Maxwell says. (Leader D1)

Task-oriented Followership Competencies Desired by Followers

Fourteen concepts emerged during open coding about task-oriented competencies of followership desired by followers. Six themes emerged during axial coding: work hard, follow the leader, be goal-oriented, work together, understand the work, and make decisions. (See Appendix D, Table D8)

Work Hard

The followers considered working hard to be the most important task-oriented quality of followership. Working hard connoted a follower who was capable of doing, and responsible for his work:

> Also capable person and responsible person. A capable person means capable in his area and work. For example, … I am supposed to be capable in finance and also know how to evaluate, …how to analyze data to understand a project. The necessarily skills the follower should have to fill up the role. (Follower C4)

However, an Asian follower expressed that hard work in SIL was less important than hard work in her own country:

Follower E8
    Hard work is less important [in this organization]. Productivity is less important. While in our culture, hard work and efficiency is very important. According to my experience, in this organizational setting, productivity, efficiency and hard work is not as important as in my country (my home organization).

Researcher
    What do you mean by efficiency?

Follower E8
    Like you can meet the target, I mean, you don't waste time. You can use your time well. For example, you don't have to reply to your emails immediately [in this organization]. You can wait. In my country, you usually almost always reply to emails immediately. And also like …a piece of writing, if I am asked to do [that] in my country, I usually have to do that within like two weeks. But here I

can finish that in four weeks. So it's more relaxed, more, yeah, I have more time to do the same kind of job.

Another Asian follower noticed that sometimes when there was pressure to complete a project, work quality was sacrificed instead of personal life:

> Westerners tend to like individual satisfaction, but I want to accomplish things together, group accomplishment. For example, if there is a tight due date, rather than the goal being considered most important, the individual's life is sometimes considered more important [in this organization]. I don't want to lower the standard under high pressure but this organization seems to allow lowering standards for the sake of releasing the tension of the individual. I want an individual to willingly sacrifice some personal things to meet the goal. (Follower E12)

Interview data indicated that some Asians had different understanding of hard work based on their countries. Unless expectations were understood, there was potential misunderstanding about the concept of working hard.

Follow a Leader

The term follower was chosen for this research rather than using subordinate, team member, teammate, or staff. That might have influenced why the term *follow* was ranked high in the task-oriented competencies for followership. Follow could be categorized as a relational quality as well as task-oriented quality. In this research, I categorized it as a task-oriented quality because the data was related more to work than to relational issues.

A follower is expected to understand the directions that a leader suggested and follow their directions to accomplish the work:

> I follow him, probably the same way that I try to get from him the direction we are going. And try to understand what he wants to see happening in our area. And then figure out what is my part in making that happen, how does my department serve the group so that we can achieve the goals that the leader has. (Leader E1)

One follower expressed that followers in general should be careful about whom they follow; do their best to produce results; and help the leader to accomplish the goal:

> I think the Bible actually talks a lot more about following than it does about leading. I think a good follower, first of all, is very careful about whom he follows. In English, if we say a follower, we mean it as an insult. A person would just go along with whatever he is told by anybody. But a really good follower chooses very carefully who his leader is. He considers if this person is a good leader and if they are leading in a good direction. So I think a good follower is careful about the people he follows. I think also a good follower follows to the best of his ability. He doesn't simply go in the same direction but he seeks to assist, he seeks to aid, he seeks to further the goals of the leader that he's following. And I think also that the good follower is willing and able to put aside his own desire and his own opinions and trust his leadership even he doesn't completely understand or agree with what they are doing. (Follower H5)

One American follower expressed that American followers in SIL and its partner organizations have a tendency to not be good followers, because they ask too many questions rather than follow what has been decided upon:

> He [a follower] has to be willing to follow, I mean, the problem with lots of us Americans is that we question too many things sometimes and we are all individualistic so we grow more and more self-centered, you know. We want our way. The leader can't lead. And that's the problem. An ideal follower is someone who is going to be led. Trust the person who is leading them to do the right thing. (Follower B8)

In contrast another Western follower stated that asking questions was important so as not to become "a blind follower:"

> A good follower is somebody who does follow for the things that are clearly set out to do, they are expected to do, but they do them. But also to be a good follower, you have to be prepared to ask questions. If you are being asked to do something and you don't think it's right, I think you need to be prepared to say so. (Follower C5)

One Asian follower expressed that, even though she would give her own opinion, she was willing to follow leader's direction even if the leader's direction was not what she wanted:

I myself understand to work as a team, being a follower. I follow the direction. The wider direction of the team is very important. I will give my opinion and input but I will not insist on my opinion and idea. If I see something where I have another viewpoint or perspective, I will say that instead of hiding it. That's only maybe my attitude, my character only. The important thing is I will follow what they instruct and how they lead us. (Follower C4)

It appeared that there were different understandings about the concept of what it meant to follow. These were both culturally and personally based. Some people wanted to know where they were going before they followed a leader but others were willing to follow even if the direction a leader was taking was not the direction they wanted to go. Unless the definition of follow was understood by a team, it could create tension and misunderstanding.

Goal Oriented

Followers explained that they needed to work for the same goal—not a personal goal, but a shared goal:

It's not doing our own program or our own idea, our own agenda. No, I don't want them just to follow our own agenda, but we all have the same goals. We have the same plan as far as the work goes. So that's what we work together to follow. It's not necessarily that one person is the leader. I mean there are leaders per se but not, he is not the leader who always makes the decision. Everybody has to follow, but the team knows that they all have the same, they are working at the same goal. (Follower G7)

Followers expressed that organizational goals should be internalized:

A follower is usually a responder, and the follower would make the team goals his own personal goals. He would subsume them all, whatever the term will be. A follower would make a good effort to fulfill those goals and would pull his share of the load. (Follower D8)

Work Together

In addition to having the same goal, it is important for followers to do their part with a collaborative spirit because people have different skills:

> The teammates have collaborative spirit to work together, because we know we need each other. It's very important. I can't fill my co-worker's role. (laughter) I can assume that the other person cannot fill my role. We know our responsibilities. Teammates understand their gifts and capabilities, and friendship among us is very important. (Follower C4)

Understand Work

Followers need to understand the work. It is important to clarify the requirements with their leader until they understand their work:

> If a follower doesn't understand something that the leader [said, like] "This is what I'd like you to do" They don't understand. We don't say "I don't know what you mean. Please [explain it to me.]" I think that the follower needs to communicate—"Help me understand what you want me to do, or where we're headed." I think that if they just say, "Well, I didn't understand, so I am not going to do anything." That's not a good follower. (Follower D3)

Followers take initiative in understanding their work and communicate with their leader for clarification:

> A follower needs to understand. So if he doesn't understand, he should know that he needs to understand. And that's where the follower should take initiative to get that understanding. Or even make a correction if information might be given out by the leader that doesn't seem to match the goals, that were agreed upon by the group and if the follower can detect that, he should ask what's going on and either make a correction or ask for clarification. (Follower D8)

Make Decisions

In addition to understanding the work a follower needs to make decisions. If a follower did not make decisions on their regular work and passed that responsibility to a leader, the follower contributed to making their leader a micro-manager: "On the other side of that, though, the follower has to not make the leader a micro-manager. … I need to make my decisions" (Follower B3).

One follower experienced that SIL required her to make her own decision about her project:

Researcher
>In what way does SIL want you to be independent?

Follower H7
>Independent in decisions. For me, learn to be more independent in making decisions. Setting your own goals.

Normally in her own culture, other people made a decision for her. She had to learn to make a decision about her work in SIL.

Chapter 5 Summary

In terms of task-oriented competencies in leadership, both leaders and followers considered developing followers and having vision to be very important. Leaders emphasized their role in developing followers more while followers wanted a leader to have vision. Followers highlighted the importance of their leader not being a micro-manager. Both leaders and followers wanted to have a supportive or an administrative type of leadership with vision in SIL.

While leaders wanted followers to take initiative and to be responsible, followers saw being hardworking, following the leader, and focusing on the goals as being the most important task-oriented followership qualities. Leaders wanted followers foremost to be self-starters, but followers considered executing the work to be the most important task-oriented followership quality.

CHAPTER 6

CHARACTER-RELATED QUALITIES IN LEADERSHIP AND FOLLOWERSHIP

In addition to the task-oriented competencies of leadership and followership presented in the previous chapter, interviewees in this research included character-related qualities as desirable for leadership and followership.

The following character-related qualities emerged from data collected from leaders and followers. Followers explained that their leader should have certain character qualities while leaders did not mention many character-related qualities for followership. Humility was one quality that was desired for both leadership and followership and was addressed by both leaders and followers. Table 4 depicts a summary of character-related qualities for both leadership and followership.

Character-Related Leadership Qualities Desired by Leaders

Four concepts related to character-related qualities emerged during open coding. In the other section, when a theme occurred once, I did not include it. However, I included themes that occurred once in this section due to scarcity and also appropriateness of data. Leaders did not mention many character-related qualities that they thought leaders should have. Humility was mentioned twice, and willingness to learn, being transparent, and having integrity were mentioned once.

Table 4

Overall Character-Related Qualities of Leadership and Followership

	Leader	Follower
Leadership	Humility Willing to learn Transparency Integrity	Personal characteristics Interpersonal skills Work related competencies Background and ability
Followership	Humility Flexibility	Independence Obedience Integrity Loyal Humility

Humility

Two leaders expressed that humility was a desirable character quality for a leader to possess. One leader confessed that he realized there were many things he did not know about working in cross-cultural situations, which demonstrated his own humble attitude:

> Honestly, I would say the experience I myself gain by working here, having to do with all these different partners and even government, university, etcetera, etcetera, help me to understand how to work in a cross-cultural context more and more each day, as well as help me to acknowledge that there is only very little I know and there is much more that I don't know. (Leader C1)

Willing to Learn

When one leader helped nationals to form a board, he had difficulties teaching them to actually function as a board. He studied to learn what was needed to produce a good working board:

Husband (Leader B2)
> I haven't sat on American boards. I've read the books—people, policy, governance— there are lots of boards that just rubber stamp what has already, had taken place, not thinking of the future…

Wife (Leader B1)
> (Laughter) He studied about this for a while and read some books.

Transparency

One leader stated that a leader must be open and transparent. The definition of transparency according to him was to share information openly so that the followers understood how the decision had been made and so that the followers had enough information about their work to do the job:

Researcher
> What do you mean by transparent?

Leader C1
> I would say information is shared openly with staff in regard to what they should know and what they are allowed to know. But by transparent, I don't mean that you share everything. There is information that needs to be restricted and that need to be confined it to either a small group or just those who are in leadership, or even those who are involved in the issue. And so by that I don't mean by being transparent you share everything, but I guess it's defined also on the receptive side. Who this person is working with in the field or hear from him and feel like they have sufficient information to do the job, and understand how the decisions were made.

Have Integrity

One leader stated that integrity was a quality a leader must have, especially in a Christian organization. Integrity to him meant that a leader's actions matched his words even if his actions and words worked to his disadvantage:

> What I admire in him and what I said, first word was integrity or self-discipline. [It] doesn't matter for him whom he is working with and where he is working, and he will be always making stand [for the right thing]. His words and deeds are he is always trying to match up. I've seen in his leadership. People questioning because of where he is making stands and people make questions. And he is not afraid to confront in the way that he knows it could hurt them, but he has to make that stand. I've seen that, and he suffered because of that in his leadership because sometimes people didn't like him. Because of the way he was truthful about what he believed. Which is always, I felt that he was right. (Leader G1)

The above examples gave actual instances where leaders practiced these qualities that they listed as important leadership attributes.

Character-Related Leadership Qualities Desired by Followers

The followers described many qualities related to character that they wanted to see in leadership. Thirty seven concepts emerged from the initial coding (open coding) which I categorized (axial coding) into four themes: personal characteristics, interpersonal skills, work-related competencies, and leader's background and abilities. See Appendix D, Table D9.

Personal Characteristics

Followers whom I interviewed described many character traits that they wanted to see in leadership. Wisdom, humility, honesty, patience, integrity, and a positive attitude were the themes that occurred most frequently.

Wisdom. A leader should be wise in understanding timing and making decisions:

> Leader should know the moment of action…The time of action means this is the time for me to make some decision, but I postpone it to tomorrow. By that habit, I can make a lot of chaos. So the time of action is the wisdom of the leader. It's very, very important in leadership. You need to act, not tomorrow, but today. There are certain tasks but there are certain times you can postpone, just give it more time. (Follower G2)

Humility. Followers valued a humble leader because, they said, that is what Jesus demonstrated:

> Another thing, maybe the last thing, the important ingredient for a Christian leader that I would suggest in this organization is humility. The fact that God can use a leader is the quality of humility that he can find in him or her. Humility and humbleness. Maybe I don't know how to explain that. The greatest example that I find in the example of humility is Jesus. He humbled himself. He was God and he came down. That's why he was able to win many people. (Follower G2)

Although leaders usually attended to high-level tasks of leadership, followers wanted their leaders to be willing to do what was considered a lower-level job because this willingness demonstrated a humble heart:

> A director or whatever, they are usually doing the high-level things, and you wouldn't see the director outside working on the lawn at the center. That would be beneath him, but someone who would have the willingness to do that, I think, is really a neat thing to see. If I see that, that to me makes an impact because I see that person, I say, "Wow, even though he is in this high position, he's willing to do what would be considered one of the lower jobs and it's not beneath him to do that." So to me that shows a real sign of character. So I think that's also a key thing that I like to see in a leader, but you can't expect that to happen when leaders are in positions where they don't really have time for those kinds of things. But just the willingness to do something like that, to me, demonstrates humility. (Follower H4)

Honesty. Six followers identified honesty as an important quality for leadership. One follower noted:

> Honesty makes a leader admit his strengths and weaknesses and more importantly honest to admit in his heart and by action that he can't do it without the help of God and other people. An honest leader is also transparent about his life and shares it to people who are close to him. (Follower E9)

Another follower explained it this way:

> Concerning "honesty", I think I just value this as a character trait and therefore would also like to see it in a leader. A leader is or should be an example to others, and honesty will inspire trust. I know that people in leadership cannot always tell everyone what's going on, and that sometimes they have to be somewhat diplomatic in how they say things. Obviously, one also doesn't want to hurt people. Wanting to be honest will still have to be adapted to the particular cultural one is working in. But one can still seek a way to say the truth in love, or in a culturally appropriate way. (Follower H3)

Patience. Some followers wanted their leader to be patient to the point that if they, the leader, were misunderstood, they did not defend themselves. Instead, they waited for the followers to clear up the misunderstanding: "He is patient, if people speak against him; he is just silent, quiet. It doesn't seem to matter what people think. And those are clear visual examples people can follow. He has [a] lot of patience" (Follower G5).

Integrity. Followers wanted a leader who was a person of integrity, whose action matched his speech:

> I think that a leader will have personal integrity. I think that even if it's in a secular, like a football team or something, a leader's going to have integrity that other people will respect. For us all the more in a Christian context, we desire that a leader has personal integrity and moral integrity. (Follower D3)

Positive attitude. There were ample opportunities for a leader to be discouraged. Having a positive attitude was another good quality a leader should have:

> There is going to be every one of available opportunities to deviate and also to discourage. Because it's almost impossible to meet the expectation of all the people involved. It is also almost impossible to please everybody in the group. So commitment and that giftedness to say, "I know I didn't please them, but I was still keeping on. I am not going to be defeated." Almost every single day there is always something that is going to make you feel like "I really want to quit." (Follower G6)

Interpersonal Skills

In addition to the personal characteristics that were enumerated, the followers wanted the leaders to have interpersonal skills. Fairness, trustworthiness, accountability, selflessness, and being respectful were qualities that were mentioned multiple times.

Fair. Some followers stated they wanted their leader to treat them fairly and objectively regardless of their cultural background: "A leader should not be biased because there are people who are from many different cultural backgrounds. Treat people equally" (Follower C9). Sometimes they recognized that a leader was being unfair by protecting a weaker person rather than trying to see the whole situation objectively:

> In this case he was very much trying to sympathize and take employee's [side], I think it was [an] employee versus member kind of thing. He was always taking

employee's side. And for the national's perspectives, he was spoiling the employees by allowing them to take out loans, large amount. I am not an expert on loans but according to other local people. They led given too much leeway and he was enabling that kind of thing. (Follower D2)

Fairness was mentioned mostly by Asians and Africans. I was suspicious that if the follower's cultural norm was different from organizational culture of SIL and its partner organizations, even if they were treated fairly, according to the organization's norms, they would not recognize or acknowledge it. It was also possible that a leader might not know how to express fairness to a follower in a culturally appropriate way, or it was hard to tell whether or not a follower truly experienced unfair treatment.

Trustworthy. Having a leader that they could trust was considered important: "In SIL it should be a person, you want to be able to trust that person, because it's a Christian organization and we are translating the word of God" (Follower H3).

Accountable. Being willing to be accountable was another important quality a leader should have. A follower observed that a leader might fall away from his commitment to God and ministry if he did not have clear accountability:

> In general and in our context, having clear accountability, for me that comes out of just being on a mission field for a long time, and then seeing the different things happen, with people did not have clear accountability, how many good intentions and good people really go astray in various ways. That's why He made us; we are part of the body of Christ. Accountability to first God, for then also to the people who we lead and that we are serving. (Follower C7)

Selfless. Followers did not want a leader to pursue their own personal interest. One leader observed that another leader sacrificed his family to pursue the right decision: "Even though we as all family suffered by some of the decisions he made, he knew what he was doing was right even though his family suffered by that" (Leader G1).

Respectful. A leader should be respectful: "A leader has wisdom and character and can get respect from all the staff" (Follower F9). When an Australian follower observed how followers treated a leader in an Asian organization, she noticed that the followers wanted a leader whom they could respect and keep distance from: "They are looking for someone who they can respect. Not such a close relationship with a leader maybe, a little bit more distance [between follower and a leader], expectations to respect an elder" (Follower F3).

Work-Related Competencies

The most desired work-related competencies that followers wanted to see in leadership were: leading by example, being flexible, accepting criticism, and having authority.

Leads by example. A follower wanted a leader to demonstrate the work rather than just order the followers to do the work:

> I would add number one, a leader that leads by example. Someone who doesn't just say nice things and say, "This is how we need to work and this is what we are going to do and et cetera, et cetera, and you have great people who work with you." But the fact is a leader that will actually lead by example, of being the first one to step forward and really put himself first on the line, or herself. To me, that speaks very highly of that person. (Follower H6)

Flexible. Flexibility became important when situations changed rapidly:

> Also very flexible. With comprehensive plan, one time with this model, next time it was another model, I mean they are really flexible, trying to adopt, and what fits better. I mean sometimes it can also be frustrating because there is one change after another. But I think it also shows their flexibility and willingness to think outside of the box and accommodate the opinions of other people. (Follower H3)

Accepts criticism. Followers expressed that a leader must be able to accept criticism. The leader should reflect on his own life and work, and the followers could give helpful criticism. A leader should ponder the criticism to see if he could learn from it:

> Another quality as a leader is, a leader should be able to accept criticism. He can accept criticisms for good and bad things that he does. Either way he should be ready to accept it, not just retaliating for people who criticize, but take it positively. What I can ask a leader, I can learn from those criticism, learn and try to better me. Not to retaliating, or pouring out my revenge on the people who criticize me. As a leader, it is the common denominator that I get criticized. (Follower G2)

Also when the things did not work, a leader should accept the blame: "Share glory when the organization is doing well and accept the blame also when things don't work" (Follower G6).

Exercises authority properly. Some followers wanted a leader to exercise authority properly, which comes from experiences and ability: "Someone who's with authority becomes a leader, that'll be great. People who don't have authority are hard to follow" (Follower F11).

Leader's Background and Abilities

Some followers stated they wanted their leaders to have experience in field situations, life in general, and linguistic ability.

Experience. Having field and life experience enabled a leader to identify with followers and to understand their lives:

> One that had field experience already. Then they know what we are dealing with. They have to understand where we are coming from. We said that we want them to have a field experience. For example, our leaders, they have not been the translators but they have experiences. They have been here for a long time. They know about the culture. They know about the unique problems with language projects. They know lots of stuff. So we really feel like we can trust them. Even our director, he hasn't been a translator but he knows what it's like there. So that helps. (Follower B3)

A follower had an easier time following an experienced leader but had a hard time working under an inexperienced leader:

> A leader should be an expert and experienced, but SIL picked a pilot or a teacher to be a leader, who had never experienced the village life. I think they have a position in terms of authority, but it's hard for me to give authority because they don't have experience in what we are going through. So there is a tendency to lead without previous experience. Therefore, it's hard to give authority and respect. I wonder how well this person will lead. SIL selected a young leader, to whom it's hard for me to give respect. …The current leader has vision for the Bible translation, is experienced in many different aspects of village life, is exposed to the foreigners, so I can accept his advice wholeheartedly. I like a leader who is experienced, has many life experiences, and also has a good track record. (Follower F11)

SIL intentionally tried to build up national leaders. In doing so, some inexperienced and immature leaders were appointed. That created some difficulties with followers:

> Since SIL is trying to give leadership to the nationals, the nationals are in the leadership role. But it is hard to work with younger and inexperienced leaders. They ask me opinions but they protect their leadership. If they are experienced and mature, they should have known my intentions. But they only have their level of understanding and tendency of misunderstanding me. Sometimes they cannot make decisions and pass it to others and that was hard. One national leader forgets what I tell him, which frustrates me. (Follower D4)

Linguistic ability. Linguistic ability was considered a good skill to have as a cross-cultural worker, especially with SIL because SIL is a linguistic organization. Learning the follower's language promoted openness and trust between a leader and a follower:

> And they also try to learn our language, when they were very good at our language, and if they use our language, they are more close to me… If they used my language, I feel good to communicate with them and the relationship is very good. (Follower A5)

Character-Related Followership Qualities Desired by Leaders

Just as leaders did not state many character-related qualities for leadership, they only provided two desired character-related qualities for followers: humility and flexibility.

Humility

A leader wanted a humble follower who was teachable:

> I would rather have a humble, teachable person than a brilliant know-it-all with high ambitions for personal success and the abilities to achieve it. It seems to me that often humility comes hand-in-hand with humility and teachableness. Not always, but usually. (Leader E1)

Humility not only impacted the personal relationship between a leader and a follower, it also impacted the follower's work:

> They must be willing to see their inadequacies and be willing to accept help, and not insist on their own way. We have had difficulties with the two remaining teams. Both have had slow progress in translation over many years. Both are resistant to change. One couple becomes angry, talks loudly and visibly stressed out in meetings, but eventually they change. The other couple says, yes, yes, yes, but then there are no actual changes… However, the one couple is spoken of as selfish or stingy, and so their words and actions reflect this to the leader, to the national co-missionaries, and to the language people themselves. (Leader B1)

Flexibility

Flexibility was even more necessary when the organization was going through major change:

> Especially right now, it's important for people to be flexible, to trust their leaders, because there's a lot of change going on. And if you are not flexible, you won't last very long. Because everything keeps changing…We have to be flexible and we have to trust our leaders. (Leader D1)

Character-Related Followership Qualities Desired by Followers

Sixteen concepts emerged in open coding regarding character qualities the followers I interviewed desired to see in followership. During the axial coding they were summarized as five themes: independence, obedience, integrity, loyal, and humility. I removed four concepts that occurred only once during the axial coding. (See Appendix D, Table D10)

Independence

When interviewees talked about being independent during the interviews, being independent was associated with both character qualities and task-oriented qualities. However, I categorized independency under the character qualities because it was more related to character than task in this research.

The reason being independent was valued highly by followers in SIL was related to their work environment. Historically two translators were assigned in a remote and harsh place, and had to manage their life and language work without much help from other people. To survive in that environment people had to be very independent; this is why, historically, independent people were drawn to work with SIL:

> If you are not independent-minded and strong-willed, you won't get here, or you won't get to the field. My home organization seems to be fairly laid back and let you make your own way. You have to be determined to get there… It's easier to do something else, not, if you really don't feel God called me. So people are determined, strong willed. Some places are isolated. They have to be self-sufficient and used to making their own decisions. So they are not used to really someone else telling them to do something... People still manage their own projects. SIL's given a certain amount of independence in that project. I mean that's now changing somewhat. That's challenging. But in the past, it seemed to be a lot of independence about how you did things, maybe because communication wasn't so easy. (Follower C8)

150

Another reason independence was highly valued by followers was because the language workers (the followers) were the experts on their project and their leader was not. They handled their own project autonomously and their leader supported their work:

> In SIL, it's different from most organizations because your supervisor doesn't necessarily know your situation. More often than not, he hasn't even been to where you live. He doesn't know the people that you deal with. He doesn't know the language. He doesn't really know the situation. So it's a different kind of situation than if you are in the same place where you are working in an office and your supervisor is in the next office. It's different. So in SIL, your supervisor is very dependent on what you tell him or her. Because all he knows is what you told him. So we don't want them to be interfering with us much. We want them to be more enabling us. I guess the difference is if you are in the office or the factory, then the supervisor is the boss and you are doing work for him. In SIL you're doing the work for God and you want the supervisor to be there to help you to do your work. In other words, it's a little bit upside down from the normal relationship of the supervisor to a team member. (Follower B7)

Unlike some other organizations, in SIL, followers figured out what needed to be done and reported to the leader of their work. In this way, followers practiced their independence and had freedom in handling their project. Sometimes, they did not feel that they had a leader, or even when they had one, the leader served more as an administrator or support person:

> SILers are given lots of freedom, … they don't have a supervisor always looks what are you doing. So I think an ideal follower needs to have their own motivation and own standard to achieve and to do what our job is. (Follower H3)

Because SIL's organizational culture encouraged members to be very independent, people who were not naturally independent due to personality or culture had to learn to be independent to work in SIL:

> We were brought up like that [being dependent or just following a leader without saying no] so we are applying that way. But there's a difference in a way that they want us to be independent, so we learn also to become independent. The way they train us. But actually we just follow our own culture; we are just like very dependent followers; just listening, hearing, just like whatever they say, we just

follow; because that's our way. But that is not very good [in SIL], you know, you need to give your opinion. Don't say yes and yes. Think about it and you can still say no. (laughter) But learning to say no is very [hard], it really takes time for us. You always say, "Oh, yes, that's okay." Even though it's not so okay [in my culture]. (Follower H7)

Since people took remote assignments, even if they were not language workers, not being able to see the leaders frequently and not having colleagues they could talk with face-to-face necessitated that they work independently:

I can tell it's very different from our culture, not the same. In a multicultural team like that, I feel that the boss expects you to be more active, always taking initiative to do anything. You don't have to wait for the orders. You have to be very independent. And my experience is, for example, I only can see my boss just several, or once every two or three months. So doing that longer period, I have to plan my work ahead myself. I cannot just wait for the orders. Also working like in a, you still have to be working but if you are not, nobody will complain to you. (laughter) Nobody will say no. … Yeah, independent. So far it's the biggest difference I notice from my own country in an office setting, instead of now working remotely. And also in a multicultural team, the only boss I have to report to is my supervisor, and there is no colleague on the same level. So I'm just there and then I have to drive myself to push myself forward. (Follower E8)

Obedience

The next character-related quality the followers thought important in followership was obedience. Since the follower already had made a decision to be submissive to the rightful authority when they joined the organization, they were expected to submit to the authority:

An ideal follower if they are indeed working within the system, and under rightful authority then they would complying with what they are being asked to do… Moving into other relationships, organization-wise, if the person has chosen to become a follower in the organization, they will have already agreed to submit to their leaders, and then it would be their responsibility to follow through on the decisions that their leaders have made. Here again I would hope that the leader would be listening to the follower, but the follower's job would then be to be compliant. (Follower B4)

One Asian follower expressed that he would obey even if a leader went in a wrong direction:

Follower E9
> I think a good follower won't be complaining too much about leadership, about direction, where we are going. So I guess the attitude of being ready, always being ready to be able to serve and looking for opportunities to be able to serve no matter what.

Researcher
> No matter even if a leader goes to a wrong direction?

Follower E9
> Yeah,

Researcher
> In your organization? (surprised voice)

Follower E9
> Yeah, because I believe in submitting to authority. I can always have my own way of thinking. This is the best direction. This is the best way we should be going. But then again, it's just me. God didn't put me in authority. So God takes up someone else. But I can always share my point of view. But then again, I would still have to submit.

Integrity

Integrity was a more important issue with leadership than followership as shown from the data described in the previous section. However, integrity was important with followership too: "A leader should have integrity, so does the follower" (Follower C5).

Loyal and Being Faithful

Followers considered being loyal and faithful important for followers: "A good follower at this organization, like I said, Christ-like character. He is faithful and he is honest" (Follower G3).

Humility

Another desirable characteristic for a follower to have was humility. Some people are naturally humble but some have to learn to be humble:

Follower A8
    Humbleness for everyone, and there will be a different level of humbleness and it depends on the culture too.

Researcher
    What do you mean by 'different level of humbleness?'

Follower A8
    There are people who are naturally humble. There are others who need to really learn to be humble. Sometimes they are forced to be humble. It's not really their personality.

Chapter 6 Summary

Both leaders and followers had similar expectations that leaders would possess both humility and integrity. One difference between leaders and followers on leadership was that leaders identified willingness to learn as an important quality, followers named being fair, leading by example, and being experienced as important qualities to be found in leadership.

Expectations leaders and followers had for followership were very different. Leaders said humility and integrity were the most important qualities for followers to have and would be expressed by followers being obedient to leaders. However, followers expressed that being able to work independently was the most desirable characteristic for the followers to possess. Historically SIL followers have worked in difficult environments in isolation from leaders and from the other colleagues. Followers indicated that self-motivation with integrity was the most desirable quality for followership in SIL and its partner organizations.

CHAPTER 7

SPIRITUAL QUALITIES IN LEADERSHIP AND FOLLOWERSHIP

In addition to the relational, task-oriented, and character-related leadership and followership qualities, the importance interviewees placed on spiritual qualities[1] they expected in leadership and followership became evident from the data collected. This chapter reports the desired spiritual qualities for leadership and followership that emerged from the interviews. It seemed that the priority interviewees gave to spiritual qualities in both leadership and followership was the result of their own Christian faith and how it was embedded in their thought process.

I divided the leaders' data from the followers' data to further analyze how leaders and followers responded to questions about leadership and followership. In the initial interview, the leaders did not mention spiritual qualities for the followers. To obtain data about the leaders' expectations for spiritual qualities to be found in the followers, I contacted the leaders again and asked the following question: "What spiritual qualities do you desire from the followers?"

The major spiritual qualities desired in leadership and followership were very similar. The spiritual qualities for both leadership and followership were based on one's relationship with God, which required an active prayer life. Because of that spiritual relationship one had with God, spiritual fruit would be demonstrated in their personal life, in relationships with other people, and in their ministries. The differences between leadership and followership were related to the role of leaders and followers. What followers desired in spiritual qualities for leadership was more focused on the leader's personal spiritual life, while leaders expected other leaders to understand the spiritual purpose of the organization[2] and to recognize God as the ultimate authority over all aspects of leadership, in addition to having a strong personal relationship with God[3]. Leaders were expected to lead with a vision from God or lead with the direction set by another leader, which should be in line with the Word; followers should obey their leaders because God put their leaders in that position and their obedience demonstrated spiritual maturity. It behooved the followers to examine and decide for themselves if their leaders were in line with God and His Word. Table 5 summarizes the findings of spiritual qualities in leadership and followership.

Table 5

Summary of Spiritual Qualities in Leadership and Followership

Leadership		Followership	
Leader's description	Follower's description	Leader's description	Follower's description
Relationship with God	Relationship with God	Bear spiritual fruit	Person of prayer
Understand God's call for the organization.	Bear spiritual fruit	Relationship with God	Relationship with God
	Person of prayer		
Recognize God's authority			

Leaders' Description of Spiritual Qualities in Leadership

Participating leaders indicated that a strong relationship with God, an understanding of the spiritual purpose of the organization, and recognition of God's ultimate authority were important spiritual qualities in leadership.

Relationship with God

Leaders in this study articulated that leaders must have a good relationship with God in order to lead their teams well in the work of their organization, which is largely spiritual in nature: "Someone [leader] who loves God, who fears God" (Leader A1).

Understand God's Calling for the Organization

Leaders in this study expected leaders to have an understanding of God's call for the organization[4], and be confident of setting direction for the organization:

> When I talk about the visionary, in all networks of the organization, this person [leader] has to be able to express that spiritually. So it is not just one person's ambitious drive to get things done. But it is being done on the firm belief, with lots of support, that this is God's calling for our organization. (Leader H2)

Recognize God's Authority

Leaders working for Christian organizations are expected to recognize God as the ultimate authority. Therefore, leaders at SIL and its partner organizations must recognize that God is their ultimate boss and they must be accountable to God in what they do:

> The things that make that easier, of course, is when a leader is able to articulate honestly ways in which they are responsive to the authority of God. And when that is understood all the way around, it just makes such a big difference. (Leader H1)

Followers' Description of Spiritual Qualities in Leadership

As leaders in this study articulated spiritual qualities in leadership, so the followers in this research also identified spiritual qualities they hoped to see in leadership. Followers wanted leaders to have a relationship with God, to bear spiritual fruit in their lives and in their ministry, and to be persons of prayer.

Relationship with God

Three facets regarding a leader's relationship with God emerged from the followers' data about spiritual qualities in leadership: having the right attitude toward God, seeking or being led by God, and understanding the Word.

Attitude toward God. The followers described the leader's attitude toward God as "love God," "close to God," "have a heart for God," "premium on the relationship with the Lord," and "God-fearing." One follower expressed his appreciation for leaders who had a good relationship with God and sought God in life and ministry: "Within our organization, I have observed that the majority of leaders have a connection with the Lord. I'm blessed by that. They seek God more than anything else" (Follower E2).

Another follower expressed how a leader's spirituality was practiced in his leadership:

> Just as I mentioned before, he should be a person who has a very close relationship with God, like he prays a lot, he knows the teaching of the Bible well so that he could lead the team biblically according to the teaching of God. (Follower E8)

Led by and listen to God. The followers wanted their leaders listening to God in their personal lives as well as in the work they were leading. Without understanding God's leading, a leader could not lead the team in the direction God wanted: "We hope and trust that that person is being led by the Lord really on what they are doing. Personal prayer, because how could they lead us, if they aren't being led by the Lord?" (Follower B3)

A leader must be sensitive to God's guidance and listen to God's voice to serve the body of Christ:

> Listening for God's voice, and knowing that people are part of that, as the part of a body of Christ. It's very different from a secular organization. So you have to listen for God's voice wherever you are leading. And in some ways that's going to look different. You need a person of prayer. It's interesting, it should come out before too, but (laughter) really seeking God again. He's recognizing God's guidance in different ways. All of the guidance has to come from Him. (Follower C7)

A leader should understand God's vision and direction, not be skewed by the worldly business model, but to focus on what God has for the organization:

> I also would like it if I think the person should really always listening to God and his voice, because there are a lot of things that we picked up from the business model that it relies on our own strategies more than what God is going to prevail to us. So I think [an] organizational leader always has to listen to what God has to say because He is the only one that knows the future. The secret things belong to God, both the future and also the heart of man, what other people are thinking, or how people accept the rebukes or correction. Those things all depends on God. We don't have control over the heart of man. So that's kind of my Christian point of view. (Follower E7)

Understand the Word. The followers articulated that their leaders should understand God's Word, believe in God's Word, apply biblical truth to their life, and demonstrate a changed life through God's Word because they were involved in translating the Bible:

> So we think it's important for someone to be competent with in God's Word. And we think it's important that a leader not only knows God's Word but applies it to their life, not just have heart knowledge but to know that it changed their life. (Follower G5)

The followers desired their leaders to learn from leaders in the Bible and to demonstrate biblical leadership in their work:

> As a Bible translation organization, I would say that the leader should be very faithful to the Scripture, because the Scripture gives a lot of qualities that a leader should have. Jesus as a leader, there are many leaders that we can see in the Bible, like Joshua, Moses, and Paul himself as a leader. Timothy was a leader. We can take the leadership qualities from the Bible. That's what I mean. A leader in this organization must be very faithful to the Bible. He should be a Bible-believing leader, a leader who follows what the Bible says. (Follower G2)

Bear Spiritual Fruit

Followers wanted leaders to bear spiritual fruit in their personal lives as well as in relationships with the followers.

In personal life. The followers wanted their leaders to be spiritually mature and to demonstrate godly character in their lives: "But definitely for our organization, [it] requires [a leader] a lot of spiritual maturity, that's probably [goes] first for the most. That's almost given. That's why probably I didn't say that at the first" (Follower E7).

In relationships with the followers. The followers wanted the leaders to recognize God's call on their life because they had received God's call to be placed where they were and were provided funds for their work:

> One [a leader] who really respects the calling of each person, not referring to God called them to do work among the Bugabuga people, that respect the fact that God has called them. God is working in the lives that they have come on a journey to be where they are. So respecting that in those he is leading, in that he is respecting the fact that everyone is a volunteer. They raise their support. They have their church relations. They are sent as missionaries as well and [he is] respecting that. (Follower C6)

Person of Prayer

The followers wanted their leaders to pray for God's guidance about important issues[5] as well as their normal work:

> Well, for my part, I guess the characteristics I mentioned earlier and that individual would have an act of lot of going, walk with the Lord, and be spiritually alive, which would enable them to live out those characteristics that I mentioned. A leader that would maybe, out of conversation, might conclude with, "I would pray about that, would you pray about that?" something like that. And those kind of like that when we had, we call "Updates,[6]" and we would go through our disciplines, and successes, not finish what we planned, all of that kind of thing, program planning, and then commend it to the Lord in prayer, perhaps led by the leader. That seems very natural, for me, being part of this organization, being involved in a fulltime very actively Christian organization. That prayer means a lot. That would be included, or for me for an SIL or Wycliffe leader. That's just, I would assume it's because that is what I would expect from them. (Follower B5)

When the followers detected that the leaders were praying, they were willing to change their perspectives and to follow the leader:

> They were praying with their hands open and just earnestly seeking, whatever God wants. It's okay, we can agree with our leaders if we change our perspective. We're willing to have our perspective changed. … So we were praying, in our view, with a humble attitude, that was willing to have our hearts changed. And our leaders were telling us that they were also very much praying about the situation. (Follower B2)

Followers wanted leaders to pray for what they were going through in personal life and in ministry: "She always listens to us, when we talked about ourselves. She always listened and prayed for us" (Follower A5).

Leaders' Description of Spiritual Qualities in Followership

Leaders noted that, without faith, it would not be possible to be involved in the work of SIL and its partner organizations, and without spiritual maturity, the followers would not be able to grow in their spiritual life. The leaders stated that the spiritual maturity of the follower was demonstrated by bearing spiritual fruit[7], and the follower should have a relationship with God.

Bear Spiritual Fruit

The leaders articulated that followers should bear spiritual fruit in relationships with leaders and the people they were working with. They should demonstrate mature behavior, and grow in understanding themselves through other people's feedback.

In relationships. Spiritually mature followers demonstrated their maturity by following a leader:

> I would say that a good follower needs to have spiritual maturity in order to recognize the importance of following the leader. People who are not spiritually mature don't realize or maybe don't accept the fact that they need to follow their leaders. In an organization like ours, it just doesn't work if people want to do their own thing and not follow the leaders. Sometimes, though, the leader is not a good leader and is hard to follow. Again, it takes spiritual maturity to recognize that we still need to follow the leaders in a way that helps them to lead well. (Leader D1)

Spiritual maturity in the followers resulted in good relationships with a leader:

> I would of course enjoy spiritual maturity in followers, and find them to be easier to work with because they already have the self-discipline to set aside personal ambitions and seek success beyond their own personal goals. They would take instruction and correction better than others, I suspect. All things being equal (talent, training, experience) I would choose a spiritually mature person over a lesser one, to be sure. ... Even if they are spiritually immature [if they] at least have a desire to grow spiritually and will therefore be moldable, I believe I could help spiritually immature teammates to grow as we work together. (Leader E1)

Spiritually mature followers became a good role models to the people they were ministering to. Otherwise, their work and their relationships were impacted in a negative way:

> They must display spiritual and mature character towards the culture whom [which] they are serving. They should be an example of a Christian role model... It takes great spiritual and mature character to put aside one's own plan and to try a new and different plan, especially if the ideas come from non-translation people.

Translators must be followers of the Lord. He is the One who has placed them in this environment… If only they could see what their lives reflect, and are actually hurting the cause of Christ in their long time language assistant, rather than kindly drawing him to the Lord. (Leader B1)

In personal life. Spiritually mature followers demonstrate mature behavior in their lives, and produce the fruits of the Spirit:

In fact, if they are spiritual and mature, they would know how to conduct themselves and address the issue in a mature manner. If the follower is spiritually strong and close with God, they know they would be accountable to a higher being and hence speak and act appropriately. They would exhibit the gifts of the Spirit and be patient and not be quick in provoking an argument. (Leader A1)

Spiritual maturity based on one's identity in Christ was the single most important quality for both followers and leaders to grow in many aspects of life:

I would say from my experience that the single most important quality for both followers and leaders relates to spiritual maturity. A person that does not grasp his identity in Christ is simply not secure enough to be a learner, to be able to recognize ways in which he or she could have handled a situation differently...the impetus and will to offer an authentic apology and ask for help from the LORD and others to handle a relationship or situation in a better way also relates closely to maturity. The input from others may give insight into cultural sensitivities, but the willingness to modify one's interpersonal style relates to spiritual maturity. (Leader H1)

Relationship with God

As a Christian worker, the follower was expected to have a relationship with God: "Somebody who is struggling with the faith try to engage in the work, and I think very soon we'll lost [lose] shared value, and they just want to get the work done, but not focusing on Christ-centered ministry" (Leader C1).

Follower's Description of Spiritual Qualities in Followership

Not only the leaders had an expectation of spiritual maturity for their followers, but followers also wanted other followers to have a prayer life, to have a good relationship with God, and to bear spiritual fruit.

Person of Prayer[8]

The SIL follower pray for the leaders and the organization, and practice corporate prayer.

Pray for the leaders and the organization. The followers pray for the leaders, because they were given an important task:

> I think part of the ideal follower is to pray for their leaders. I think that's really, really important.... Also, the leader's going to pray for his follower. There's mutual prayer but I think particularly for the followers because leaders have the key roles in setting the goals, and vision, and interacting with the high level officials and things like that. I think especially for the follower. It's to pray for the leaders is the part of ideal role of the follower. (Follower D3)

The followers prayed for their leaders and tried to discern whether the leaders were going in the correct direction:

> We prayed every morning about this: "What do you want, God? What is your will? How would you use us?" And it was very difficult because the Bible says, obey your leaders, respect your leaders. God puts the leaders there. And so are we supposed to obey God's rule that we should obey this person up here? Or is God giving us a different message and we should not listen to him (laughter)? (Leader B1)

The followers also prayed that the leaders would make good decisions, and for the organization as a whole, and for fellow workers:

> A good follower would be prayerfully praying for the leaders, for the organization, and also for the staff, for the whole organizations. Good followers would have a heart to serve God and the leader. We are different attitudes. We are different characters. We are different culture. And that will not be a hindrance to following the leader because sometimes you will frustrate, or upset about the

attitude of some of your co-followers, but it will not be a hindrance to serve the organization, but it will be tools to serve more. And pray more for the team. (Follower E6)

The followers prayed for their work because they were working in a Christian organization:

If the team is from Christian background, they should start to work with prayer. I've never work[ed] with other organizations. When I start[ed] my career, I just joined SIL members. I like them very much, understand the work, started with prayer. (Follower A5)

Practice corporate prayer time. The followers were actively involved in corporate times of prayer to encourage the people they work with:

We also have SIL meetings to worship together and pray together. That's also a part of the team in terms of SIL. Our SIL culture, it's good to worship together and pray together. It's part of the body of Christ. Most of us are part of the local churches but also another body of Christ to pray together, carry each other's burdens. (Follower D3)

Relationship with God

Followers stated that recognizing God's authority[9] and honoring God in relationships were expressions of having a relationship with God.

Recognize God's authority. Followers recognized God's authority in the position they are in: "I was obedient to God's push. ... He asked me to come and work and I obeyed. Obedience to God's call, and God's leading that brings happiness in me" (Follower G2). Followers acknowledged God's authority by serving God with a ministry that was in line with God's Word and being diligent in the work:

As we believe in God and we are serving God, we will be in tune with what the Bible says. Like for example, this project requires this, and it's consistent with God's Word. Or what God is saying then for me. That's a good SIL follower. Someone who is accountable to God, and who is serving God above anyone else. (Follower E2)

The followers acknowledged a leader as having God's authority: "If somebody is in the leadership position, we have to trust that God put them there and we need to submit to him out of reverence of Christ" (Follower D5).

Honor God in relationships. The followers identified that honoring God first would provide the basis for a good relationship with a leader:

> The person should have a heart that seeks to honor God first. Because if that would be your motivation, then it's going to be easy to follow your leaders. It's like looking at your work and seeing God as your big boss, so that even if your boss is not around, you would still perform at your best because you know that there's someone who sees what you do. (Follower E3)

Having good relationships with fellow followers from many different cultures would honor God:

> Because especially with our department set-up, we are really diverse in culture. Plus the fact that we have different backgrounds, plus we are diverse in personality. So if you put that together, it's kind of messy in a way because there are instances that you may not intentionally want to offend people by your action or by your words or by your working style, but you are just wired to it. But you will try to be less offendable, you would not take things personally, but you will try to see how Jesus would look at things if Jesus is in my position, how would He treat this person. I think that's the ground for people to be more understanding, to be giving mercy to other people, and try to work things out, so that we come up with something that will honor God. (Follower E3)

Bear Spiritual Fruit

The followers could demonstrate bearing spiritual fruit in their relationships with team members and in the work they were involved in.

In relationships. A close relationship with God brought unity among team members: "If we are close to God first, then we have harmony, but if work is the first, not God first, it maybe is separate" (Follower A3).

In work. Interview participants wanted to serve in unity:

> We bring to the table all the best that we can offer to God.... We met just two weeks ago, and it's beautiful like, you know, this is God's team like. This is how God has been envisioning it like, no barriers, no labels but we are all together. We want to serve God with our best. So that for me is a good working team. I am not saying my department is perfect but for me the way we have been working together: we have disagreements; we have difficult times but we pray and we seek God about it; and we go through that together; and you never feel that you are alone. (Follower E2)

Chapter 7 Summary

The spiritual qualities for both leadership and followership were identified in the following areas:

1. Having a relationship with God

2. Being a person of prayer

3. Bearing spiritual fruit in relationships and in ministry

People in SIL and its partner organizations desired to be used by God in their work or felt called by God in their involvement with the Bible translation ministry. Therefore, the spiritual aspects of their lives were connected to their Christian identity and the work they were doing. Whether one was a leader or a follower, it was assumed that he or she would have spiritual vitality in his or her life and ministry.

One thing that stood out was that the leaders did not mention spiritual qualities of followership during the initial interview. It may be that leaders simply assumed or forgot to mention the spiritual aspects of followership, but it also could be that spiritual qualities were desired more for leadership than for followership in general. The spiritual qualities were discussed when I contacted leaders for the second time.

---

[1] Spiritual qualities in this research means any qualities resulting from having a relationship with God.

2 One of SIL's goals is to translate the Bible into languages that have no translation. Because SIL considers the Bible to be God's Word, SIL's existence has a spiritual element and purpose.

3 Acceptance of Jesus as one's own personal Savior and Lord is the beginning of a relationship with God. Christians communicate with God through prayer and by reading the Word of God.

4 SIL believes that all men are created equal under God, so everyone should have God's Word in their language. SIL exists to meet this need, so that God's grace and mercy can be manifested through His Word. Understanding God's call for the organization involves understanding the unique roles in the organization and the methods needed to solve specific social needs.

5 Important issues of SIL are related to major decisions regarding the organization. Sometimes they are personnel issues such as placing people in the right places; sometimes they are strategy issues such as how to go about doing the work; and sometimes they are about how to form partnerships in order to accelerate the work.

6 "Updates" was a regional quarterly meeting of SIL Philippines to keep people to be updated with various projects in the region.

7 The Holy Spirit dwells in a Christian's life and produces fruit. Galatians 5:22-23 lists the fruits of the Holy Spirit: love, joy, peace, patience, kindness, goodness, faithfulness, gentleness, and self-control.

8 A person of prayer in this research means someone who communicates with God through prayer.

9 The Bible indicates that all authorities in the world are approved by God (2 Peter 2: 13-14). Therefore, SIL Christians believe that God is the final authority for their work and they are under His leadership.

CHAPTER 8

CULTURAL INTELLEGENCE IN LEADERSHIP AND FOLLOWERSHIP

The preceding four chapters examined the relational, task-oriented, character-related, and spiritual qualities of leadership and followership which were mentioned by the interviewees. In addition to those qualities, as I analyzed the interview data, the ability to understand and work well in a multicultural environment, defined as cultural intelligence (CQ) qualities in Chapter 2 emerged as well. This chapter reports the CQ qualities of leadership and followership that the interviewees in this research articulated.

It is important to note that I used the same questions that were used for Chapters 4 to 7, and did not ask the interviewees specific questions about CQ. During the initial interviews, the leaders did not mention what CQ qualities they desired in followership. I did a followup interview with the leaders and asked the leaders the following question in order to collect the CQ data on followership: What cultural abilities do you desire for a follower to have?

Three major categories of CQ qualities emerged from the interview data as desirable in both leadership and followership: cognition qualities, behavior qualities, and an indefinable something that I decided to label *cultural savvy*.

The primary qualities in the cognitive dimension were cultural understanding and cultural sensitivity for both leadership and followership. The key element in the behavior dimension was communication for both leadership and followership. The leaders and followers desired to communicate in culturally appropriate ways. The qualities I labeled cultural savvy pertaining to both the cognitive and behavioral dimensions were different for leadership and followership. Table 6 summarizes the CQ qualities in leadership and followership.

Leaders on CQ in Leadership

I analyzed leaders' CQ data and three categories of CQ qualities emerged: cognition, behavior, and cultural savvy. Table 7 summarizes the findings of CQ qualities in leadership desired by the leaders.

Cognition

As leaders in this study faced challenges of comprehending cultural differences, they identified three CQ qualities that leaders should have in the cognitive dimension: understand culture, understand cultural similarities, and open-mindedness in understanding culture.

Understand culture. Leaders shared their struggles of not understanding the cultures of the followers. One American leader in this research shared his challenges of not being able to understand Asian colleagues: "I don't know if you're going to ask later about Asian style, but that's different, because we don't always know what our Asian colleagues are thinking. I'm not saying that's right or wrong. As an American that's a challenge" (Leader D1). Another leader had a chance to learn about multicultural team issues in the previous year, which was helpful to her, but she expressed that it was still hard for her to comprehend cultural differences:

> Every time I have a meeting with one of my followers, while I am in a meeting, I'm praying to God, "Open my brain to understand what he is trying to tell me

Table 6

Summary Chart of the Cultural Intelligence Qualities of Leadership and Followership

	Leaders	Followers

Leadership	Cognition
	  Understand culture
	  Understand cultural similarities
	  Open-mindedness in understanding culture
	
	Behavior
	  Communicate through a third party
	  Communicate in direct/ indirect way
	
	Cultural Savvy
	  Understand and respond to team dynamics
	  Be a cultural mediator
	  Promote cultural strengths
		Cognition
		  Understand culture
		  Have cultural sensitivity
		  Consider other cultures
		
		Behavior
		  Demonstrate proper behavior
		
		Cultural Savvy
		  Leader's cultural background and ability
		  Cultural learner
		  Cultural adaptation
		  Attitude toward culture

Followership	Cognition
	  Understand culture
	  Have cultural sensitivity
	
	Behavior
	  Communicate properly
	
	Cultural savvy
	  Danger of misusing culture
	  Overcome cultural weakness
	  Seek cultural maturity
	  Cultural advantage
		Cognition
		  Understand leader's culture
		  Understand colleague's culture
		  Understand organizational culture
		
		Behavior
		  Communicate properly
		
		Cultural savvy
		  Have cultural ability
		  Attitude toward culture
		  Promote cultural strengths
		  Be a cultural mediator

Table 7

Summary Chart of Leaders on Cultural Intelligences in Leadership

Cognition	Behavior	Cultural savvy
Understand culture	Communicate through a third party.	Understand and respond to team dynamics
Understand cultural similarities	Communicate in direct/indirect way.	Be a cultural mediator
Open-mindedness in understanding culture		Promote cultural strengths

right now because I am confident this man is really very smart. He's got a lot of wise things to offer to me to hear. But I'm not understanding why he's telling me the story right now. I am not seeing how it fits into the topic we are talking about. [God,] Help me to understand." I only know that because I learned about high context and low context last year at the multicultural team workshop. Otherwise, I would be sitting there going, "What on earth are you talking about? I asked you [follower] this question, and you are telling me this story, and I am not seeing at all." Well, now that I even know that, but it still doesn't make it easy. I still don't understand when I asked him [follower] about this and he told me that. And I am thinking, "Okay he's doing his high context thing, but I still don't see the connection." So just knowing that is not enough. It's so hard to get down below that and to understand. It's one thing to know things, but to live differently with that knowledge is very hard. Very hard to do. You just have to marvel at the whole body of Christ thing. "Wow, God. What were you thinking? (laughter) How do you imagine unity of the body of Christ? I mean look at us, we are a mess." It's a miraculous thing (laughter). (Leader E1)

SIL leaders often communicated and worked with partner organizations and other SIL entity leaders and department heads. They also communicated with government officials, researchers, and local SIL staff members. The leaders had many layers of cultures to work with and to understand: organizational cultures of different geographic areas, internal subcultures of certain groups they were working with, local contexts in which they were working, and different cultures that their followers brought. This created a complex mix of cultures that the leaders needed to understand:

> Since SIL is becoming more and more multicultural, there is no way that a good leader, no matter in what setting of SIL, can work without the consideration of being able to understand different cultural contexts, and different ways of people from different cultures—how they perform and function. Like what to do in a meeting, whether you ask them to give you input or allow them to volunteer their input, or what does it mean by, when people are trying to say no without saying so. How far can you push, and ask verification or you just have to face on your experience and knowledge and take that as a no before you make a wrong decision. And there are, on the other hand, internal subcultures of our own organization, not to mention overall as an organization, even in different areas, like working in Asia might be very different from working in Africa, South America, or in Dallas. So as a good leader, I think, you also need to understand the local context of our own groups. Each unit will be different. (Leader C1)

Understand cultural similarities. Member of different cultures exemplified different idiosyncracies. In general, Asians were sensitive to people's facial expressions or unspoken words. One leader pointed out that Asians had more cultural sensitivity and Asians understood other Asians better than Westerners: "The cultural sensitivity as an Asian will be stronger than a Westerner. We can sense how other Asians think or speak. It is harder for a Westerner and they tend to be missing the 'blind spots'" (Leader A1).

One leader expressed difficulty with working in a similar but different cultural setting. In this case, an Asian leader was working in an Asian country different from his country. He knew what he could do and what he could not do because he understood the cultural expectations of that culture. He limited himself and did not cross boundaries in terms of what was expected. Understanding similar culture did not make him easy:

> I think the hierarchy system is the hardest. It is the cultural thing. Because I am an Asian, I know that [there are] certain boundaries—I can do and I can't do... I know that if I step out of my boundary, and do things, I could affect [our] relationship. And it did affect [our] relationship. (Leader A1)

Open-mindedness in understanding culture. If a leader is working in a multicultural environment, he should be open to other cultures, so that people from various cultures would feel included and their leadership styles affirmed:

> I see more and more people coming from different cultures engaging in leadership, and especially when we try to encourage that, we as an organization need to have a more open gesture of embracing different ways of leading and following rather than just work only. We might say we embrace all different cultures and hope that some of them can be in the leadership, but at the end when we carry our responsibility and try to function very easily, we'll look back to our own culture because that's where we are comfortable. So I think we need to have a more open gesture, not just saying but willing to respond to people behaving in different cultures and taking it with grace and trying to understand what they are trying to do. (Leader C1)

Behavior

One leader I talked to had the experience of being treated as if he were invisible when his status was lower than his counterpart in an Asian context:

> As a young Asian leader it was very difficult to access to the most senior national leaders in this Asian country, very difficult. They will not entertain you if you are in those meeting. I had an incident with a very senior national leader, a director of this national organization. He didn't talk to me at all. I am like irrelevant to him. When another Wycliffe director older than me, Asian too, came, he shook his hand, and he invited him to speak in church. That frustrates me a lot... I tried to communicate with you [the national leader], I show respect to you and all that. I do everything. He tries to prove, to say that I am this level; you are this level. (showing the high and low level with his hand) You play the hierarchy game. That is the culture in this country, very strong. (Leader A1)

Communicate through a third party. The leaders in this study identified communicating through a third party and communicating directly or indirectly as the desired CQ qualities in the behavior dimension. There are various ways to communicate in a cross-cultural environment. One leader stated that some Asians communicated by action rather than verbally when they disagreed with a leader. This leader used a third party both to understand the nonverbal communication and to respond:

Leader A1
> In this Asian organization, no, they don't [disagree with a leader]. (laughter) They will show it in action. So you must find your resource, feedback from another way...

Researcher

    How do you get the feedback from your Asian followers?

Leader A1

    From another person, the third party.

Researcher

    After you got feedback from the third party, how did you approach the issue?

Leader A1

    When I knew about it, I would try to talk to the person individually, not in a group. If we do realize that it's a big issue, it has to be done by another person too, someone who is more middle ground.

The same leader indicated that if a leader was younger in a hierarchical culture, he should bring a third party to communicate with an older leader:

> The other challenge is, always be a hierarchy system. You respect the elders, leaders who are older. And then it was very difficult because we couldn't, we have to be very tactful [about] how to address issues in that high level. So you need to know how to go about bringing a third party in to mediate, things like this. (Leader A1)

Another leader expressed the benefit of using and getting help from a third party when he did not understand the situation:

> In both of those cases the solution, which was basically the same, was to get help from a third party. I have done that with multiple occasions with Asian members where I got help from a third party or insider or someone who understood better… So the third party cultural insider has always been helpful. If you are asking, what in the future, how to make that easier, I would say involve the third party from the beginning. For my part, if I know or if I expect that I'll run into a cultural barrier, it would be helpful to get some help from the very beginning, just to alleviate that. (Leader D1)

The same leader suggested using a third party to deal with conflict when open communication was not possible or culturally inappropriate:

> Actual methods [of handling conflict in cross-cultural situation] are varied. Again, I think open communication is the best way possible. But if that is not appropriate for one of the people involved, I have to go with the third party thing. (Leader D1)

Leaders were expected to communicate properly in cross-cultural situations. Involving a third party brought many benefits like communicating without losing face, leveling status, and handling conflict.

Communicate directly or indirectly. Leaders should know when to be direct or indirect in communicating with followers and behave properly according to the situation:

> One of the challenges that just keeps recurring is to find the balance between being straight forward and saying what you know needs to be said. And then to be able to interpret how that's being responded to. I think I am getting better then I realize that I am not (laughter). I have an Asian friend saying "Please be straight forward with me. And I can pick up this. I want you to be." And then when you do and even when you feel like you being gentle, really gentle, there is defensiveness. But I think I do that in my own culture too. So I don't think it's just Asian. But there's comes to a point of not knowing how to sort out how straight forward to be and then how to follow up a conversation, when you needed to be straight forward, that proves that you are still a friend, that you still respect and appreciate. (Leader H1)

Cultural Savvy

SIL leaders in this research identified four CQ qualities that pertain to cultural savvy dimensions: understand and respond to team dynamics, be a cultural mediator, promote cultural strengths, and have cultural flexibility.

Understand and respond to team dynamics. If the leader's team members consisted of people from many different countries, the leader should understand the dynamics of a multicultural team and should be able to respond properly in a multicultural situation. One leader who I interviewed expressed difficulty in understanding many different cultures and in behaving properly when he was leading his own team:

> It's really hard when you put the cultural side on top of that. Because it's very different in everyone. Just across Asia, all the different cultures in Asia, it's very, very different. And trying to figure out for me now being a leader, trying to figure

out how to appropriately connect with each people on my team different cultures they are to insure not being culturally insensitive but still needing to get the work done needs to get done. (Follower H6)

Knowledge was not enough, but action should reflect that knowledge: "Understanding multicultural team dynamics is difficult. We don't know what we don't know. Knowing is one thing but living by understanding is another" (Leader E1). Therefore, the leader in a multicultural environment must be able to understand cultural differences and act properly according to the values of the cultures they are dealing with.

Be a cultural mediator. One leader observed the communication between two of his followers, an older American and a younger Filipino. He realized that the younger Filipino follower was not able to say what he wanted to say to the older American follower because it was not culturally appropriate for a younger Filipino to express different opinions to an older person. When the leader saw this, he communicated to the older American follower what the younger Filipino follower wanted to say:

> One of my Filipino followers is perceptive enough. He will know what the old American translator really wants. And so he will make the right decision based on what he knows, in response. We have to interact sometimes. And so in one case, like my wife was talking about, we knew that he [the American] was really going to put my follower [the Filipino] in a difficult spot. But that old man was not picking up on the cues. And so I had to interfere and tell him straight in an email, and say, "What my follower cannot tell you because of culture, I will tell you." And so I told him straight what the real story was, and said, "This is really how my follower feels, even though he can't tell you that." And immediately this older guy, he capitulated and said, "Okay, then we'll do it this way." Because then he knew what the real story was, that he wasn't hearing from my follower because my follower, culturally, couldn't tell him. But he could tell me. So I could intermediate. (Leader B2)

When necessary, leaders acted as cultural mediators to smooth relationships among the followers, to prevent potential conflicts, or to bridge different cultures among the followers.

Promote cultural strengths. An Asian leader who had ample experience working with Westerners expressed that there were ways to incorporate cultural strengths both from the East and the West:

> Yeah, maybe because I'm from an Asian country, but very westernized in the way we do business. I'm in between; I've seen the East and the West. I've seen how a certain culture in the West has helped the society develop, push forward for the good. I've seen also the East culture, how good it is to maintain it so that we don't go back to corrupt society... So try to marry the two together. (Leader A1)

Followers on CQ in Leadership

Followers stated that they wanted a leader who was "able to work cross-culturally" (Follower D5) and "someone who had very good intercultural skills" (Follower A8). Followers wanted the same three dimensions of CQ qualities in leadership as the leaders wanted: cognition, behavior, and cultural savvy. Table 8 summarizes the CQ qualities that the followers desired in leadership.

Cognition

Followers wanted their leaders to understand culture, to have cultural sensitivity, and to consider other cultures. The data articulated by the followers was very similar to that of the leaders in cognitive qualities of CQ.

Understand culture. It was important for a leader to understand cultural dynamics because SIL and its partner organizations are very culturally diverse:

> It's a very complicated environment here. With different expectations from different cultures and groups, and the dynamics are slightly different. A person working in this organization, I think understanding of cross-cultural dynamics is really important. The expectations from each of the cultural groups, that understanding is really important... The leader needs first to understand the cultures, and the backgrounds of the groups involved. (Follower G6)

Table 8

Summary Chart of Followers on Cultural Intelligence (CQ) in Leadership

Cognition	Behavior	Cultural savvy
Understand culture	Demonstrate proper behavior	Leader's background and ability
Have cultural sensitivity		Cultural similarity
Consider other culture		Exposure to different cultures
		Cultural learner
		Cultural adaptation
		Attitude toward culture

One follower stated: "My leader knows my culture, which is very important" (Follower A3). Another follower said a leader should be someone "who can understand you even culturally" (Follower G4). Another follower appreciated that leaders made an effort to understand her culture: "And they [leaders] tried to understand other culture. They cared for other people's culture" (Follower A5).

Be culturally sensitive. Followers wanted leaders to be culturally sensitive: "First of all, someone [a leader] who understands multicultural situation, aware of and be sensitive to that" (Follower D7). In other words, leaders needed to learn to be sensitive to nonverbal expressions: "The other one is also to learn to ask and learn to be sensitive, sensitive not just whatever he hears. He needs to be sensitive on the facial expressions" (Follower H7).

A follower who was from a minority culture of the organization expressed that a leader should be sensitive enough to care about people from the minority cultures of the organization: "In SIL somebody [a leader] normally from North America, I would expect to be a person who is sensitive to cross-cultural settings, but not fake, sincerely care of this section of the organization, I mean, the international members" (Follower H9).

Consider other cultures. Due to the cultural differences in a multicultural environment, there were different cultural norms practiced:

> Now I am thinking a little bit cross-culturally, I am an American and I know the majority has in the past been Americans. Lots of Koreans now (laughter). But I know that it will be easy for just thinking in our own culture all the time, and so the leader needs to really think about other cultures the way things are now, which is a big job. (Follower B3)

When a follower's culture was not taken into consideration and they were treated differently than the dominant culture of the organization, the follower was hurt and felt misunderstood. It seemed to her that Westerners in SIL wanted her to relate to the people on the field as professionals, but she related to them as family members because of her cultural background:

> I guess that was real cultural, I think that, SIL, Americans, or the Westerners, there's not really understanding that I value our relationship with the people. Because I am treating them like my family and they treat me like family too. So when I get upset and when I scold them, in the sense, when they do wrong, it is in the capacity of a sister. I am training them in doing things correctly and all these things. So (sniffling) but I guess SIL concept is that I have to be there as a professional. (Follower B9)

Behavior

People demonstrated their cultural norms through their actions. Actions that are considered proper behavior in one culture may bring about a different reaction in another culture. One follower stated that the practice of her leader's cultural norm was a surprise to her and made her uncomfortable: "Americans put a high value on transparency. To keep his transparency, he copies some emails to people when I wanted to keep it private" (Follower D4).

One follower watched a leader handling a very difficult issue in a culturally appropriate way:

> In one case there was some wrong doing involved in the part of the staff member, and at least the way I heard it. There was some very harsh words spoken and a lot of anger and he [staff member] just left.... He [the leader] was concerned not about making everything public, and getting his staff member in trouble but about trying to make the relationship good again, and save face, which is very important here in this country and other Asian cultures. He was concerned about that even if it meant loss of money or loss of some other things that were less important to him... he was concerning about maintaining the relationship with these people, the personal relationship even though organizational relationship ended up being broken off. That was a real value to him. (Follower F6)

Another follower observed a leader who respected the local culture and behaved properly to the point of putting his life in danger:

> Yeah, he amazes me on how much he [the leader] can bear. Yeah, I think from the depth of my heart, not taking because he is my boss or what. I recommend him; I think he has good understanding of all these things. I traveled with him to Ghana, on the third day; he was admitted to a hospital because of food poisoning, because of eating. Over the couple of days we were visiting a Ghana family. He doesn't care. He eats... Actually, he was in a danger. We rushed him to a hospital. The fellow [leader] was in critical condition. (Follower G6)

Cultural Savvy

The followers in this research identified four CQ qualities that have cultural savvy dimension: leader's background and ability, being a cultural learner, cultural adaptation, and attitude toward culture.

Leader's background and abilities. Followers were able to see high CQ in leaders who had a lot of cultural exposure and experiences. Followers observed that cultural similarities brought easier cultural understanding, and a person exposed to different cultures tended to be a better multicultural leader.

Cultural similarity. Several followers who had experienced working with a leader from a similar cultural background expressed that cultural similarities were helpful in both personal and working relationships. The following African follower was comparing an African leader from another African country with an Asian leader, and expressed appreciation for the African leader who could understand African culture:

> For my leader, he knows everything. He can relate to them [followers]. He knows the way in which he can explain things to them with respect. But for the other cultural way [Asian], they are not really sure how African way is low [Asian leader's understanding on Africal culture is low level]. They can't really come together. (Follower G8)

An Asian follower stated that it was easy for him to work with another Asian leader because of cultural similarities: "For my leader, it's very easy because I'm Filipino-Chinese, and there are very common things with Korean and with Chinese culture. So it's easier for me to be able to relate with my leader" (Follower E9). Another Asian follower expressed that she preferred working for an Asian leader because of the cultural similarities:

Follower A5
> Some [leaders whom I have worked with] are from the West, some are from Asia. Asians have similar culture. …

Researcher
> In what aspect do you think Asian cultures are similar?

Follower A5
> Especially emotionally, when we talk about some things, bad or good, they feel the same thing. They don't pretend like Western people, I think. When they feeling something, they tell us. …

Researcher
> Between the Western and Asian leader, who do you feel easier to be connected with?

Follower A5
> For sure it's an Asian leader because they look the same (laughter). (Follower A5)

Another Asian follower expressed that having an Asian leader was helpful because Asian leaders understood and adapted to his culture well: "Understand and adapt to our culture, being an Asian helps" (Follower A6). Another Asian follower expressed the same about the cultural similarity:

Follower C2
> Right now we have a director from an Asian country, I think he is a good X [national language of the field] speaking person, and his country is also from Asia. It's little bit easier for us to work with him.

Researcher
> In what way it's easier?

Follower C2
> He knows our culture better. Asian culture sometimes similar culture with Asian people.

One Western follower observed an Asian leader working in Asia and handling the work in an Asian way and witnessed the effectiveness of cultural similarity:

> Asian leadership is much more relational, which I think has been very good here. My leader understands the importance of relationships, meeting people, getting to know them, just even casually, because he also does lot of business over meals, which is not so British. We have meetings in the office; he has meetings in the restaurant. (laughter) That's something I struggle with a little bit. Because we spend a lot of money on meetings. So the budget for the meetings is quite large. You can do this at the office with a cup of tea. But that's not the way it gets done. But here it really pays benefits because he's gone out, he made the contacts, he's cultivated people. Because he's done this PR work in this country, it's like he sends gifts, that encourage government relationships, and we now work with some of these people and have good partnerships so that for this country. Working in Asia, it's very important that someone understands the Asian way of doing business, particularly if you want to open up national partners, and work well, I think that's important. (Follower C8)

When a leader did not understand cultural similarities among the followers, the followers had a difficult time because of lack of comprehension from the leader: "I told her [leader] 'Asian understands other Asians better than the Westerners.' But she did not know that" (Follower F4).

Exposure to different cultures. One follower stated that leaders who were exposed to different cultures while they were growing up had the potential to be good multicultural leaders:

> Someone who grew up bicultural. In my experience, an MK person makes an excellent candidate. I appreciate the leaders who are MKs. MK has totally different level of attitude about another culture compare to a missionary who grew up in mono cultural setting and spent very little time in cultural emersion in another culture. (Follower E7)

Another follower pointed out that his leader's culturally-diverse background made him a good multicultural leader:

> He [an Asian leader] is very exposed. (laughter) I met him and he worked in Kenya over ten years. (laughter) ... He's first of all married to an American. So he has an advantage over the natural unexposed leader. That mixed with a blend of some American aspect coming from his wife, …having stayed in Africa, makes him a multicultural leader. (Follower G6)

Another follower stated that her boss was a good multicultural leader because of his ample exposure to the different cultures he was working with: "My boss is not a typical Y [nationality] because has been working with many different cultures so many years. So he considers the foreigners and listens well" (Follower F4). Another follower observed several leaders who had worked with multiple cultures and became good multicultural leaders. "Those leaders that I can see are very flexible leaders because they are working in the different places and different cultures so they should be flexible. And also sensitive to the people, to the cultures they are working" (Follower H7).

Cultural learner. One follower witnessed how his leader was learning the local culture. In the process of her learning the local culture, sometimes it was awkward for her to ask the follower questions. My understanding of this situation was that, when the leader asked the follower questions, that put the follower in a higher or authority position. However, asking questions demonstrated the leader's learning process:

Follower E9
    Being an American, my leader I think she is very careful whenever she talks, and she asks lots of questions about, maybe because she is not exposed to Asia.... I felt initially like that was my boss at the first. Although it's good that she was asking questions and saying that very careful in not offending. So sometimes I felt that it was awkward. But nowadays I told her that she's becoming more Asian.

Researcher
    What situations did you feel awkward?

Follower E9
    In our conversation, all of sudden she would say "Is it okay for me to say this way?" She would always ask what would be the proper way. But in a way it's good because she's asking. She is not guessing. She wants to learn.

One follower noticed that her leaders learned her culture well: "Maybe our expectation is that since they are in the country they learn to the way we are, our way here in the Philippines... Americans [her current leaders] are very successful and very good in learning our cultures. They learn our way" (Follower H7).

The same follower also stated that both she and her leaders learned each other's culture:

> As the years go by we learn about each other and be more close to each other, something like that. Until we become more open to them as I learn about their culture they are also sensitive to us, as they learn our culture. Because in the confrontation we also telling them, you know our culture is that way. They are also learning. And also they are telling me that until you tell us we don't have a clue. We also learn that they are like this. So we always learn [from] each other. (Follower H7)

Cultural adaptation. Followers wanted their leaders to have the ability to adapt and to adjust culturally. One follower saw how his leader was struggling to adjust to the culture:

> He was good because he tried to learn our culture and he tried to adjust to our culture in the way that he can do. I think he fought inside because the different cultures but he tried to learn and adjust his life to our culture. (Follower A7)

Another follower observed how his leader adapted to his culture: "I think my [American] leader right now is beginning to be more Asian, not like from the first... I think she has adapted very well already" (Follower E9). Another follower observed that not all the leaders adapted to the culture well: "I think their experience in the past they [three leaders] had already several years' already experience working amongst other culture people. This other director had it [adopted to the culture well] but somehow it did not affect him. He didn't change" (Follower D7).

Attitude toward culture. Followers observed some positive attitudes leaders had. One follower appreciated his leader who demonstrated fairness in dealing with culture: "He doesn't show favor over one culture" (Follower G6). Another follower expressed his appreciation for a leader who respected other cultures: "So [a leader] respecting someone else's culture, and we want to help people understand God in their own way" (Follower G5).

Leaders on CQ in Followership

Just like leaders needed CQ, followers also needed to have CQ to work effectively in SIL and its partner organizations. Leaders in this study expressed their desire for the followers to have CQ while working in a multicultural environment. The list of CQ qualities desired in followership were categorized into three dimensions: cognition, behavior, and cultural savvy. These were the same dimensions as for the CQ qualities desired in leadership. Table 9 summarizes the CQ qualities desired in followership which were identified by the leaders.

Table 9

Summary Chart of Leaders on Cultural Intelligence in Followership

Cognition	Behavior	Cultural savvy
Understand culture	Communicate properly	Danger of misusing culture
Have cultural sensitivity		Overcome cultural weakness
		Seek cultural maturity
		Cultural advantage

Cognition

Leaders in this research wanted their followers to have cultural understanding and cultural sensitivity in terms of the cognition dimension of CQ qualities.

Understand culture. One leader stressed the importance of followers to understand other cultures, and specified that the follower needed to understand the leader's culture as well as the culture they were working in:

> Cultural understanding is also very important in an organization like this, because the leader/follower relationships are often cross-cultural and the work context is almost always cross-cultural. People who can't understand or appreciate cultures other than their own just won't make it very far, either as leaders or followers. So, thinking especially about followers, in response to your question, I would say that in our context, cultural understanding is more important than in many other work contexts. The people who work under my leadership need to understand my own culture as well as the cultural context in which we work. (Leader D1)

Another leader said she preferred to work with a follower who had cultural understanding over someone who was insensitive to culture, even if he or she was a gifted person:

> I would very much rather has someone with cultural understanding on my team than someone with great talent and little understanding [of culture]. I have found that talented people who are culturally insensitive have actually caused me more trouble -- dividing the team, offending clients, [and] being insubordinate. No, I'd rather live without help than have culturally-insensitive workers. (Leader E1)

Have cultural sensitivity. Leaders desired their followers to be culturally sensitive: "Nonetheless, a leader definitely would like a follower who is spiritually mature and culturally sensitive" (Leader A1). The followers needed to be sensitive to culture because their leaders were from diverse cultures:

Leader C1
> To be a follower, especially in the context of SIL, I think being culturally sensitive is very important. Because very often we have supervisor coming from different cultural background, especially nowadays, if you look at, our leadership team is so diverse. We have people, even not to mention about Asia, Europe. Within Europe and North America, we know that they are different. And the style of communication, [and] way of dealing with conflict and confrontation [are different]. And as a follower, I think it's even more important sometimes, we have to understand the mind of leaders so that we will not create unnecessary confrontation because of cultural differences. That can be avoided.

Researcher
> Can you give me an example of what you observed?

Leader C1
> Say for example, several of us in the team right now are from Netherlands. And I think they all admitted they are more direct, confrontational, not that they are aggressive, but the way of expressing themselves. And so we work together, and the follower having a supervisor like that, and we either don't understand it or find it harsh or we don't understand it and don't know how to respond. Sometimes it might be, our good intention might be misinterpreted. So I guess on the other hand, they need to be sensitive as well. But focusing on the follower part, I think we need to know our supervisor, not just who they are, but the way they express themselves, and the way they give instructions, and even the way

they care for their people. Sometimes they might be trying to care for the people, but the way they present it would be very different. (Leader C1)

Another reason for being culturally sensitive was so that the followers could properly communicate with the leader instead of creating miscommunication:

> If the follower is aware or sensitive to the culture of the leader, he or she would know the ways of how to communicate more effectively and the boundaries to avoid. The cause of friction and disagreement can most often be derived from cultural misunderstanding. (Leader A1)

Behavior

Leaders in this research identified one CQ quality in the behavior dimension: proper communication. The CQ qualities in the behavior dimension which were mentioned in the leadership section were also related to communication. One leader expressed his frustration at not knowing why followers did not give a response. Leaders desired followers to respond in a way that they could understand:

> In general with Asian members, it's hard sometimes because I don't know what they are thinking. When there's a different communication style, and they are silent because they do not want to share bad news. I am waiting for a response from someone and it doesn't come. Simply because they have bad news. That happens occasionally. (Leader D1)

One Asian leader wanted his followers to change their way of communication and to express their ideas and opinions in the SIL context:

> And if there are disagreements, it can put on the table, and discuss but it should not affect the work being done. But if people coming from my [Asian] background, don't feel like he agree or she refuse to do the job or he doesn't listen to my instruction then he keep on doing it things on his own way, not willing to bring it up front and talk about it openly and try to avoid it. Then I think this is not a good follower. So I do not expect people who work for me would not have their own thinking. And I am very concerned if someone coming from our [Asian] background, we have hesitation try to bring out our differences and discuss with our leaders. And I think that would not work well in the context of SIL because when you don't speak up, people don't know that you don't agree. (Leader C1)

Another leader observed that her follower was insensitive to culture and communicated with people of her language group very directly. The leader wanted her follower to communicate with people in a culturally proper way:

> Because if she thinks something, she will tell you, straight. She loves you but she's going to tell you. (laughter) And she has done this with her partner. But her partner is older than she is, you know, it's not like she's younger, no. But she is very straight, very clear, very confrontational with her partner. She is also very confrontational with the people group that she is working with. "YOU DON'T DO THAT." (raised voice, emphasis added), you know. And at times she is not cultural, if there's other people around. "YOU CAN'T DO THAT." (raised voice, emphasis added). Other people are listening. Then that person is embarrassed because she shamed them in front of other people. (Leader B1)

Cultural Savvy

Leaders in this study identified four CQ qualities in the areas of cultural savvy: danger of misusing culture, overcoming cultural weakness, seeking cultural maturity, and cultural advantage.

Danger of misusing culture. One leader observed that a few of her followers isolated themselves culturally from the people they were working with, and created a subculture of their own. She acknowledged that creating subculture in that way was not healthy. She wanted her followers to embrace the different cultures they were working with instead of creating an unhealthy subculture:

> These couple has created their own culture of just the two of them, which sometimes jives with the host culture, sometimes with the home culture, and sometime just their own private culture. Their evolved view leads them to rigid decisions and actions that fit with their own perceived norm of culture. (Leader B1)

Overcome cultural weaknesses. An Asian leader in this research recognized that Asians respect the older person as someone with authority. However, he desired that the Asian cultural trait would not hinder the follower's work:

> That person [follower] would also be humble and be willing to support the leader in areas that he is good at. This would especially difficult for many Asians who are older in age as compared with their younger leaders, bosses. There would be conflict if the older follower would not want to accede to the leadership of the supervisor and creates dissension among the colleagues. They may have more life and job experiences but because of the cultural trait [age and hierarchy], they are not matured enough to handle the loss of "face." (Leader A1)

A leader wanted the followers to show proper respect to the leader and trust the leader appropriately. In some cultures, the followers did not seem to respect the leaders:

> And that kind of thing is destructive and I think something that has come out of North American culture perhaps or worse some other cultures, Australians. They feel like it's their inherited right to distrust. And what is the word that they use? It's almost sports for them. But when I've heard from them, it's been embarrassing. So that's what I am looking for in followership. It's not going to just say "Yes sir." I don't want that. But somebody who can grasps the idea of general direction and here's how we think, we can approve that. (Leader H2)

Seek cultural maturity. One team in this study had a multicultural team workshop the previous year and the leader of that team reviewed what they had learned from the workshop as a group. She realized that understanding was one thing, but behavior change from cultural understanding was another. The leader wanted the team to process more of what they had learned:

> Cultural things really are tough. I mean, I know we talked about this, and we tried to prepare for this, but they are very real, and we reviewed what we learned last year [at the multicultural team workshop]. And the team [followers] was great at remembering so many things. But then when we were getting to our meetings. I'm still watching them communicate to each other, thinking "Okay, list those things on the board now." Have they gone from the list on the board to changing the way I am going to think about your response? I'm going to choose not to get upset about that because I am going to understand what I've learned. Or I am just still going to react emotionally. It takes a long time for people to take information and let it influence instinct. So I think we are still responding out of instinct. (Leader E1)

Cultural advantage and disadvantage. SIL language workers had the advantage in learning culture because studying language and culture was part of their work.

However, if they spoke the language fluently but did not understand culture, it had a negative influence on relationships:

> Because of their study of the language and culture, they should be knowledgeable about understanding that culture. However, often times, it's easier to study and mimic the language rather than the culture, which can then result in a gap in the social standards, and lead to misunderstandings. (Leader B1)

Followers on CQ in Followership

As with the leaders earlier in the chapter, the followers had the same three dimensions of CQ qualities desired in followership: cognition, behavior and cultural savvy. Table 10 summarizes CQ qualities desired in followership by the followers.

Table 10

Summary of Followers on Cultural Intelligence in Followership

Cognition	Behavior	Cultural savvy
Understand leader's culture	Communicate properly	Have cultural ability
		Attitude toward culture
Understand colleague's culture		Promote cultural strengths
Understand organizational culture		Be a cultural mediator

Cognition

Followers in this research identified three categories of culture that they should understand: the leader's, the colleague's, and the organizational culture.

Understand leader's culture. One follower realized that the meaning of her leader's response was different from what she would normally understand in her culture:

Usually I am very agreeable with administrators and all that, you know. I am not a very rebellious type. (laughter) But there was once that, because of my work, and we had to attend the conference. It is supposed to be compulsory, right? (laughter) But of course there are always exceptions. And so I have requested to be exempted. In the beginning when I asked, "Can I be excused?" the leader said, "Okay, give me some good reason. Write to me a good reason." Maybe for Asians, when someone says, "Okay write to me," I could consider that, I would would that as very positive. I did write and gave my reasons. But later he said that "No, that was not a good reason. You have to come." (Follower B9)

Another follower recognized that it was important to understand the leader's culture: "We are from different cultures. We should know our leaders' cultures, where he or she is from. So we try to know their background, and try to understand them" (Follower A5). Followers were more careful when they worked with a leader from a culture other than their own: "Sometimes I have remembered that my leader is not from my country and I need a little bit more to be sensitive, maybe" (Follower F3).

Several followers recognized cultural differences of leaders from different cultural backgrounds. One follower commented on the cultural differences between Korean, Chinese, Filipino, and American leaders:

I would expect a Korean to be more demanding, especially in an Asian context. I have been working with Chinese, and with Filipinos. A Filipino is usually relaxed, doesn't have very high expectations, although it depends on background. But if I work with a Chinese, then I would definitely expect higher expectations than with a Filipino, a Westernized Filipino. American people tend to be sometimes very lenient or maybe more diplomatic, maybe it's not the word, diplomatic, maybe more gives you a lot of space, gives you a lot of time, too. (Follower E9)

Another follower compared his understanding of cultural differences between Western and Asian leaders:

I think the Westerner usually doesn't understand how things are handled in an Asian context. Among Asians, a leader usually order things to the followers but the Westerners make things formalized, and ask people to report things in a formal report, which is very hard. There are so many writings to do, [and] many reports to fill out. That's not necessary for the Asians. When Asians meet, they know what's needed. But Westerners only realize things if the issues were addressed in a report. Asian followers feel isolated when they don't get attention from the leaders. (Follower F10)

One American follower recognized that having an Asian leader required him to be more flexible and ambiguous:

> Flexibility and ambiguity. And they're going into a training program with Filipino involvement in leadership, just a lot of changes. I know a little bit, one who is a little older, and I am not so keen on all those changes. I mean I kind of get used to my patterns I like to follow. And maybe more so than average, and as I'm getting a little older and set my ways, and the name of the game these years is flexibility and ambiguity. And that's a whole lot of stretch. Not just literally. Just kind of on all the time, so it's an exciting ride. (Follower B5)

Understanding colleague's culture. One follower shared that followers needed to work hard to understand the culture of the other followers: "They strive hard to understand cultural differences, share their culture, and understand each other" (Follower D4). One follower stated that working with his colleague for ten years, he understood his colleague's culture well:

> We got on well with other American family. We would sometimes think of different ways of doing things. But both of our families, certainly after ten years both of our families knew about the other culture so we would expect that. I would tease him and he would understand that that's a Kiwi thing. (Follower B7)

Understanding organizational culture. One follower addressed the issue of understanding the organizational culture: "So I need to know how they [followers] perceive the organization, what the rules are, and try to understand culture of organization and how they do things" (Follower H9).

Behavior

The behavioral CQ qualities which were articulated by followers were related to communication. Some followers who came from a culture where a follower did not talk to a leader directly were having difficulties expressing their thoughts:

> My communication always goes indirectly. Until now, I really don't have that courage, even after fifteen years, and they, even the guy that I was working with. I'm almost like a son to him. He really loves me. He did not think of me as another person. But I still don't have the courage through express everything I want. I don't know. I just want to understand that. Even the way I act, I want to do it. I really don't want to offend. If I have a boss, I really don't want to offend my boss. Because for me, it is not healthy. It is not the way of Christian people, to offend somebody. So if I communicate the message I wanted to communicate, I want to find the best way. I'd rather delay my communication rather than do, give my reaction right away, which I know it will just bring out some high level of attention. (Follower B6)

But another follower who was not used to telling what she was thinking to a leader in her culture learned to express her opinions adequately while working in SIL:

> If I have something not in line whatever, I'm just telling it. If they are not that so much agreeing with that. But I believe that, what I in my mind, just fight for it. So I learn to fight for my opinion if I am convinced that and learn to respect the opinion of other people. In our culture, it's not like that. Even though you want it, once the leader is not approving it, then you must respect him. So that's the way we are. (Follower H7)

Followers should be patient in communication because people from different cultures might have different concepts: "… like you've been more patient with, like, communication is not that straight. You need to have more patience when you communicate, because we might have different concepts" (Follower A8).

Cultural Savvy

Followers in this study identified four CQ qualities that pertain to the cultural savvy dimension: have cultural ability, attitude toward culture, promote cultural strength, and be a cultural mediator.

Have cultural ability. Followers were expected to have cross-cultural skills: "who [followers] has cross-cultural skills, usually it's cross-cultural in SIL" (Follower A8). Followers were also expected to adjust to the culture where they work:

Just last week, we were required to be interviewed by someone for, I think the intent was to find out how we were adjusting to cross-cultural life of mission. You wouldn't be required to do that in the business world, I don't think. (Follower C3)

Attitude toward culture. Followers understood they should embrace other cultures and not stereotype people based on their nationalities:

Since we are multicultural organization, someone who sees people as God's people, and not just putting a label on them, "Oh, She is an American so she must be like this or something." … That's how, like I know that as followers of God, we need to embrace other cultures and other ways of doing things, other cultures' way of doing things. (Follower E2)

Followers knew they should respect other cultures. One way of respecting culture was not asking nationals they were working with to adjust to their culture:

We have a tendency for the nationals change to our culture. Having expectation but not realizing that you have one that others change according to your culture because yours are right. I see that in lot of mission cultures that has been happen whether it's intentional or not intentional. I assume that it was not intentional. But we all do that. We need to be sensitive. (Follower H4)

Promote cultural strengths. Some followers detected cultural strengths of other cultures and tried to promote them:

Western culture is better with organizational skills and administration, which I need to learn. The national organization is good at contextualization and spiritual authority. If those gifts are used, that would be good. … So if we can use the strengths from both sides, it will be good. If we are open-minded about other cultures, and acknowledge our own weaknesses, that would be good. Indonesians are very spiritual. (Follower F10)

Be a cultural mediator. A follower could be a cultural mediator when he detected a need to bridge cultures between other followers and the leader:

Husband (Follower B8)
    A couple of years ago, a Korean colleague here, he had been trying to get some help with a certain thing that they haven't done here at this office. He wasn't getting anywhere with the leaders.

Wife (Follower B3)
> But he had not told his leader. He had tried indirectly. He tried to communicate in an Asian way. But it didn't get anywhere. He tried in an Asian way.

Husband (Follower B8)
> So I wrote some letters and finally we got the facility.

Chapter 8 Summary

The findings revealed that participants considered CQ necessary for both the leaders and the followers to work in a multicultural organization like SIL. Although I organized the leaders' data separately from the followers' data, there were no apparent CQ qualities specific to just the leaders or to just the followers. Rather, similar CQ qualities were desired, regardless of the individual's position. The leaders and followers in this research listed three dimensions of CQ qualities for leadership and followership: cognition, behavior, and cultural savvy. In terms of cognition CQ, understanding culture and being culturally sensitive were considered important for both leadership and followership. The primary area for behavioral CQ was communication. Both leaders and followers wanted to communicate in culturally appropriate ways.

In terms of cultural savvy CQ, there were various aspects of CQ identified. In leadership, while the leaders placed importance in understanding team dynamics, the followers identified the cultural background and ability of a leader. Followers detected that leaders who previously had ample exposure to other cultures were more likely to become great multicultural leaders. With followership, leaders noted the danger of misusing culture, overcoming cultural weakness, seeking cultural maturity, and cultural advantages. The followers desired to have cultural ability, to possess a proper attitude toward culture, to promote cultural strengths, and to be a cultural mediator in followership.

CHAPTER 9

COMMUNICATION METHODS' EFFECT ON LEADERSHIP AND FOLLOWERSHIP

Some interview participants took remote assignments in their home country or in other countries for various reasons. Communication by computer made these remote assignments possible. People who took remote assignments did not have many occasions to have face-to-face meetings with their leaders. Leaders in this study traveled frequently to attend meetings or for other work related occasions. In those cases, even though a leader and a follower were located in the same place, when a leader was travelling, face-to-face meetings were not possible with a follower.

Many SIL people, especially language workers whom I interviewed, were independent self starters. Because of this quality, language workers could usually determine on their own what they needed to do for their project; they did not need much communication with a leader as far as their work was concerned. However, they were still required to report on their tasks and be accountable.

Other SIL people working in support roles, such as computer specialists, teachers, and others in non-language work, needed more directive communication with leaders. For example, if a team worked together on a project, then communication among the team members and with their leader was essential for the successful completion of the project.

Because each method of communication has its strengths and weaknesses, the methods used affected the relationship between the sender and the receiver. Findings regarding methods and communication tools used within SIL and its partner organizations and how those methods and tools affected the working relationships between leaders and followers are reported in this chapter.

The data indicated that SIL and its partner organization personnel used email, face-to-face, phone, SMS, and Skype for communication. One team in this research used Facebook and Pronto[1]. Three themes emerged from the data for every communication tool: usage, strength and weakness. Table 11 describes what communication methods were used by the leaders and followers. The communication tools used by the interviewees are given with those that were reported the most frequently listed first.

Table 11

Summary of Communication Tools Used by the Leaders and the Followers

	Leader	Follower
Email		
Usage	Regular work Urgent issues Confrontation	Send reports and information Regular work communication Simple things Important issues
Strengths	Document Monitoring time and organizing thoughts Straight talk	Document Expressive Organize thoughts Convenient

--continued on next page--

--continued from previous page--

	Leader	Follower
Weaknesses	More miscommunication and conflict Time related issue Depend on the recipient Language issue Not expressive Technical challenge	Relational issues Time related issues Not suitable for certain situations Miscommunication Language issue Cultural issues

Face-to-face

	Leader	Follower
Usage	Sensitive issues or conflict Lengthy discussion	Sensitive issues or conflict Lengthy discussion Important issues Cultural reasons
Strengths	Clearer communication Add relational component Shorten communication time	Clearer communication Relational Language issues Flexibility Cultural
Weaknesses	Too much exposure	No documentation Language issues

Phone call

	Leader	Follower
Usage	Handling conflict Making an appointment	Important issues Time related issues Secondary option
Strengths	Tone of voice	Clear communication Tone of voice

--continued on next page--

--continued from previous page--

	Leader	Follower
Weaknesses	Interruption	Interruption Economic reason
SMS		
Usage	Traveling	Urgent, Secondary method Encourage
Strengths	Connecting people	Inexpensive Not interrupting a recipient
Weaknesses	Technical difficulty	Unclear message Not available without roaming overseas
Skype		
Strengths	Able to see facial expression	Know when other person is online Leave documentation - chat
Weaknesses		Technology Easily distracted Crossing time zone issues
Facebook		
Usage		Building relations
Strengths	Sense of community	Informal social activity Team morale Encourage

--continued on next page--

--continued from previous page--

	Leader	Follower
Weaknesses	Not available in some parts of the world Not proper for work	Passive in communication
Pronto		
Usage		Team discussion
Strengths		Team building Accountability
Weaknesses		Language issue Speed of typing Controlled by Internet speed

Leader's Description of Communication Methods

After data was collected, I divided the data into two major categories: communication methods leaders used and those followers used. I further analyzed the data obtained from the leaders and identified the following communication methods as being the ones they used: email, face-to-face communication, phone call, SMS, Skype, and Facebook. As I further studied the data for each of the communication methods, three categories emerged for each method: usage of the communication, strengths, and weaknesses. Then, using the three emerging categories, I described each communication tool with the items for which I had the most data listed first. Table 12 describes usage, strengths and weaknesses of communication methods used by the leaders.

At the time of data collection, the major communication method used in SIL and its partner organizations was email, even though people preferred to communicate face-to-face:

> For me, I am a face-to-face person. But you cannot have those things frequently. Although I like face-to-face communication, you don't have a choice. Because of the geographical location, you have to contact people with cell phone, email, and those things. (Follower H8)

Leaders stated that the greatest strength of email communication was documentation; the biggest problem with email communication was that it could create misunderstandings. Leaders noted that the biggest benefit in having face-to-face communication was clear communication, but one drawback to that could be showing too much transparency in facial expression.

Phone calls, SMS, Skype, and Facebook communication were mentioned significantly less than email and face-to-face. Because SIL and its partner organizations used email for their primary communication method, the relationship between a leader and a follower was most affected by the email communication.

Email

Email was the most common method of communication in SIL and its partner organizations: "Even if I am in the office, I email" (Leader F1). For some people, email was their communication of choice:

> Writing is my bread and butter. It's the easiest thing I do so I communicate best through writing. Even when I am talking to God, a lot of times I write my prayers, just because I communicate that way. So for me it's email. (Leader E1)

But for another leader email was not his first choice of communication: "I take pride in writing a good email that's well-understood, but my earlier points stand: it's never the first option, given a choice" (Leader B2). Regardless of writing being a personal choice or not, leaders had to communicate with their followers through email most of the time.

Table 12

Overall Chart of the Communication Tools Used by the Leaders

	Usage	Strengths	Weaknesses
Email	Regular work Urgent issues Confrontation	Document Monitoring time and organizing thoughts Straight talk	Miscommunication & conflict Time related issues Dependence on recipient Language issue Not expressive Technical challenge
Face-to-face	Sensitive issues or conflict Lengthy discussion	Clearer communication Add relational component Shorten communication time	Too much exposure
Phone call	Handling conflict Making appointment	Tone of voice	Interruption
SMS	Traveling	Connecting people	Technical difficulty
Skype		Seeing facial expression	
Facebook		Sense of community	Not universally available Not proper for work

In addition to normal communication, a leader used email for urgent matters when he was traveling:

> If it's an urgent task to attend to, for example, we have a program there's something missing, I will email back. I will also cc to another person, which is my

manager who's here. So cc the next highest person in the office, and the person can help to ensure that things are done. (Leader A1)

Strengths of email communication. Leaders contacted in this research noted that the benefits of email communication included having the communication documented, being able to monitor time and organize thoughts, and being able to have a straight talk without being hindered by cultural issues. Sometimes email was also a preferred choice for dealing with conflict because email provided time to carefully craft the content:

> Face-to-face is absolutely my preferred mode, if that can happen, I would much prefer face-to-face, to anything except confrontation. I would rather write my confrontation but I know those have to happen face-to-face, and that's always a killer for me because I would much rather write it, because in addressing delicate, sensitive or hot issues, sometimes doing it in print instead of face-to-face gives people time to kind of just be hit with the information, get over with your initial reaction, think about how you want to respond, you can write the email and you can look at it and say, "Is this really how I want to say it? What's the tone of this? Is this the tone I want?" You can change words. (Leader E1)

Documentation. Leaders pointed out that the primary strength of email communication was to document the communication: "I would say email is good for a certain kind of task which is required, like for doing finances, or doing other things that need to have a written record" (Leader C1). Because of written record, the communication could be reviewed any time: "We can go back. We have a history of this conversation, for future reference" (Leader E1).

Summarizing a meeting and sending it though email was a good way to have a written record so that people could go back to the previous conversation if necessary:

> He [follower] always says, "Okay, I will write down; I will put it in an email." That's what I appreciate. Just to make sure that we have anything we discussed verbally but we have something written. Whether it will be a personal plan or it will be a project plan, whatever. If I am doing that with some other people, I usually follow by writing an email…. So let's make sure that when we get confused two-three weeks later, we go back to the email. And what we were talking last three weeks ago, I would say at most in the email. (Leader F1)

Monitoring time and organizing thoughts. In addition to documentation, email made it possible to manage time and organize thoughts on what to communicate:

> I like email because I can open it when I am ready to sit, and think and work and engage with the group. It's kind of like being able to monitor my own time, and investment in the group. I like email because we have a record of what we are talking about, and we look through the threads, and we can look at the two lists and make sure that all the right people are getting the right information…. It's always a little more of a safety net to write because I can pause. I can walk away, come back an hour later and fix it before I send it out. I could be more careful about my communication. (Leader E1)

Email allowed time to think through how to craft the content without being pressured by time: "But it is helpful sometimes, when we're not together, we can consider the right words to use and take a long time, thinking about how to say it" (Leader B1).

Straight talk. One Asian leader, who normally did not confront directly, was able to confront his follower through email, which was against his culture. My understanding of this situation was that when this Asian leader did not have the person in front of him, he did not have to think about saving face for the follower and was able to write forthrightly to her about the issue:

> I did a straight talk by an email to the Westerners, "This is not what this organization wants to see happen, the policy of this organization to do like this. But you are already doing this." After I did that, I just felt it's not something wrong according to her culture or his culture. But it's against my way; I mean it's against my culture. I know what I did is right, but later after I wrote that and she wrote back to me and apologized me for that, I just feel I also made a mistake. Why should I open straight like that to her? So, because that's against my behavior, my culture and my way of doing that. (Leader F1)

Weaknesses of email communication. Even though it was not always ideal to handle difficult issues through email, sometimes email was the only choice: "So email is a necessary method of communication. If there are issues between the parties, or if the subject matter is difficult, it is never a good way. It is sometimes the only way" (Leader B2). The leaders explained that the weaknesses of email were that it sometimes created miscommunication and conflict; it was not timely; how it was received depended on the recipient; it was hard for the non-native speaker of the language to understand; it was not expressive; and it had technical challenges.

More miscommunication and conflict. The leaders in this study stated that the greatest weakness of email was that it was prone to cause miscommunication and conflict. One leader noted that fast speed of email exchange accelerated the level of conflict and miscommunication:

> Less conflict thirty years ago where there's no good communication systems like now. Because right now people are tempted to write things when they read: blah, blah, blah, blah and send. After the email went, that person reading from the other side, okay, then he responded. Blah, blah. And then conflict arose… Thirty years ago where there was no conflict, I would say, where there was no email and phone and those kind of like we have right now. Conflict was there, but not as many and as faster as now. Because if he sends a mail, it takes one week or two weeks before it reached the United States, or reached Korea or Manila, it's fine. When they respond to us, it needs time. During the time their mail is in the air or on the ship, people's hearts change. So when they receive the mail, attitude and the way of thinking has been changed. So that's why I am saying thirty years ago, the conflict not as faster and greater than right now (laughter). (Leader F1)

Another leader preferred traveling to where the followers were to avoid miscommunication from email:

> I cannot communicate through email, because email communication can create a lot of speculations. It's still not clearly communicating sometimes … If I can wait, I will just say "Wait, I will come, then we'll talk about it face-to-face." (Leader G1)

When one leader received an email from her follower written in bold, she felt like her follower was shouting at her. Later she realized that her follower had some problems with the computer:

Wife (Leader B1)
> The problem was once again between the two translators, and two followers, and also us, and the font was big, and it looked like it was large, and it looked like it was in bold…

Husband (Leader B2)
> It looked like she was shouting.

Wife (Leader B1)
> Oh was it capital letters, too? It was capital letters, maybe even. And I thought, "Oh boy, this is going to make the other follower very mad (very loud voice) when she sees this." Because it did, it felt like she was shouting at us all (very loud voice). Because we could almost hear her voice as we read those, plus the style of the email. And so I wrote her and I said, "In that message, it seemed like you were shouting at us because, I don't know if it was capital, but it was very large and bold. And it just felt like you were shouting at us." And it's good that I wrote her because she wrote back and said, "Oh, it's some problem with my computer."

Not only the bold letters but copying someone mistakenly created a problem too:

> It was by accident I emailing her for something, but I copied somebody else but she was mentioned to me that "Oh, I was so embarrassed because you copied somebody else." I said "Okay, I apologize. Please forgive me for that. Next time if I write something it will be more confidential." (Leader F1)

Time related issue. Composing email took time: "Emails can take hours to write, and more hours the next day to go over it again and to rehash it" (Leader B2). When a difficult email needed to be written, it took a long time and the writer needed to be very careful:

> I don't shy away from email. I'm willing to tackle the difficult Emails. You can't do that fast. And I try to put myself in the other person's position. I reread it probably ten times before it's sent. And I'm always thinking, "Okay, how will they understand that? How will they understand this? Am I getting across what I'm trying to get across?" (Leader B2)

For complicated issues, it took many email exchanges to explain things while the situation could have been explained easily in one sitting in a face-to-face meeting:

> If it is needed more of a discussion, dialogue back and forth, in order to solve the problem, sometimes you have to send ten emails back and forth before you can

solve it. ... I always prefer if it can be wait, then it is always good to have a face-to-face meeting. (Leader G1)

Sometimes, not getting an instant reply was another drawback of email communication due to time difference or delayed reply: "The con is that it's not as instant as it used to be." (Leader E1).

Depended on the recipient. Email communication required an assumption of good will of both parties for mutual understanding:

> Email communications are a necessary evil. They are never a good substitute for face-to-face. They are often the only alternative that is available, because face-to-face is not possible. But when everything is fine, and the relationship between the people that are communicating is great, and there is an assumption of good will going both directions, then there is no trouble with email, there's never any trouble with email. Because you don't have to worry about how your message is going to be understood. Because there is an assumption of good will. (Leader B2)

Language issue. Not only did email communication depend on attitude of the recipient, but also language was a potential drawback. One leader had noticed that people whose mother tongue was not English had a hard time communicating with their leader by email:

> If you wait for an email reply from them, I know that I will never get it from my Asian colleague because he struggles. Honestly he told us that he struggles writing, not that his English is not good. Sometimes he hesitates because, whether he is not sure because he is expressing himself in an appropriate way or if it's offensive. So I don't get reply. (Leader C1)

Not expressive. In addition to the language issue, written forms of communication were deficient in expressing what people wanted to communicate:

> Honestly, I think email is a written form of communication. Despite we all use English, and no matter whether they are even mother-tongue English speaker, I still believe that the communication through email is not the best that can express 100 percent what they want to say. Or we can be on the receptive end [and] can understand 100 percent what was intended in the email. (Leader C1)

Technical challenge. Some people were not used to using a computer for communication. In this case, technology was a challenge:

> One of the things I realized for people in the north [side of this country] is that their computer skill is not good. And it's not their fault. They don't have that kind of opportunity to use this kind of email systems, Skype things like this. You have to train them from the beginning how to use Skype, how to use emails, how to use team viewer, things like this. So I don't put very high expectations. I personally help them to see how to training, a lot of training. Then emphasis again and again, that it's important that they check emails. (Leader A1)

Face-to-Face Communication

The majority of leaders expressed that their most preferable communication method was face-to-face. However, they were not able to communicate face-to-face with their followers as much as they wanted because some followers were working in different locations:

> The biggest challenge is personal face-to-face interaction. … Even just communicating in general is challenging. On the other hand though, it's a lot easier than it used to be. It's Skype and email. It's easy to communicate. It's just hard to communicate face-to-face. (Leader D1)

Another leader expressed that he put face-to-face meeting as his priority as he visited different locations where his followers were working:

> And if possible, we are in the same location, I would try my best to talk to them face-to-face. If that is possible…, when I travel to Kathmandu or when I go to Bangkok, when I go to Hong Kong, or to other places and I know my team are there, I would try my best to meet with them and talk to them face-to-face. That is my highest and first priority. (Leader C1)

Use of face-to-face communication. Leaders stated that for handling sensitive issues or conflict, and lengthy discussions it was very necessary to have face-to-face communication.

Sensitive issues or conflict. Leaders stated that face-to-face communication was the best way when they handled sensitive issues or conflict. One leader articulated her experience of dealing with a sensitive issue with face-to-face, which brought positive results:

> I remember …organizationally we had an Asian member that was terribly distressed about the way she was being handled in a Western organization. That's the way it's been described. And I remember going to a director and saying. "Please give me the budget to go and sit with her. This must be worked out. We cannot leave this kind of festering sore here." That was allowed. By God's grace we spent four days together. It was the most beautiful fellowship I've ever had with anybody in any culture. At the end the Asian director who's known to be prickly, for being very difficult, said "I have never felt so cared for by a Western colleague. You came here to listen. You came here to make something work out." So there was a reestablishment of fellowship. It was wonderful. (laughter) It was one of my highlights of my career, actually. (Leader H1)

The same leader reflected how she worked with organizational conflict with face-to-face meeting:

> I found myself in an informal, and at times formal, liaison role between those three organizations. I learned a lot but it was very challenging, very challenging indeed. Number one I would say history. Negative history – when you are trying to forge an organizational cooperation, it's very, very hard to undo, because [when their] woundedness is that when way back and they tended to carry over to assumptions that we really couldn't change [assumptions]. And that was difficult. In the case of one of the organizations, they had such a rich way of doing things that when you look for flexibility to be able to collaborate better, it just wasn't there. And for that challenge, what we did try to help was to actually insist on face-to-face meetings instead of all of the writings back and forth. So there was a relationship base that had not been there before. We went through seven memorandums of understanding before we could come to a point on a single decision that three had to do together. But I think it was worth the efforts. But it took face-to-face meetings and it took a proactive gentleness that said we can't go on the way we were going. (Leader H1)

Lengthy discussion. Leaders articulated that they preferred to have face-to-face communication with the follower when they had lengthy discussions like a debrief or planning session. One leader described how she debriefed face-to-face with the followers who were with the language project for couple of months:

> But we would have them for meals, when they come in, so we can listen. And before they go out and pray for them. And one thing about having people when they first come in is that it's all fresh and new. And they will talk and talk and talk. I call it Englishitis. Meaning, they have to talk English. They've been talking M language for two months now. They're tired of M language. And it feels so good to speak English.... And it's how God made us. But if you come, if you catch those people when they first come in, you can hear a lot of stories and a lot of emotion. (Leader B1)

Another leader expressed that face-to-face talk was obviously necessary when she planned work with her followers: "But just work-related things, talking about projects or, certainly brainstorming ideas, writing a project plans and things. Oh, that has to be face-to-face" (Leader E1).

Strengths of face-to-face communication. The leaders articulated that face-to-face communication made it possible to achieve clear communication, to build relationships, and to communicate in a shorter amount of time. The leaders explained that body language in face-to-face communication aided clear communication; helped to clarify previous miscommunication; and made it easier for people whose mother tongue was not English to communicate.

Clear communication. Body language could communicate things that words could not communicate. Posture could communicate good will with face-to-face communication:

> I think it's [face-to-face] always an advantage because I have the opportunity to communicate my good will. And that cannot be misunderstood if we're face-to-face, because I can express my appreciation, my respect, with humility to that person. Whatever the situation is, there's always room to approach somebody lowly and slowly, humbly. So yes, there may not be good will on the other side and there may not be agreement and the meeting is over. That may be a given. But

especially if there is no good will, the best chance you have is to be face-to-face. (Leader B2)

Face-to-face meetings could clear up miscommunication that had been caused by previous written communication:

> There was a conflict in between two parties. And we started corresponding by emails: blah, blah from the other organization. The more we wrote, I've seen the more conflict, the more gaps developed. Finally I talked to the chief pilot. I said, "Stop correspondence by mail, making a plan, all of us going to the United States, sitting in the meetings, in person talking face-to-face." So we did. The problem solved. (Leader F1)

People whose mother tongue was not English had an easier time talking face-to-face than writing, because of quick responses and ability to ask questions:

> It's just so much contacts that you have to bring into that, that you can't cover it with written words, especially for whom English isn't their first language. I mean it's asking a lot of them to fully communicate what they're trying to say in written words. For them, sometimes face-to-face is easier because it gives them a chance to just keep saying it until they've communicated what they are trying to communicate. And I can ask questions, and we get to the issues that way. So in the context of work, face-to-face is the best. (Leader E1)

Adds relational component. Face-to-face brought a relational component to interaction between leaders and followers. One leader shared that living close to the followers and having face-to-face meetings often built up relations and provided the leader with a chance to pray with the followers:

> What a delight to be with these people! We can see each other's lights turn on and off. We just get a text from each other saying, "We need to pray with you." We just can hop over there. It is such a pleasure… And we've done that a couple of times. We've got to do a little more. I'd like to do it more. So face-to-face, whatever and whenever possible. (laughter) (Leader H1)

Visiting the followers and having face-to-face time with the followers brought more understanding of the followers:

> We have traveled sometimes to do things face-to-face or sometimes just to have a visit also, because it's always good to go there. Because there, you get a better

understanding of the situation in that environment. It's always good to go. Better idea of what the Lord is doing there. And all the personalities, and you know, as they come to the door and then leave, all the people. It's always good to go. (Leader B1)

Shortens communication time. One leader shared his experience with a follower who was not replying to his email. He travelled to where his follower was and handled the work in a very short time:

> I need to do in one of my trip and sit down. Within two hours, everything was done. But I have to accept it. I can't say "No, you have to reply in an email." I know I will never get a reply back from him (laughter). (Leader C1)

Weaknesses of face-to-face communication. Even though there were many strengths identified, there were weaknesses in face-to-face communication. One leader explained that she habitually showed too much of her emotions by her facial expression. When she dealt with difficult issues, she wished she could write rather than talk face-to-face:

> Whereas you are face-to-face there's a lot of body language and stuff that feeds into it that can send messages. For example, I am really frustrated with one of my followers for example. Just, I have this issue with the follower right now that I have to deal with. So I badly want to write to him but instead, but I think I have to Skype with him with the camera on, because that's the appropriate way to deal with it. But when that happens, he responds to what I say. I know my face gives me away. I know that some of my emotions show and I need to try to be careful of how I, guard what I say. (Leader E1)

Phone Call

Due to the digital age providing many different methods of communication, the phone was not considered a primary communication tool in SIL and its partner organizations. One leader said that people seldom used a phone to communicate: "Because now in this digital age, people are corresponding through emails, no more picking up the phone and calling you" (Leader A1).

Usage. A phone call was more desirable to deal with conflict than email if face-to-face time was impossible:

> So I just called them. This is kind of expensive, just to call from here to there. But in that case, it was worth it. So the same would apply in a conflict situation. Don't try to deal with the conflict with just words, either texted or email. I would go, minimally voice contact, if not actual in person. You need to be able to hear their voice when you deal with conflict. And part of that is because written communication leaves too much room for misunderstanding. If someone writes an email, telling me about a problem, I can't hear their voice. I can't pick up all their emotions. It's not clear exactly what the seriousness of this is. (Leader D1).

Another leader who lived close to followers stated that she called followers to make an appointment: "But we still can show up at their gate by, in 15 minutes, of a call" (Leader H1).

Strengths and weaknesses of phone calls. Phone calls had both strengths and weaknesses as communication tools. Being able to hear the tone of voice was an advantage phone calls had over written communication:

> Oh, whenever possible, face-to-face. Voice to voice is pretty good too, because you can get inflection, you can get a tone of voice that you just can't get with an email message, certainly that you can't get from a quarterly report. (Leader H1)

At the same time calling might interrupt a recipient. Instead of calling, sending email or SMS message did not interrupt a recipient:

> But he is very busy. He is Asia Area director. I am not going to call him unless, or even text him, unless I have to. Cause he's got hundreds of people. But if it's really urgent, you know, and I will just rather sending him an email that it's going to get buried in the stack of emails, I will send him a brief message. So again, it depends on the person involved, and it's good to have options. (Leader D1)

SMS Communication

One leader who was based in the Philippines noticed that her followers were communicating frequently with SMS and realized that she should participate more actively with their SMS communication:

> And a lot of communication happens that way [SMS] and I wasn't participating in that. They made a joke of it for a long time. "We know our leader does not use the phones." But I think they would really appreciate that. So I have to make more of an effort to when I am here, to participate with their text conversations or just talk to people. (Leader E1)

Strengths of SMS communication. When a leader could not access email during travel, then SMS became a primary method of communication: "When I'm travelling for the staff in the office, I am mostly using both: email and SMS. But places I cannot access email, then I use SMS" (Leader F1). Using SMS could improve communication and build relationships: "Text messaging is big, especially for people in the Philippines, and that was another issue with me as director because the team is very connected by text here in the Philippines" (Leader E1).

Weaknesses of SMS communication. Technical failure or delay caused inconvenience of not being able to receive SMS in a timely manner: "Because sometimes SMS, my mobile, like you SMS'ed to me yesterday afternoon, but I just got it this morning (laughter)" (Leader F1).

Skype

Skype was not actively utilized in communication between leaders and followers in this research. However, one leader stated Skype video did have benefits for communication:

About, we've done Skype with the one team in the south part of the country, a few times also. That helps because we can see the tension and the emotion on their faces. You can hear it. And you know we have a problem. (Leader B1)

Facebook Communication

One team in this research used Facebook to get to know each other better. Facebook provided a sense of community, connection, and morale but some people could not use Facebook because it was not available in their country. While Facebook was good for social interaction, it was not appropriate for work:

> The pros are that it has much more sense of community and talking to each other, and they seemed to like it. They all connect well with it. Believe it or not, even someone who is in a remote area and doesn't have real strong Internet connection is able to get on Facebook. And so he keeps up with the team a lot better through Facebook than we ever do with email cc'ing everybody. The con is that one follower located where can't get onto Facebook connected to a group like ours. So it does limit some people from being part of the group conversation. That's too bad. Another con with Facebook I think is, Facebook would be the equivalent of all of us being on the same floor together, and having that community, but Facebook is not where I see us getting work done. It's too casual, too chatty, and it's not where we are going to really progress. (Leader E1)

Finding Out the Best Way to Communicate

Leaders were aware of the strengths and weaknesses of different communication tools. Leaders tried using the best tools based on personal and cultural choices of the recipient:

> If there are cross-cultural communications, I am learning all the time better how to do that. For example, with my Indonesian people, texting is much more effective than emailing... He [Indonesian] does read his email, but it's a lot quicker and more effective just sending him a text. If I just need an answer to a question, it's normal for him. If he is in a meeting, he is always texting. That's no problem. Now with my American contact, they would feel bothered by that. Let's say: "Why do you keep bothering me by sending those texts? Just write me an email. When I get home, you know, I'll answer it." With Indonesians, it works better with text, and Filipinos too. So I am learning that cultural difference. Basically there's a wide variety of tools. I can run down the list... I have probably six or seven options. I don't know that I can explain it. I kind of can in my mind.

"Okay, this is the best way for this person, that's for that person." As I get to know people, I just figure out what's the best way to communicate with that person. With this person, I text; with that person, I Skype... So I have to keep my audience in mind. (Leader D1)

Another leader stated:

Sometimes I might have to test and find out which is the best, and keep telling my people that I carry phones around Asia that work no matter where I go. So they call me or send me SMS and I try to get back to them as soon as I can. Of course sometimes systems fail and it doesn't work. So I would try to test and maintain channel of communication so that whenever they need to talk to me, they would not have a problem finding me and be able to talk to me. (Leader C1)

Followers' Description of Communication Methods

The followers in this research listed all the communication methods and tools the leaders described above but added one more —Pronto. Also with the data obtained, the same three categories (usage, strengths, and weaknesses) emerged for most of the communication methods used by the followers. The order of the communication methods as listed below reflects the frequency each method was mentioned by the followers. Table 13 describes usage, strengths and weaknesses of the communication methods used by the followers.

Email

The same as the leaders, email was the primary communication tool used by followers in this research: "My supervisor visits two times a year. Even though he visits here, we talk only when I make an appointment with him. I communicate with my supervisor more than 90 percent using email" (Follower D4). Another follower said that he also communicated about 90 percent of time with his leader through email: "Most of time I communicate with my leader through email, probably about 90 percent" (Follower

Table 13

Overall Chart of the Communication Tools Used by the Followers

	Usage	Strengths	Weaknesses
Email	Send reports and information Regular work communication Simple things Important issues	Document Expressive Organize thoughts Convenient	Relational issues Time related issues Not suitable for certain situations Miscommunication Language issue Cultural issues
Face-to-face	Sensitive issues or conflict Lengthy discussion Important issues Cultural reasons	Clearer communication Relational Language issues Flexibility Cultural	No documentation Language issues
Phone call	Important issues Time related issues Secondary option	Clear communication Tone of voice	Interruption Economic reason
SMS	Urgent Secondary method Encourage	Inexpensive Not interrupting the recipient	Unclear message Not available without roaming overseas
Skype	Contacting traveling leader Urgent Connecting with team members	Know when other person is online Leave documentation - chat	Technology Easily distracted Crossing time zone issues
Facebook	Building relations	Informal social activity Team morale Encourage	Passive in communication
Pronto	Team discussion	Team building Accountability	Language issue Speed of typing Controlled by Internet speed

F10). The followers in this research explained the usage of email, and its strengths and weaknesses. Interestingly, followers said the biggest drawback to email communication was not lack of clarity, as noted by the leaders, but the lack of a relationship engendered by email communication.

Use of email communication. Followers in this research identified four areas when they used email for communication: reports, regular work, simple things, and important issues.

Send reports and information. One follower stated that she sent her leader a monthly report to account for her activities, and used it for herself to plan her work. She was satisfied with email exchanges about her monthly report to her leader:

> I send him my monthly report and get email responses. I am very thankful for the monthly report. For me, it's an accountability thing, and also when I wrote back and I see what I have done over that month. It can be quite amazing sometimes (laughter) and I use it too for planning for the next month. I don't use it just for my leader and whoever he sends it to. I use it for myself to help myself plan, keep me focused, keep me on track, but also if I had special need, like when I had that font issue. The font I was given, I needed to have special characters. I finally wrote something to my leader on that report. (Follower D6)

Regular work communication. Followers in this research communicated with their leaders through email for regular work:

> I email him for a visa issue and email him for the literacy materials. When I have prayer request, I sent him email, like when I had malaria or dengue fever or the medical reports I get from the country I was in. I explain my situation and give updates. (Follower F4)

Another follower also stated that his regular communication with his leader was email:

> But in terms of just keeping in touch, email is fine with reports. … Keeping in touch with him, our director, and to say, "Here is what we did, here is what we are planning, what do you think?" A lot of that is okay by email. (Follower D3)

Email was used not only to communicate with the leaders but also to communicate with the colleagues: "Better to keep record, and to let other colleagues to know that I use email. It's more official" (Follower C4).

Simple things. Some followers limited their email communication to simple issues that were easy and convenient to communicate through email: "So I don't communicate anything important through email. I only email simple things, or things already decided. I email for the factual things" (Follower F7).

Important issues. Conversely, another follower sent important issues through email: "Important matters, I do email him" (Follower G2). My understanding with this case was that he emailed important issues because with email he could keep a written record.

Strengths of email communication. Followers identified the strengths of email communication: documentation, freedom of expression, organization, and convenience.

Documentation. Like the leaders indicated, the followers in this research stated that the biggest asset of email communication was having a written document:

> I also like email because next month when I am trying to remember what I said, I can go back to my email and look it up. "Oh yes, this is what they said because I've got a written record." So I like email because I have a written record. (Follower B7)

Because a written document was created, people could refer back to it if clarification was necessary:

> Email is recorded. So whatever was communicated is there. But the content of the face-to-face dialogue is not recorded. When the content is changed later, I have no proof of the previous communication. I have experienced that several times already. When things were confirmed by face-to-face communication, he had another plan and he was not able to do the things planned with me, but he did not notify me. When I addressed that incident, he said that he had other urgent thing

came in and decided to do that instead. Even though he had valid reason, I could not understand why he did not communicate to me. If it had been communicated through email, those things would not happen because there is proof of the conversation. That is why I prefer communicating through email. (Follower F10)

Freedom of expression. Some people expressed themselves freely in writing. One Asian follower stated: "I started to do it [expressing] in writing. I feel that in writing I could express myself. So actually in email, and chat is good for me (laughter)" (Follower B6).

One follower observed that her Asian leader was very expressive through email although he was not that expressive when he was with people:

> I think he is more direct in emails, but in face-to-face he's more personal. He can express his true meaning other than sometimes coming close to passing emails or missing things. Sometimes when he writes an email, he doesn't think too much. He just says what he wants to say. (Follower F3)

One Asian follower also was able to express herself more freely when she disagreed with a teammate through email. She realized that by writing email she was able to control her emotions, express what she wanted to say, and have a written record of it:

> I had an incident where I disagreed with a person in a team. I argue with him through email. Even though we could not come up with a solution, due to the difference in perspectives about how to approach the nationals, I expressed what I thought, even though he didn't understand. It was easier to do it through email, because I was able to control my emotions…Through email, I could think through the issues, control emotions and have written records. So I learned that I needed a written document for the important issues. (Follower C9)

One Western follower also said that she was able to express herself through email with controlled emotion: "But sometimes an email allows you, especially if it's emotional, (laughter) allows you to put out all your reasons and wherefores without crying (laughter)" (Follower F5).

One Asian follower said that he was able to express what he wanted to say to a top leader in email while he could not do that face-to-face because of their difference in status:

> In email, if you are thinking, to something in authority, for example, the top leader, it's hard to communicate face-to-face. Because you wanted to make sure that everything you were saying, you really have to have something in your mind to support your statement. In writing you can do that. I write this because I know this is the right rationale behind. And you are talking to the top leader. (Follower B6)

Organize thoughts. Email provided time to think through an issue and to organize thoughts:

> If I was trying to explain something or give a response, I would much rather email than say it... So the pros of email, that you can have time to think about it before saying it, you can say everything you want to say without being interrupted by someone else. (Follower F3)

Some people whose native language was not English preferred writing email because it gave them time to organize their thoughts and to edit the writing:

> I prefer using email. Because English is my second language, writing helps me to keep my thinking organized and corrected before sending. Most of our communication is about work, so I usually do not need to see him [leader] face-to-face. (Follower D4)

Convenience. Email was convenient because the sender did not need to worry about where the recipient was located: "With email you don't worry about wherever he [leader] is, because he is always traveling" (Follower F3). Unlike a face-to-face conversation or a phone call, email did not interrupt a recipient. Emails were easy to send and could be answered whenever the person wanted: "It's easier to just email a question and it's also, it can be answered at their convenience" (Follower D2).

Weaknesses of email communication. As the followers noted many strengths of email, they also articulated many more weakness. Six themes emerged through analysis: relational issues, time issues, not suitable for certain situations, prone to miscommunication, language issue, and cultural issues.

Relational issues. When people wrote emails, they had tendency to write only business matters and not necessarily try to build relationships:

> Sure, we do electronic stuff. But there hasn't been as much, and consequently the relationship…up close and personal. You sit down together with a cup of coffee, or something to drink and have some merienda [snack], and just kind of relaxing, share stories, what're your kids doing, and it's got all business, electronic stuff. That's kind of sterile. There's not a life to it. I mean it's all business. (Follower B5)

When email was used among friends, it was sometimes unsatisfactory: "Email is somewhat impersonal, even with friends of mine. When I email my friends, I have to tell him my email is just business-like" (Follower H5). When email was exchanged with a leader who was only an acquaintance, the content of the email was very formal and handled only work: "It was a very formal one. I knew him before. We've met in few meetings... We didn't have that close a relationship. But still, email was something, kind of a more formal way of doing things" (Follower G4).

Communicating discontent to a leader through email might result in worsening the relationship rather than fixing the problem:

> Sometimes I expressed my frustration over virtual communication, speaking about my leader, of course, that doesn't work or did not work well. It ended up complicated things more beyond where it started. And it took more hours trying to fix the relationship other than trying to communicate. (Follower E7)

Emails could be understood as offensive when they were not carefully crafted and there was no quick way to find out how they were received:

I have to make sure it's clear that I'm saying it. I am not offending anybody. You do it in English, too. Email can be very offensive sometimes. I mean someone can throw out an email without rereading it and thinking it through. This is among Americans. The guy at the other end feels offended, so the way it was stated. So within the same culture, email can be a problem. Whereas talking, you have an opportunity to correct. If you see you are being misunderstood, you have the opportunity to correct it immediately. (Follower D3)

One follower said that when he wrote an email, he was very careful not to offend the recipient:

If I am very concerned about causing offense, or if there is a very delicate or immediate issue, being able to write something out allows me to think through my words very carefully and consider modifications. And I think, reduce the chances of causing some offense. (Follower H5)

If there was no relationship between a sender and a receiver, email communication might be difficult. Usually email communication worked best with people who already had established a relationship:

Probably for most cultures, face-to-face is good. When you are working with someone you have never met, you correspond through email or something, it's always a little bit different if you met that person, then you know them. It's just a better bonding connection there. Or if you are just doing email, if you never met the person face-to-face, then it's really hard. It's a different type of interaction. So if you had that opportunity to meet, people get to know you. That's better. That works well and that works better. (Follower H4)

Another follower recognized that her leader did not answer her email if she did not have a personal relationship with him: "When I did not have a relationship with my leader, he did not reply to my email well. But after building a relationship, he promptly replies to me" (Follower F4).

Time related issues. One follower stated that it took long time to write an email that would not cause offence:

I am very aware when I email that email comes cross very bluntly. It's very hard to write an email that I think won't upset people around, particularly when it's across culture. So it takes me a long time to write emails. (Follower C5)

Another follower explained that it took a long time for him to write a good Email because English was not his mother tongue:

> It takes forever to craft a nice email, explain the issues nicely. We spend so much energy. If you could just say, "I need this." It's easier. If you didn't understand, "Oh, what do you mean," you ask again. It's easier. English is not my first language. ….. Putting the thoughts really clearly in another language, and where do you get time to read all those emails, and where do you get time to write whatever. (Follower G6)

Sometimes, people must communicate through email across multiple time zones. Time zones added difficulty in getting a reply in a timely manner: "Because with the time difference for email, it will take a while before somebody responds" (Follower E4).

When the followers did not get feedback as quickly as they needed it, they tried to do their work without adequate information:

> One supervisor had to be evacuated because of illness and he has communicated through email. I saw a need of that team, and then I started to help them with replacing the primer. I experienced the difficulty--things lacking in long-distance relationships. When the local people made a primer, since they could not get feedback frequently, they almost copied a primer of the other language group. The primer should have a principle to know which letter to teach first. There needs to be an analysis of which letter is used the most. Without having those understanding, they just copied a primer of the other language and followed the sequence of the letters of the other language. I explained to them that their language is unique and different from other languages, so the language has to be analyzed. (Follower F3)

Unsuitability. In addition to the issues with time, email was not suitable for building relationships or expressing things in detail. Email was only good for announcing a meeting or to say something simple:

> In our relationship, it is just very much friendship, so their emails are short like, "Hello, how are you? I am praying for this and that. All this happened with your teammate or I wanted you to know this and that." Just trying to open up a conversation, but we don't talk in details in the email. Mostly [we communicate simple things] like a call for a prayer. And maybe set up time that we can meet some place to talk about it. (Follower H9)

With email communication you need to present one idea at a time rather than jump from topic to topic:

> Whereas written communication tends to much more linear, you have to go in a particular direction and it's harder to introduce a new topic, and it's even harder to come back to get to the old topic whereas in conversation it's much more free-flowing. (Follower H5)

Email communication was not suitable for talking about sensitive issues that dealt with people's feelings or personal issues: "Also in this context, there are certain sensitive issues, it's probably not good to put it into writing..." (Follower D2).

Email was not suitable for having a long discussion because it took a lot of time to compose the emails:

> It's hard to hold long discussions by email. It takes a lot of time, and sometimes email isn't, especially when I am travelling, it's not always reliable. I mean, I've been in places where I can send an email. I made time to compose it. Also, when you compose an Email, you have to think a lot more and how you say it. (Follower D2)

Email was not suitable for communicating the whole picture of complex situations:

> Even though I feel inadequate in some aspects, because I am in the country, I could contact people, listen to them, and try to struggle with them. If a supervisor is outside of the country, a local person is impossible to communicate to the supervisor through email [and explain their complex situation]. (Follower F3)

Email was not suitable for village living where there was no Internet unless a satellite was utilized to get Internet connection: "It will be very expensive because of satellite" (Follower F5).

Miscommunication. Email communication could be unclear because there was no body language, which would have added meaning to the communication:

Email is the poorest method of communication. And I have a deep concern, not that I am going to voice this to the organization, because I think everybody is aware of that. I hope everybody is aware of that. It is so poor in the way that we are having more interpersonal conflict created over email than the generation before, in the pre-email era. When I talk to someone face-to-face using the same language, the stats I heard is 70 to 80 percent of communication. So it leaves 20-30 percent of miscommunication. So let's subtract from them, from 70-80 that is left, so not face-to-face, not having live chat, not having the tone of voice, relying a lot on somebody speaking English as a second language, people coming from different cultures, where they don't really need to offend people, because their value system is different. Other people take it as an offense, and it doesn't give you time to clarify in 5 seconds, so they just, everyone of these things. So it's the poorest method of communication but everybody depends on that. (Follower E7)

One of the reasons that email caused miscommunication was because of its one-way communication aspect:

Yeah, it depends on which kinds of roles or aspects we are thinking of. It's not usually as effective as I think it's going to be. That's one way of saying. What more things are not communicated that I think probably should have been. It's quite a bit of miscommunication that happens through email. (Follower C6)

Another reason email caused miscommunication is that people did not take adequate time to compose and analyze the content of their email before sending it:

Email works well also, actually email might be more efficient if its matters to deal with that can't be dealt with quickly. Maybe just not with my leaders, but in general my experience with email is sometimes messages have to be written and then carefully reread, and re-edited and then maybe keep them overnight because so much can be misunderstood in printed form, in my experience. (Follower B4)

Some people were more willing to share details about a situation in face-to-face communication than in email. In that case, email communication caused misunderstanding because background information was not shared:

I think it's better with him to write to clarify. Sometimes in emails, he is a bit vague about why he feels a certain way. He wouldn't just say it. But in person he will explain why he feels a certain way. Recently there was an email to our team leader, and I knew some of the background, but she (leader) didn't. So she was very confused about his email. Whereas I talked to him face-to-face about the issue, and got a lot more understanding. (Follower F3)

Email could be lost in cyber space so it never arrived. It was also possible that the recipient did not truly understand the message as it was intended. If this occurred it required effort to clear up the situation:

> An email can go astray, not too often, but that can happen. It just doesn't arrive, very seldom. Even if you try hard to say exactly what you want to say in an email, people can still misunderstand it. Fortunately, not too often, and then you actually got back and you got to work that out. (Follower F6)

Language issues. Added difficulty arose when one or both parties wrote in a second language. In those cases, the sender and the receiver both needed to work hard to overcome language barriers:

> We do a lot of communication either by typing, chat or by email. That does the cross-cultural differences as well as language difference there. So in that sense it's more the language barrier that's a barrier than the culture. It's the language and the medium, having to put things in writing when it's your second language. Writing English is awkward. I have to be careful how I write things so it would be understood clearly. (Follower C6)

One follower expressed his struggle with the language barrier when he was working with people whose mother tongue was not English:

Follower E9
    If I would be working with just Americans, then it might work. But since we work with people with different cultures, it's very hard.

Researcher
    In what context do you mean by 'it might work with just American?'

Follower E9
    The clarity of the email message. Especially because we always talk about projects, and we really go into detail. It's very important to get details, very specific. So I am always struggling with my colleagues not using the proper words and not using the correct term.

Another follower shared his concern about his English level; he was willing to put things in writing but still wanted to go over the items face-to-face to make sure things were communicated clearly:

> I will not put in email everything. Because I know that I do not have the ability to express in the language that will communicate clearly, because it is not my language. I could speak English but I could not really determine whether the vocabulary I am using would bring out the same meaning, what I have in mind. But I can put maybe, could something, the issue in general there and discuss with them in person. (Follower B6)

One follower articulated that, when his leader was out of the country, he would not email about an important issue because of the language difficulty:

> In his [leader's] absence, if it is a major decision, I will wait for him. Because once he is away it is not easy to just connect to him. If it is an emergency thing, ... he might just give me an answer. If it is something I and he need to sit together to discuss, he will not just email. Because email uses English, which is not our first language. So if the communication is not very clear, the decision that is going to be taken will be affected. (Follower G2)

Cultural issues. Beside language issues, email was difficult when it was used cross-culturally. As people communicated through email, they communicated with people from different cultures without knowing the cultural norms of the other culture:

> Suddenly our global leadership or everybody assumes that, hey, we can talk to each other. We can talk to someone in Africa. We can talk to somebody in Papua New Guinea. Yeah, and we can. We can start to talk to someone we've never met and the cultural background that I've never studied. The kind of seasons, the kind of economy, economic crisis, and the church climate that they are going through, that I never had any idea of. And I have to start to communicate with them. So how much assumption I have to have to put when I start talking to this person. That never happened before. If I am meeting somebody in Canada face-to-face in the traditional communication, after a few years, I learn to be a Canadian, or I learn what's expected in Canadian protocol so there even if I am talking to, say, those Chinese person and I over the years learn to know what the Canadian protocols are, so we can communicate with certain standards. We totally broke that. (Follower E7)

Email communication was not a proper form of communication in some cultures. When interview participants worked in those cultures, they had to consider cultural aspects:

> In my perspective about trying to communicate with Indonesians, my observation is that face-to-face is still the best. It's their culture. ... Even today, with wedding invitations, people still have them personally delivered it to you. They don't send it through mail, or email it to you or announce it. Announcing it at a church is not enough. They go individually to people's houses to invite them. You are allowed to ignore written communications but when it's personal, you have to pay attention. That's in Indonesia. (Follower D2)

Therefore, more caution had to be taken take when communicating with people from other cultures through email: "It's very hard to write an email that I think won't upset people around, particularly when it's across culture" (Follower C5).

Face-to-Face

Most of the followers expressed that they wanted to have more face-to-face meeting with their leaders. Followers covered usage, strengths, and weaknesses of face-to-face communication.

Use of face-to-face communication. For face-to-face communication, the followers in this research identified the same two areas as the leaders: dealing with sensitive issues or conflict and important issues. They also added two more areas: lengthy discussion and cultural issues.

Sensitive issues or conflict. When there were personal issues, difficult issues, or conflicts, the follower wanted to communicate with leaders and team members face-to-face: "Face-to-face, definitely, if there are interpersonal issues on the team. We need to see their nonverbal expressions" (Follower B3). Another follower expressed the similar opinion: "Anything that has to do with personnel or with other people, you don't like to write that on the email, if you're discussing some personal sort of issue. That's a bit of face-to-face" (Follower B7). Another follower expressed that handling conflict should be done by face-to-face communication: "If there were ever a conflict or personal problem or something, I would think that would be face-to-face, if possible" (Follower D3).

Lengthy discussion. When a certain issue required a lengthy discussion, it was best to discuss it face-to-face rather than emailing back and forth many times:

> If it's going to be a lengthy discussion about something, it's just easier to be face-to-face to talk about it, than to try to write it all out. Writing is not a strong point for me. So to me it has to do with the length of, or if it's complicated, I would prefer to be able to talk face-to-face with somebody about it than to write an email or a letter. (Follower F6)

One follower gave his opinion that a face-to-face meeting was required or at least a voice conversation was desired to cover a lengthy discussion:

> Sometimes it's good to at least talk on the phone, because sometimes things need to be discussed, and it's too much effort. You don't need to say all this. If up here the answer would be a certain way, then you would not go that direction. Sometimes discussing something, it's better to be able to either it's talk face-to-face. (Follower D2)

Another follower identified that a face-to-face group meeting was very beneficial when the leader updated them with a lot of information:

> Last week, we had two days of meetings here. My leader asked us to come over for some updates and talking about some topics. That was really good. I appreciated face-to-face and it was in a group. So we had interaction, and he had some power points so you could see what he was talking about and see the pictures of people he was talking about. I think that's helpful to me, to see people's faces. So I really appreciate occupational meetings like that. I really think that was helpful. Even though it took time, it was a chunk of time of those two days, but for occasional meetings like that, it was very good, to be there together. (Follower D3)

Important issues. Followers wanted to communicate about important issues with their leaders face-to-face: "That's [face-to-face] the best probably but it's not always possible. If something is important, it's face-to-face… If you want to suggest something, then… you can present to the person. That's more like to be accepted" (Follower C3).

Another follower explained that he would call his leader for important issues when the leader was traveling for the leader to be updated but would wait for a face-to-face encounter for a real discussion: "It is very important that I call my leader. When my leader is traveling, I wait until he comes back for the important issues" (Follower A6).

Cultural reasons. One Asian follower expressed that her preference for all communication was face-to-face, but realized that the Westerners wanted certain types of communication to be written:

> I prefer face-to-face but when I say something face-to-face, the Westerners tell me to email them. They may think that they may forget or not official unless it's written. When I share something, sometimes they tell me to write a certain person on that issue. I think my communication is about 50 percent email and 50 percent face-to-face. I prefer face-to-face communication with difficult issues or sharing feelings and use email for sharing information. But when I share information, I prefer inviting people over a meal and talk about it more than just writing an email. (Follower F11)

One follower stated that face-to-face conversation was important in her culture, and she communicated that to her leaders: "We tell the Americans face-to-face conversation is very important" (Follower H7). Another follower experienced that, when she dealt with an Asian colleague, communicating with them face-to-face was honoring them: "Better to wait for sensitive issues to face-to-face to honor them" (Follower D5).

Strengths of face-to-face communication. The followers in this research identified the same two strengths that the leaders stated—clear communication and being relational. In addition to those, they added language issues, being flexible, and cultural issues.

Clear communication. In terms of clear communication, face-to-face communication could utilize body language and facial expression which did provide more understanding.

Body language and facial expression. The strength of face-to-face communication was holistic communicating by using facial expression, tone of voice, and body language:

> I don't have to write (laughter) for lazy person like me. I don't have to write a piece of message. I just talk. I just speak up, and also I can see both of us. We can see each other facial expression, gesture, tone, everything all together. So it's easier. It's a holistic communication, not just words. I can almost feel how she [her leader] is feeling and thinking. That is something usually I cannot tell just from words. (Follower E8)

One Asian follower said what he truly wanted to communicate was done through his facial expressions not with his verbal communication, which was sometimes contradicted his facial expression. He appreciated the leaders who understood his nonverbal communication:

> With my leaders, with many SIL people, I love to do it face-to-face, because something you could express, you could support your language with your facial expression. Sometimes in Asia, you may say yes but you express it in your body, say no. (laughter) The advantage of having face-to-face is that you can really show them. This is what you really feel. People in SIL, you don't need to explain deeply and they could just get it. I think they were trained. When they hear the language, where they could see someone, they could determine whether he is saying it's true or not. That's our people in SIL. (Follower B6)

This particular Asian follower said that SIL people were good at understanding body language. However, some of the leaders specifically expressed that understanding nonverbal language was a challenge as reported earlier. Therefore, this area should be examined more.

Another follower stated that even though she knew her leader was busy, she still wanted to communicate with her leader face-to-face because she wanted to have clear communication by seeing facial expressions:

> You can get a better idea of how you each are feeling, facial expressions. With our leader, like what I said, it's easier to me what is feeling with face-to-face. He is very busy. Even if he is there, sometimes I feel like I steal his time. (Follower F3)

More understanding. Face-to-face communication brought more understanding about what people intended to communicate:

> When people are not able to talk face-to-face, that makes things much more difficult, much easier for misunderstanding. And in our cases, when we make assumptions, and we make a whole lot of decisions based upon assumptions. We find that can be very disastrous. (Follower B5)

Face-to-face communication made it possible to clarify conversation instantly by asking questions:

> For me there is nothing that replaces face-to-face conversation. Nothing. So much can be misunderstood even in a face-to-face conversation, there can be misunderstanding. There constantly needs to be clarification: "What did you mean by that?" In my experience, because there's so much high need for that, my feeling is that nothing replaces face-to-face. (Follower B4)

Relational. In addition to having clear communication, face-to-face communication added the relational aspect, while written communication could not add it as much: "The other thing is also when you talk face-to-face is like that you feel the relation, closeness" (Follower G2). Face-to-face communication provided meaningful interaction: "The pro of meeting face-to-face is, I think, it's more meaningful interaction" (Follower D3). Face-to-face meetings encouraged people: "It encourages people around with face-to-face" (Follower E3). Also face-to-face meetings provided enjoyable social time: "When we are together, we joke and laugh…and tease each other. It's more enjoyable face-to-face" (Follower H5).

Language issues. In the previous section, it was noted that some English-as-a-second-language people desired to communicate through email because it gave them time to think about what to say and to be able to edit their writing before sending it. However, many more people whose mother tongue was not English appreciated face-to-face communication because body language could compensate for their lack of language:

> For people in SIL, when you talk face-to-face, they have full consideration, especially for Asians. Because sometimes Filipinos could really not express everything you want. We are not that expert in language. We could not really communicate like Western people. Our expression is different. Sometimes the vocabulary we use is not clear. So most of us have that kind of fear, "If I say that, is this correct? Do I need to use dictionary to be able to communicate and use the right vocabulary? So that I could tell them what I feel inside." There is that kind of fear actually in communication. But in SIL, even if you speak a little bit ambiguous, the way you articulate your message, they can understand you. (Follower B6)

Another follower, whose mother tongue was not English, stated that speaking was easier than writing: "And also because of the fact that both of us are, English is not our first language, and that's the language we use. That becomes a factor also. Talking in English is easier than writing" (Follower G6).

Flexibility. Face-to-face communication added flexibility in knowing when it was the right time to approach people and to pray for other people:

> I think you are able to read what this person is going through. So it makes it easier to pray for them, or you are able to find the right words, and in a way, you can put a time, the right timing for you to approach them, the best time to approach them. If they look tired, maybe this is not. (Follower E3)

In face-to-face communication participants could change topics, but people could easily return to previous topics if they needed to:

And also in a conversation, if somebody says something and thinks of something else, you want to change the direction of the conversation, then it's very easy to do that. And then you come back to where you were before. (Follower H5)

Cultural. The followers in this research identified that there were cultural aspects of face-to-face communication: "It's Indonesian culture to talk to face-to-face when dealing with important issues" (Follower F2). Another follower stated that because he did not use technology for communication in his culture, most of communication was done face-to-face:

Well the other factor is, I've been to this email and this Internet and all this sophisticated system only for few years. Before in my country also, the communication system was almost like face-to-face, before telephone came and all these things. Growing up in that environment, you know, not used this system of Internet and communicating through email and all those things for many years until I was like maybe 25 years old or 23 years old. Only from that time I started using Internet, email and all those things. I probably only use it in unavoidable situations. (Follower G2)

Weaknesses of face-to-face communication. Every method of communication had weaknesses. Even though face-to-face communication was the most desirable according to the interview participants, it still had weaknesses. The followers in this research identified two areas: no documentation and language issues.

No documentation. One follower had a hard time when her boss changed a decision they had made earlier, without notification, and the follower wished he had written documentation about their previous communication:

When the usage is changed later, I have no proof of the previous communication. I have experienced that several times already. When things were confirmed by face-to-face communication, he had another plan and he was not able to do the things planned with me, but he did not notify me. When I addressed that incident, he said that he had other urgent things that came in and decided to do that instead. Even though he had a valid reason, I could not understand why he did not communicate to me. (Follower F10)

Language issues. One follower whose mother tongue was not English stated that it was hard for her to choose the right words when she communicated face-to-face:

> But the bad thing is, of course, my broken English, I have to think, "What are the right words to express something?" And then "Yeah, yeah," and she was looking at me and you know, she is kind and she just looks at me, patiently waiting for an answer, something like that. (Follower E8)

It appeared that the language issue was identified as both a strength and a weakness.

Phone Call

The phone call was significantly less addressed in comparison to the email and face-to-face usage in communication among followers also. The followers articulated usage, strengths, and weaknesses of phone calls in communicating with their leaders.

Phone call use. The followers used the phone call to discuss important matters with the leaders, to get a timely response from the leaders, and to use it as a secondary method of communication.

Important issues. Followers called their leader about important issues when the leader was traveling: "Telephone is about the talk about the issue. … If it's very important issues, then call my leader [when he is traveling]" (Follower A3). Another follower also expressed that he called his leader for important issues: "I called him when he was in India. There was some important to decide on" (Follower G6).

Time-related issues. When the followers needed immediate response from the leader, they called the leader: "If you want to get a response immediately, then call him on the phone" (Follower B8). A follower called his leader during the off hours for communication: "Phone is if away, off-duty period, off-business hours" (Follower A2).

Secondary option. When one method of communication did not work, the followers tried a phone call as a secondary option: "He might forget about my email. Or he maybe didn't understand my email so that he did not reply. Then I call him" (Follower F7). Another follower texted her leader but when the text did not work, she called her leader: "When text did not work then I call" (Follower F8).

Strengths of phone calls. Phone calls were often used to discuss email communication that already had been sent: "If I am far away, for example, when I was in US for couple of months, and I had to email a certain subject and follow up with a phone call later to make sure he was understanding" (Follower D5). Another benefit of the phone call was to hear the tone of voice: "Maybe telephone because I can hear each other's voice" (Follower D5).

Weaknesses of phone calls. One drawback was the potential interruption of a recipient: "I am reluctant to call because I don't know he might be in a meeting" (Follower D2). The other drawback a follower identified was an economic issue: "The telephone call is really rare because it was expensive" (Follower B9).

SMS

SMS was a relatively new method in communication. The followers explained when they used SMS, and what the strengths and weaknesses were using SMS in their communication.

Use of SMS communication. The followers used SMS for urgent issues, as a secondary way of communication, and to encourage other team members: "If he [her leader] is travelling, he is usually available email or text. I have texted him, when I had emergency finance situation, and he helped with that" (Follower D6). One follower stated that he used SMS when he did not have an Internet connection: "When I don't have Internet connection, I text a lot. When I communicate to staff who don't have Internet connection, I copy people to be in the loop, with people who are outside of the campus" (Follower G3). One follower sent Bible verses to encourage other team members: "I am sending some [Bible] verses to them" (Follower E5).

Strengths of SMS. One follower noted that texting was inexpensive, did not interrupt a receiver, did not require Internet connection:

> If I was in another country, had a concern I could've text, because it's cheaper than calling, and again I am not interrupting if he is in the middle of talking to somebody, I am not interrupting, and I don't have good email reception most of the time. (Follower D2)

Weaknesses of SMS. The followers in this research identified that the drawback of SMS communication was unclear messages due to shortened words: "SMS is less clear than phone call" (Follower F8). SMS did not work without roaming for international travel: "One time my leader was trying to communicate with her [his follower] and eventually we found out she was travelling outside of the country. So texting was not working, of course" (Follower B4).

Skype

Video communication provided another way of connecting the leader to the followers. Skype was the tool that was used the most in SIL and its partner organizations among video communication methods. Some followers used Skype video communication when their leaders were travelling, and some followers used Skype chat for sending urgent messages to their leaders, or to get connected with the other teammates located in other locations: "I am thankful for Skype, that's a second best, especially the video chat" (Follower B4).

Strengths of Skype. Some followers articulated that the Skype video communication was easier than email communication, and the visual ability provided them to communicate clearly to gain understanding:

> I used Skype with a computer person, on a computer thing that we were trying to work out and it was really great to be able to do that. We were looking at each other because he needed to look at stuff on my screen, helped me to do things but I could hear his voice, and he could hear mine, still not a hundred percent, the same as being there in person. (Follower F6)

One follower usually communicated with his leader through Skype chat because Skype was the most convenient way to catch his busy supervisor and also Skype chat provided a written record:

> When we actually have meetings, that's usually Skype, and usually Skype chat, not Skype voice. It depends on our Internet connection more than anything. And also I think this something, I want to have documentation of what happened, in writing what was decided. Sometimes you can tell ahead of time that's going to be helpful, … Things changed later on, and were different than actually what was agreed on. Therefore I was in trouble. I learned sometimes it's good to have documentation, and for everyone's sake. (Follower C7)

Weaknesses of Skype. Technology was a drawback in some of the places interview participants were working: One follower expressed that he wanted to communicate with his team members at least with an audio chat once a month, but the Internet where his team members were was not good enough for that:

> We haven't had big problems yet. Everything is going pretty smoothly. Just for morale, it will be nice just to, at least once a month, to do an audio chat. We do now, but the Internet is not good enough for that. We haven't had any issues where it would be necessary because of an issue, but just for maintaining the contact. It would be nice. Internet is not good enough in the village for audio or for video. (Follower B7)

Another follower said that it was hard to pay attention to a Skype audio group meeting and easy to be distracted:

> I think you have to be more intentional with the Skype meeting to keep the meeting moving, and to engage people who are not there. It's quite easy to get distracted, and not pay attention on Skype. They are not video Skype, they are voice Skype. And so you can have long stretches of time when you don't hear from people at all. So it hadn't been really effective. It's more difficult to get good interaction, dialogue on Skype with a group. The smaller the group, the better, the more focused, the discussion is better. (Follower C6)

When one team was having a team meeting using Skype voice communication, crossing seven different time zones was a drawback to overcome. One follower observed people who were on the Skype voice meeting and expressed difficulty of crossing time zones: "If I was on the leadership team, I would find that would be very frustrating. In fact most of my leadership team are in different countries, in seven different time zones… trying to work out time zones were difficult" (Follower C5).

Facebook

One team in this research used Facebook for their social communication. One follower of that group initiated a Facebook community to have more active communication within the team: "I suggested opening up communication channel through Facebook because when I observed our team members, I realized that there is lack of communication among team members. They have nice but not deep relationship among the team members" (Follower E11).

Use of Facebook communication. It was very effective in connecting the team members using Facebook:

> Facebook works very well because we update each other on what's going on, and people comment, and it's good. Because when we meet face-to-face, then we always have something to talk to, not just starting off with nothing then asking,

"Oh, how are you? How have you been?" Those very generic questions. Facebook is very effective and like some people, like me and my wife, I think everyone else is always on Facebook. (Follower E9)

Strengths of Facebook. The followers stated that using Facebook made it possible to share their informal social activities, to share lives, to promote team morale, and to encourage team members.

Informal social activity. Facebook communication provided a natural environment to express themselves and provided a relationship based working environment:

> Maybe the top of the list would be the Facebook my team is using, because you can be yourself in there, and still can say the same things that you would say in a formal email. For me, email is too tight. It's too task-focused, rather than relationship[-focused]. But with FB, you can have both. I think that's the top on my list. (Follower E3)

Another advantage of using Facebook was connecting the team members with their feelings and sharing their lives:

> Facebook is my favorite. You can just, if you have something like, that you are happy today, you can really post it. And it's more cheaper (laughter) than texting to everyone. And they will respond, like they will like your status, or they will like, if I am upset, they will give you a verse. That you know that you will, that will be a serve for your devotion today. That really helps even when you are in a remote area. Like we are together, we are working together. (Follower E6)

Promote team morale. Several people noted that Facebook was excellent tool for team building. People who were not interacting with other team members started sharing their lives on Facebook with other team members:

> Once there was a group on the Facebook, people who had been silent in terms of social activity with the other team members started interacting with team members proactively. Since that group is not open to the public but only open to the working team members, it received very positive responses from the team members. I encouraged people to share their personal lives not to share too many things about the work in the Facebook: jokes, ideas, life experiences and some insights about life. The best outcome of using the Facebook was that team

members who were silent and hidden came out. Because Facebook made the communication possible which was not possible through email. (Follower E11)

Encourage. Team members who were using the Facebook community encouraged prayer among the team members:

> We are using a secret group [community] in Facebook to communicate with each other. I found that that is a very good tool for us. Especially we are scattered around Asia, we are not living together in one country, in one city. So that kind of communication makes me feel that we are a team. Even though we are separate, so I, that kind of communication is not only about work, about jobs, but also like one of our teammates is sick, and then he is in the hospital. So his wife posts his picture in the hospital on Facebook, and then lists his prayer needs there. The other team members will know how to pray for him and that make me feel that we are really a team. We are not just saying hi and bye, like that. When I share what I need to pray for, then I get the responses from different team members, and that make me feel like we are really a team. (Follower E8)

Weaknesses of Facebook. One follower articulated that Facebook was not his personal choice of communication because Facebook was passive and lacked live communication:

> Facebook, I haven't gotten a chance to participate because I don't do much Facebook. I am more into chatting over text, because it's live. Facebook is very passive in terms of communication. It's like an email, because other person can check whatever they want. It's almost like in old technology, I leave a fax message. There's someone to communicate. It's up to them to check it. And I never knew if they checked it. So how can I rely to communication if I don't know if they check it or not. So Facebook is like an online fax machine. It just doesn't cost me to send stuff. (Follower E7)

Pronto

Pronto is a secure group chatting application. The same team that used Facebook also used Pronto to discuss their work. Pronto was initiated because some of their team members were not able to get on Facebook and Facebook was not suitable to discuss work. Team members were chatting thirty minutes per week to exchange ideas and to decide on work issues:

But there was a team member who could not participate in the Facebook account because the Facebook was not available in the country she was working. ... So another communication channel was opened: Pronto, which is a secure group chatting. Team members started to brainstorm and share ideas about the work every Monday morning ... for thirty minutes. (Follower E11)

Strengths of Pronto. One follower explained that a Pronto meeting helped team building and accountability:

I value Pronto meeting. It's really helping me. So since we started Pronto meetings, that helped my team with spirit building, morale, accountability with a team. And a sense of team belonging has increased. And I have talked to other remote assigned people when I meet them face-to-face. Well, there are other remote assigned people that rely on that. And it seems like they are enjoying it too, from what I can tell. (Follower E7)

Weaknesses of Pronto. However, Pronto came with weaknesses just like any other type of communication tool. Because team members typed what they thought at the moment, people whose mother tongue was not English had a hard time thinking and typing at the same time: "Pronto is just chatting. Again it's just like email. Sometimes it's very hard because the language used is English" (Follower E9).

Because everybody was typing at the same time, some of what was typed was not in order and created misunderstanding. Another problem was that Internet speed controlled the speed of communication. People located with slow Internet connection had a disadvantage in communication using Pronto:

Maybe five persons speaking at the same time, and then the chairman would lose a focus-- who is talking. And then he will miss some of the opinion, sometimes. So that may not be very good if one team member think his opinion is good but the chair person would miss that. He feels that my opinion is not taken as important, something like that. (Follower E8)

Multiple Methods

Followers in this research were using multiple methods to communicate with the leaders and co-workers, because different communication methods had different strengths:

> What I did was I sent her an Email, and then I sent her a cell text saying, "I have just sent you an Email." Later, face-to-face she said, "Yes, that was a good idea. Alert me to the fact that you sent me an Email." (Follower B4)

One follower explained that she used the most effective ones for various situations:

> Face-to-face is always good. But face-to-face, also depending on the situation, takes more time. And there's a time that text works very well. There's times when a phone call works very well, whether it's over Skype or cell phone... I will go with what the situation is. If I need more clarification, I will say, "I will call you." Or he [her leader] will do the same with me. If he needs to clarify this, he would just call me. (Follower H6)

One follower said that he used different methods for different people for effective communication: "Most of other communication is done by email. With a team, we email. When I go to the community it's face-to-face... I think email with the community is difficult. So I text them rather than email them" (Follower H8).

One team who used Facebook and Pronto in addition to the other communication tools, experienced that using multiple communication tools improved team morale:

> Email communication backed up what's been shared through Pronto communication. Since there are three different ways of communicating to the team members, people who were isolated, or quite, started to be involved in the communication with the team members very actively. (Follower E11)

People working remotely depended on various communication tools. However, when the computer did not work or Internet was not steady, communication ability suffered:

It's mostly good because we can check as an instant messaging to the team... It's hard to work with people from remote, if you have never met, but fortunately we've met... So we work by combination of email and instant messaging. The main thing is as long as computers keep going in the office. If the computers stopped, then we'll be stuck. The Internet in the office is pretty good, 90 percent, but it's very slow. At least we can instant message. We can't talk on Skype, but we can instant message. (Follower B7)

Chapter 9 Summary

Data collected from both leaders and the followers were very similar in regard to communication methods. Both identified three areas of each communication method: usage, strengths, and weaknesses. The dominant communication method in SIL and its partner organizations in this research was email, even though people wanted to have more face-to-face communication but circumstances did not allow it. Leaders noted that the strength of email was documenting and the weakness was creating miscommunication. The predominant usage of email according to followers was sending reports, and the strength of email was having a document; its greatest weakness was lack of relationship. However, there were some contrasting opinions. While the leaders stated that email was not expressive, followers stated that email was expressive because they could say whatever they wanted to say without interruption and without seeing people. Followers identified convenience as email's strength and cultural misunderstandings was its weakness while leaders did not mention these qualities.

The data about face-to-face communication from both leaders and followers was also very similar. The dominant usage of face-to-face communication was dealing with sensitive issues or conflict and lengthy discussion. The biggest strength was clear communication.

Both leaders and followers used other communication methods like phone calls, SMS, and Skype to be effective. However, the usage of phone calls, SMS, and Skype was significantly less than email communication.

One team intentionally used Facebook and Pronto to communicate with team members who were scattered in many different countries in Asia. Using both communication tools helped building relations, team morale, and team discussion for work.

Both leaders and followers used multiple communication tools and picked one tool over the other depending on the situation, person, and culture. It was wise to know which tool would be effective. The interviews I did for this research made one follower think about using video communication with her team members to improve the quality of communication: "Right now just by email, mostly, going with them, copying, and another on email. I think we need to go a step further and I think we need to do some team Skype calls or things like that" (Follower H6).

---

1 Pronto is a secure group chatting application provided by SIL.

CHAPTER 10

SUMMARY AND CONCLUSIONS

The purpose of this study was to understand and describe perceptions of good leadership and followership in a multicultural organization where computer-aided communication was the major tool for interaction. This chapter revisits the substantive theory that emerged from the data, compares the research results to other existing theories, and delineates recommendations for further research.

A Theory of Leadership and Followership in a Multicultural Organization

The main question of this research was "how do leaders and followers in a multicultural organization describe the qualities a person must possess to foster effective working relationships?" In attempting to answer the question, I interviewed 10 leaders and 65 followers who were working with SIL and its partner organizations. A substantive theory emerged from the data. Both followers and leaders in multicultural organizations where computer-aided communication is the most frequently used interaction platform perceived that effective leadership and followership derived from specific and identifiable relational qualities, task-oriented competencies, character-related qualities, spiritual qualities, cultural intelligence (CQ), and the way communication by computer is used and understood. What follows are some summary statements of the research that I explained earlier in detail.

Relational Qualities

1. Overall there were more expectations stated for leadership than for followership.
2. Both leaders and followers had similar expectations for leadership but their expectations for followership differed.
3. Leaders valued task-oriented competencies most important.
4. Followers considered relational qualities most important.
5. Among all the leadership and followership qualities, communication was the single most recurring quality named.
6. Followers emphasized the importance for a leader to listen to them.
7. Different cultural preferences for communication were detected.

Task-oriented Competencies

1. Leaders considered developing the follower the most important leadership quality.
2. Followers considered having vision was the most important leadership quality.
3. Leaders wanted followers to take initiative and be responsible.
4. Followers valued hard work more than initiative and responsibility.

Character-Related Qualities

1. Followers demanded a leader with good character.
2. Leaders wanted followers to be flexible.
3. Followers considered independence more important than flexibility.

Spiritual Qualities

1. Spiritual qualities were not mentioned very much.

2. The spiritual qualities that were mentioned were: "relationship with God" and "person of prayer." These were the same for both leadership and followership.

Cultural Intelligence (CQ)

1. The same three major categories emerged for the CQ for both leadership and followership: cognition qualities, behavioral qualities, and cultural savvy.

2. The primary qualities in the cognition dimension were cultural understanding and cultural sensitivity. The key behavior dimension was appropriate cross-cultural communication. Leaders considered understanding and responding to team dynamics important; followers stated the importance of a leader's cultural experiences and abilities.

Communication Methods

1. SIL's and its partner organizations' communication was done predominantly through email. Phone calls, SMS, and Skype were used significantly less than email for the work.

2. Most of the interviewees in this research wanted more face-to-face communication between the leaders and followers.

3. The relationship between the leaders and followers was affected by the major drawbacks of email communication, which gave rise to a lack of relationship and misunderstandings. Not having enough face-to-face communication was detrimental because the major strengths of face-to-face communication were clear communication and relationship building.

4. Both followers and leaders used multiple methods to communicate effectively based upon culture, relationships, economic realities, and specifics of the situation.

Answer to the Research Subquestions

The Chapters 4 to 9 explored the answers to subquestions. The following summarizes the answers to the subquestions listed at the beginning of this study.

Question 1 - How Do Leaders Working in SIL and Its Partner Organizations Describe Qualities of Effective Leadership?

Leaders want to achieve good communication, demonstrate care, and attain cultural understanding of the followers they worked with. Leaders listed developing followers as their most important task followed by having vision and handling conflict. They identified humility as the most important character-related quality and having a relationship with God as the most important spiritual quality.

Question 2 - How Do Followers Working in SIL and Its Partner Organizations Describe Qualities of Effective Leaders?

Followers identified communication and demonstrable care for followers as the most important relational qualities in leadership. Followers wanted a leader to have vision and develop followers but not to micromanage them. In terms of character-related qualities, followers listed wisdom, humility, being fair, and leading by example as the most important qualities. Followers wanted their leaders have a strong relationship with God and be a person of prayer. Followers expressed that a leader's cultural exposure, cultural understanding, and experiences were important indicators of being a good multicultural leader.

Question 3 - How Do Leaders Working in SIL and Its Partner Organizations Describe Qualities of Effective Followers?

The relational qualities the leaders identified were that the followers should communicate with, respect, and encourage leaders. In terms of task-oriented competencies, leaders wanted the followers to take initiative, be responsible, and follow a leader. For character qualities, leaders looked for humility and flexibility in followership. Leaders desired a follower who bore spiritual fruit from having a relationship with God. Leaders wanted the followers to communicate properly in cross-cultural situations by evidencing good cultural understanding.

Question 4 - How Do Followers Working in SIL and Its Partner Organizations Describe Qualities of Effective Followers?

Followers said communication skills and caring about the leaders and team members were the most important relational qualities they could have. In terms of task-oriented competencies, followers must work hard, follow a leader, and support the goals of the organization. Two qualities were identified as character-related qualities desired for followership: being independent, but being obedient to leadership. Followers were expected to be people of prayer and have a relationship with God. Followers should understand cultures they work with and communicate properly cross-culturally.

Question 5 - How Do Leaders and Followers in SIL and Its Partner Organizations Describe the Role of Communication Methods Affecting their Working Relationships?

Most followers wanted to have more face-to-face meetings with their leader. However remote assignments and the frequent travel of the leaders prevented this. The strengths of face-to-face meetings were clear communication and relationship. The weaknesses of email communication were miscommunication and not being relational. Because email was the dominant form of communication in SIL and its partner organizations, and because adequate face-to-face communication between a leader and a follower was sometimes impossible, relationships were affected by the drawbacks of email communication.

Application of Findings

This section gives some suggestions that can potentially provide practical help for improved leadership and followership.

Influence of Organizational Culture on Leadership and Followership

This research found that organizational culture heavily influenced the way leadership and followership play out in SIL. SIL started as a grassroots organization and, traditionally, the followers (language workers) went to a remote place for a language project and the leaders supported the followers. Therefore, independent self-starters and people who expressed themselves well were drawn to the organization, or they learned to be that way while working in SIL.

Interview data demonstrated that SIL's organizational culture influenced the concept of leadership and followership. First, the leaders' desire to develop and support followers was deeply rooted in the organizational culture. Second, SIL's preferable leadership style was supportive, administrative, or participative leadership with charismatic flavor rather than strong, charismatic, or team-oriented leadership. Third, leaders' desire for followers to initiative and be responsible echoed the same organizational culture. Fourth, the followers' desire that a leader not be a micromanager and one that gave them a lot of freedom also showed SIL's organizational culture. Fifth, followers emphasized the importance for a leader to listen to them. All the points above indicated that organizational culture influenced desired leadership and followership. Therefore, I suggest that the organizational culture should be studied together with the research on leadership and followership.

This research detected team subcultures that were different from the major organizational culture based on the composition of people or the goal of a team. Therefore, subcultures of the teams should not be assumed. I recommend a time to express leadership and followership expectations as a team exercise for SIL teams. Once the expectations are identified, the leader and the followers can adjust accordingly in order to communicate, relate, and work better with each other.

Cultural Issues

Cultural issues emerged throughout the research. First, the culture of team members influenced the concept of leadership and followership. Second, cultural preference for communication was detected. Third, at times people used the same words but the definitions were different. Fourth, people had an easier time understanding similar cultures. Fifth, minority cultures had different experiences than majority cultures. Finally, people detected cultural strengths from different cultures and wanted those cultural strengths to be practiced.

Cultural influence on leadership and followership. Several metaphors illustrated the relationship between leadership and followership. One distinctive illustration was that of a leader being a friend versus being a father. All Westerners and some non-Westerners wanted to have friendship between a leader and a follower. However, some non-Westerners clearly articulated that they wanted to have a father-child relationship with their leader.

Another cultural difference in leadership and followership was that most Westerners preferred to have administrative, supportive leadership but some non-Westerners wanted to have a strong charismatic leader. Cultural differences in leadership and followership should be communicated with the team members to avoid potential misunderstanding and conflict.

Communication. As far as cultural preference, it was evident that Westerners wanted a direct communication style and non-Westerners preferred indirect communication style especially when communicating difficult issues. Westerners struggled to understand when people communicated indirectly. At the same time, non-Westerners felt frustrated when Westerners did not comprehend the indirect way of communication. Also initiating communication with a leader was hard for the non-Western followers.

Non-Westerners needed to learn to communicate directly and to be more proactive in giving input, so they do not feel "unheard." Westerners should learn to communicate indirectly so as not to hurt the feelings of non-Westerners. It was encouraging when I saw some Westerners had learned to use a third person to understand and communicate with non-Westerners on sensitive issues.

Westerners preferred to have written communication for official matters but non-Westerners wanted to talk about work in a non-threatening environment, like mealtime. People from SIL and its partner organizations should consider a preferred way of communication with the people they are working with.

Same word with different definition. I recognized that words had different definitions based on culture. For example, "care" between a leader and a follower was very differently understood. A Thai follower stated that care for a leader meant helping with a leader's personal life like shopping, taking care of their children, performing car maintenance, or having a vacation together. This level of care was not desired in some other cultures. When expectations were unknown, some people felt over protected while others felt neglected. Therefore, unless there is time to express different ideas about the same words, relationships may suffer.

Similar culture. Interviewees identified that cultural similarity between a leader and a follower helped their relationships. They expressed that it was easier to understand similar cultures than different cultures. So people wanted to have a leader from a similar culture rather than from a very different culture. This is an important factor for SIL and its partner organizations to consider when they appoint or elect a leader.

Majority vs. minority culture. People usually behaved according to their cultural norms without any bad intentions. It appears that people from minority cultures in the organization did a lot more learning about the organizational culture than people from the majority cultures of the organization. Most of the people from minority cultures in SIL and its partner organizations were from an indirect communication and hierarchical cultural background. When they performed in a Western-dominated organization, they had a tendency toward not sharing what they thought but instead following what the leader said. Some people even felt themselves inferior to Westerners.

I recommend people from the majority culture try to understand the minority mindset in order to comprehend situations from the minority's perspective, and that people from the minority culture try to understand the majority mindset: "Working with American people, we should meet at the middle between the two cultures." (Follower H7). I recommend mutual learning.

Using cultural strengths. Organizational culture should be cultivated through fostering a multiculture friendly environment by acknowledging differences, understanding differences, appreciating differences, and encouraging the use of cultural strengths and not weaknesses. One interviewee said, "Westerners are good at planning and administration. Indonesians are more spiritual. It would be ideal to use the strengths of each culture" (Follower F11).

Paradox

Several paradoxical issues emerged from this research: independence and taking initiative versus trusting and following; and work versus relationship.

Independency and taking initiative versus trusting and following. Independent people might not necessarily trust and follow a leader automatically: "In SIL, people are pretty independent; I think it's difficult for people to follow, in some ways" (Follower C8). However, leaders in this research wanted their followers to be independent and also to follow them. Leaders also wanted followers to take the initiative and at the same time to trust them. In this case, leaders expressed that followers need to learn how to balance being independent and taking initiative with trusting and following.

Work versus relationship. Leaders valued task-oriented competencies while followers considered relational qualities more important. My interpretation of this phenomenon was that the leaders' emphasis on task was a reflection of the SIL organization itself being task-oriented as it focused on the production of the translated Bibles.

Here is a good example of balancing work and relationship. An Asian leader working in an Asian country other than his home country noticed that he should balance work and develop good personal relationships with his followers. The leader should be able to give instructions and directions but at the same time care about the followers by showing an interest in their personal life:

> I think it's very important, . . . [to have] a relationship. That's why I had built a relationship. It's a balance between, as a leader, how your relationship should be, to what level. You can be a leader, very demanding, and keep giving instructions and directives, or you could be relational. Sometimes they know that you are the leader, they're still the follower. So I could switch between two roles. ... At break time you can just talk to the person, and find out more. I have a good relationship with them so I will go even to their personal life to find out how family, children are, and then pray for them. And then they trust that you listen to them. Then they are more open. (Leader A1)

My understanding about this situation was that this leader was well aware of this particular Asian cultural practice and he balanced giving instructions and focusing on the task as a leader with building personal relationships with the followers.

Communication

Some independent followers in this research did not require much communication: "With my leader, I don't even send him email unless it's really necessary. Sometimes I wish I could talk to him whenever an issue arises. I compile issues and send them all together once at a time" (Follower C9). Another follower articulated that, due to lack of communication with his supervisor, he did not feel that he had a supervisor:

> As far as communication methods, I think communication methods could be acceptable if we had more communication. It's just, I have very little interaction with him... There's such a lack of communication and it's like, I have a supervisor, but I don't. (Follower C7)

However, it was clear that the one most desirable quality among all the qualities for both leadership and followership was communication. Therefore, both leaders and followers need to put more effort into communicating with each other.

Issues with email. Email was the most dominant way interview participants communicated. However, the drawbacks of email communication were lack of clarity in communication and relationship. Therefore, SIL and its partner organizations should look for a better way to communicate between leaders and followers. Most Asians expressed the need to build relationships through face-to-face communication. Also in some cultures, it is expected that written communication is ignored. When people work in those cultures, email should not be used for important issues.

There need to be more intentional efforts to utilize video communication or other possible communication methods that can overcome the weakness of email communication. One team's endeavor to use Facebook and Pronto demonstrated that bringing a relational component to their communication improved their relationships.

Therefore, if a team needs more effective communication between leaders and followers, they must strive to improve how they communicate.

Some Asian leaders and followers expressed that they could communicate candidly through email to Westerners while they could not do it directly face-to-face. This was a very interesting usage of email for Asians dealing with the Westerners. My interpretation was that Asians did not have to think of saving face because they were not seeing the person when they communicated through email.

Remote Assignments

Followers who were remotely assigned had few opportunities for face-to-face meetings with their leader. One follower who was remotely assigned expressed that face-to-face communication was not available to him: "Now I am in the remote assignment. So face-to-face is almost nonexistent" (Follower E7). Another follower said that:

> As people take remote assignments more these days, the followers need to be initiative and be independent with few chances of talking to a leader and less supervision without much interaction with other team members. It is harder, even though I am disciplined. (Follower E8)

Because digital communication is available, more remote assignments are doable now than before. It is my observation that remote assignments made the followers more independent. Being independent decreased the distinction between the leader and the follower. Leaders had less power and followers had more power, (Kellerman, 2008, p. 34) and less supervision from leaders due to distance promoted autonomy in work. However, benefits and drawbacks must be evaluated seriously before creating a remote assignment. "Out of mind, out of sight" still holds true. Cultural understanding might not be gained through a remote relationship. Even if the remotely assigned person knows the culture, they might not handle problems or make decisions in culturally appropriate ways, simply because it is easy to forget about the cultural implications from a distance. People from relationship-based cultures might not be as open because of the lack of the "human moment" (Hallowell, 1999) as addressed in Chapter 2, with a remote or virtual relationship. Problems do not always occur during short visits. Work might be delegated to people on-site even though they did not have the expertise that the remotely assigned people possessed. There were things that could not be understood unless one was present in person. Therefore, remote assignments should be avoided if possible, and if not, there should be plans to lessen the drawbacks.

Findings Compared to Other Theories

This section compares the existing leadership and followership theories to the research findings of this research.

Leadership Theory of Rosen, Digh, Singer, and Phillips

Rosen et al. (2000) in *Global Literacies,* identified four areas, which they named literacies, of global leadership: personal, social, business, and cultural literacy. According to Rosen et al., personal literacy was similar to character quality in this study, social literacy to relational quality, business literacy to task-oriented competencies, and cultural literacy to CQ. The major difference in categories between Rosen et al. and this study was that of spiritual quality. Spiritual quality as a category was not mentioned by Rosen et al., but it was an important part of SIL and its partner organizations because they are Christian organizations. It is also important to note that, even though the categories were similar, the content of the categories was different. See Table 14 for a comparison between the literacies of Rosen et al. and the quality categories that emerged in this study.

In terms of personal literacy versus character qualities, the importance of humility and wisdom were the same and the other points of personal literacy were in the other categories of this research. While Rosen et al. (2000) emphasized understanding business circumstances, this research put an emphasis on developing followers and providing vision and direction. Rosen et al.'s cultural literacy valued ability in dealing with cultural issues, while this research considered understanding the culture and the leader having enough cultural exposure and experience as the desirable cultural quality. Table 14 compares the data between Rosen et al. and this study.

Leadership Theory of Goldsmith, Greenberg, Robertson, and Hu-Chan

Goldsmith et al. (2003) interviewed future leaders from 120 international companies and identified the five most important characteristics of global leaders in the book *Global Leadership*: (a) thinking globally, (b) appreciating cultural diversity, (c) developing technological savvy, (d) building partnerships and alliances, and (e) sharing leadership. According to Goldsmith et al., while the first characteristic of a global leader was thinking globally, SIL interviewees did not specify this characteristic because their leaders did not handle the global level of work.

The second characteristic mentioned by Goldsmith et al. (2003) was appreciating cultural diversity, which stated that understanding other cultures was one of the key issues that promoted success. SIL interviewees identified the importance of having cultural intelligence in both leaders and followers.

Table 14

Comparison Between Literacies of Rosen, et al., and the Categories That Emerged with This Research

Literacy/Quality	Rosen et al.	This Study
Personal literacy vs. Character qualities	Aggressive insight Confident humility Authentic flexibility reflective decisiveness Realistic optimism	Humility Wisdom Fair Leads by example Experienced Honesty Integrity
Social literacy vs. Relational qualities	Pragmatic trust Urgent listening Connective teaching Collaborative individualism	Communicate Care about followers Be relational Appreciate followers Promote teamwork Understand followers
Business literacy vs. Task-oriented qualities	Chaos navigator Business geographer Historical futurist Leadership liberator Economic integrator	Develop followers Have vision and provide directions Do not be a micro manager Solve problems Attitudes toward work Delegate Motivate and Lead
Cultural literacy vs. Cultural qualities	Inquisitive internationalist respectful modernizer Culture bridger Global capitalist	Leader's cultural background and ability Understand culture

Note. Based on Rosen, Digh, Singer, & Phillips, 2000.

Third, developing technological savvy indicated that a leader should be aware of new technology related to virtual communication. The very reason this research included communication methods was the importance of understanding and using different methods communication for both leaders and followers utilizing the different communication methods for their communication and relationship building.

The fourth point of Goldsmith et al. (2003) was building partnerships and alliances. Leaders in this research addressed the complex level of partnerships they maintained.

The fifth characteristic described by Goldsmith et al. (2003) was sharing leadership. Leaders in this research did not mention sharing leadership.

I think the major differences between Goldsmith et al. (2003) and this research occurred because Goldsmith et al. gathered data from business leaders whereas SIL's and its partner organizations' data was from ministry leaders.

Leadership Theory of GLOBE

GLOBE identified six leadership styles: (a) charismatic/value based leadership; (b) team-oriented; (c) participative; (d) humane-oriented; (e) autonomous, and (f) self-protective leadership (Chhokar, Brodbeck, & House, 2007). This research identified SIL's and its partner organization's leadership as mixture of participative, charismatic, and humane-oriented leadership in order. Participative leadership was represented by the emphasis on communication and developing followers as important leadership qualities; charismatic leadership was illustrated by the importance of having clear vision and giving directions for leadership; and humane-oriented leadership was identified by an emphasis on a leader caring about, understanding, and respecting the followers.

Followership Theory of Kelley

Kelley (1992) defined five different followership typologies by using two dimensions (active engagement and critical thinking as axes): (a) exemplary (high in independent thinking score and high in active engagement score); (b) alienated (high in independent thinking score and low in active engagement score); (c) conformist (low in independent thinking score and high in active engagement score); (d) pragmatist (middle in independent thinking score and middle in active engagement score); and (e) passive (low in independent thinking score and low in active engagement score) followership.

This research identified that SIL and its partner organizations put emphasis on communication, having independence, and working hard as the most important qualities. Many interview participants expressed that they did not want to be blind followers, and watched to make sure their leader was going in the right direction. Some followers in this research, especially non-Western followers, were conformists because they wanted to follow a leader regardless of the directions and obey a leader. Kelley's followership model does not fit into the multicultural environment where people have very different understanding about followership.

Followership Theory of Chaleff

Chaleff (2009) produced four categories of the followers by using two dimensions (support and challenge): (a) Partners (high on support and high on challenge); (b) implementers (high on support and low on challenge); (c) individualists (low on support and high on challenge); and (d) resource people (low on support and low on challenge).

Using Chaleff's (2009) terminology, SIL preferred partners as the most desirable followership, because interview participants in general were high on both support and challenge. Support components from the interview data were: communicate, encourage, work hard, and follow; challenge components were: communicate and independency. Chaleff stated that followers should circle around the common purpose rather than orbit around the leader. SIL and its partner organization members were called by God for the work of translating the Bible. Therefore, interview participants do orbit around a common purpose, rather than orbit around the leader. The second dominant typology of followers in this research according to Chaleff's was individualist, because followers focused on their individual projects so much that they sometimes considered any additional work as a burden even though the additional work needed to be done for the organization.

Chaleff (2009) pointed out five points of courageous followers. The first point was that the courageous follower discovered ways to achieve their potential value to the organization, and did not anticipate that leader would provide their needs. Followers in this research were courageous followers because they strived to achieve the goals of the organization with support from the leaders.

The second point of Chaleff's (2009) courageous follower was that followers did not fear the hard work of serving a leader, and stood up for their leader in difficult times of decision making. Followers did work hard to accomplish their work rather than to serve a leader. Followers had a tendency to look at any work other than their specific project as a burden when a leader asked them to be involved. However, followers gave their leaders proper information so they could make right decisions.

Chaleff stated that "the courageous follower is willing to both comfort and confront the leader, to assume additional responsibilities to relieve the leader, or to initiate dialogue to help the leader examine her own contribution to the overload" (2009,

p. 63). I find it difficult to use Chaleff's definition of the courageous follower on this point because the concept of SIL's and its partner organization's followership was very different from what Chaleff described. The concept of leadership and followership was upside down according to Chaleff's definition of a leader and follower. In SIL the follower does the work and leaders are supportive of the followers, which means leaders relieve the workload of the followers rather than followers remove the work load from the leader.

The fourth point of Chaleff's (2009) courageous followership was respecting but transforming organizational culture. Instead of followers in this research trying to transform the organizational culture, they desired to understand leaders' and colleagues' culture.

The last point of Chaleff's (2009) courageous followership was followers being teacher to a leader and leading a leader from behind. Some leaders in this research desired followers to have a leadership mindset, which was similar to what Chaleff described. However, the followers seldom expressed a desire to have a leadership mindset, but most of them considered themselves leaders of their own projects.

The SIL's and its partner organization's followership concept was partially similar to Chaleff's concept of courageous follower but not necessarily the same. The major differences lay with SIL having a grassroots level of organizational culture where leaders supported the followers to remove the burdens of the followers as illustrated earlier.

Recommendations for Further Research

This study identified effective leadership and followership in a multicultural organization, primarily within the Asian context. It would be beneficial to have a similar study on other continents to see if there are significant differences due to cultural context.

Definitely this study recognized a need for training on multicultural issues. Training cross-cultural workers in a multicultural environment is different from training cross-cultural workers in a bicultural environment. Most of the current literature and training programs for cross-cultural workers was geared to Westerners adjusting to a field culture. There are few resources to help non-Westerners adjust to a field culture, or to help cross-cultural workers adjust to their colleague's cultures when the environment is multicultural. Therefore, a different training model should be developed to train new cross-cultural workers and re-train current cross-cultural workers for the fresh challenges of a multicultural environment.

The resources on leadership in the non-Western world are scarce. As mission agencies become more culturally diverse, and more leaders emerge from the non-Western world, it would be beneficial for Westerners to better understand the non-Western leadership style for working together in a multicultural environment. It seems apparent there is a need for more research to be done with non-Western leaders in multicultural mission agencies.

Research on followership is an infant stage. All of the followership theory has been developed in the West. Therefore, there is a need to understand the cultural norms of followership in the non-Western cultures and also to understand how different expectations of followership are played out in a multicultural environment.

Dissertation Conclusion

The central research question for participants in this study was this: How do leaders and followers in SIL and its partner organizations describe the qualities a person must possess to foster effective working relationships in an environment where computer-aided communication is used dominantly between leaders and followers? Even though my study discovered specific and identifiable qualities of leadership and followership, paradoxical qualities would emerge, reflecting people's cultural background. Therefore, a multicultural leader should be able to understand and handle paradoxical assumptions and requests from followers in addition to have general leadership qualities. I assumed that organizational culture influenced the expectations of leadership and followership but, through this study, I learned that organizational culture not only influenced the expectations of leadership and followership but also dominated them. Leadership expectations were similar between leaders and followers but expectations of followership were very different. To be an effective multicultural leader, it is important to understand different expectations of followership in addition to understand expectations of leadership. When communication is done mainly through computer-aided methods, it is critical to provide an adequate amount of face-to-face contact or any other possible method to build a strong relationship in context to the initial interactions between leaders and followers, especially in multicultural teams.

REFERENCES

Adair, R. (2008). Developing great leaders, one follower at a time. In R. Riggio, I. Chaleff, & J. Lipman-Blumen (Eds.). *The art of followership: How great followers create great leaders and organizations.* (pp. 137-153). San Francisco, CA: Jossey-Bass.

Ang, S., & Van Dyne, L. (2008). Conceptualization of cultural intelligence: Definition, distinctiveness, and nomological network. In S. Ang & L. Van Dyne (Eds.), *Handbook of cultural intelligence: Theory, measurement, and applications* (pp. 3-15). Amonk, NY: M. E. Sharpe.

Ang, S., Van Dyne, L., & Koh, C. (2008). Development and validation of the CQs: The cultural intelligence scale. In S. Ang & L. Van Dyne (Eds.), *Handbook of cultural intelligence: Theory, measurement, and applications* (pp. 3-15). Amonk, NY: M. E. Sharpe.

Auerbach, C. F., & Silverstein, L. B. (2003). *Qualitative data: An introduction to coding and analysis.* New York: New York University Press.

Bandura, A. (2002). Social cognitive theory in cultural context. *Applied Psychology: An International Review, 51*(2), 269-290.

Bass, B. M., 1985. *Leadership and performance beyond expectation.* New York, NY: Free Press.

Bolman, L. G. & Deal, T. E. (2003). *Reframing Organizations: Artistry, choice, and leadership.* San Francisco, CA: Jossey-Bass.

Broadbeck, F. C., Chhokar, J. S., & House, R. J. (2007). Culture and leadership in 25 societies: Integration, conclusions, and future directions. In J. S. Chhokar, F. C. Broadbeck, & R. J. House (Eds.), *Culture and leadership across the world: The GLOBE book of in-depth studies of 25 societies* (pp. 1023-1084). Mahwah, NJ: Lawrence Erlbaum Associates.

Bucher, R. D. (2008). *Building cultural intelligence: Nine megaskills.* Upper Saddle River, NJ: Pearson Education.

Chaleff, I. (2009). *The courageous follower: Standing up to and for our leaders.* San Francisco, CA: Berrett-Koehler.

Charmaz, K. (2006). *Constructing grounded theory: A practical guide through qualitative analysis.* Thousand Oaks, CA: Sage.

Cheverton, P. (2006). *Global account management: A complete action kit of tools and techniques for managing big customers in a shrinking world.* London, UK: Kogan Page.

Clapp-Smith, R. (2009). *Global mindset development during cultural transitions.* (Doctoral dissertation). Lincoln: University of Nebraska.

Cohen, E. (2007). *Leadership without borders: Successful strategies from world-class leaders.* Hoboken, NJ: Wiley.

Collinson, D. (2008). Rethinking followership: A post-structualist analysis of follower identities In R. Riggio, I. Chaleff, & Lipman-Blumen (Eds.). *The art of followership: How great followers create great leaders and organizations.* (pp. 179-189). San Francisco, CA: Jossey-Bass.

Corbin, J., & Strauss, A. (2008). *Basics of qualitative research: Techniques and procedures for developing grounded theory.* Los Angeles, CA: Sage.

Cramton, C. D., & Orvis, K. L. (2003). Overcoming barriers to information sharing in virtual teams. In C. B. Gibson & S. G. Cohen (Eds.), *Virtual teams that work: Creating conditions for virtual team effectiveness* (pp. 214-229). San Francisco, CA: Jossey-Bass.

Creswell, J. W. (2007). *Qualitative inquiry research design: Choosing among five approaches.* Thousand Oaks, CA: Sage.

Creswell, J. W. (2009). *Research design: Qualitative, quantitative, and mixed methods approaches.* Thousand Oaks, CA: Sage.

Crow, M. D. (2000). *Spiritual authority across cultures: The cultural contours of pneumatic leadership, east and west.* (Doctoral dissertation). Pasadena, CA: Fuller Theological Seminary.

Dalton, M., Ernst, C., Deal, J., & Leslie, J. (2002). *Success for the new global manager: How to work across distances, countries, and culture.* San Francisco, CA: Jossey-Bass.

Dean, B. P. (2007). *Cultural intelligence in global leadership: A model for developing culturally and nationally diverse teams.* (Doctoral dissertation). Virginia Beach, VA: Regent University.

DeSanctis, G., & Jiang, L. (2005). Communication and the learning effectiveness of multicultural teams. In D. L. Shapiro, M. A. Von Glinow, & J. L. Cheng (Eds.), *Managing multinational teams: Global perspectives* (pp. 97-123). Amsterdam, Netherlands: Elsevier.

Distefano, J. J., & Maxnevski, M. L. (2000). Creating value with diverse teams in global management. *Organizational Dynamics*, *29*(1), 45-63.

Dixon, D. (2008). Getting together. In R. Riggio, I. Chaleff, & Lipman-Blumen (Eds.). *The art of followership: How great followers create great leaders and organizations.* (pp. 155-177). San Francisco, CA: Jossey-Bass.

Dubrovsky, V. J., Kiesler, S. B., & Sethna, N. (1991). The equalization phenomenon: Status effects in computer-mediated and face-to-face decision making groups. *Human Computer Interaction, 6*(2), 119-146.

Earley, P. C., & Ang, S. (2003). *Cultural intelligence: Individual interactions across cultures.* Stanford, CA: Stanford University Press.

Earley, P. C., & Ang, S. & Tan, J. (2006). *CQ: Developing cultural intelligence at work.* Stanford, CA: Stanford Business Books.

Earley, P. C., & Gardner, H. K. (2005). Internal dynamics and cultural intelligence in multicultural teams. In D. L. Shapiro, M. A. Von Glinow, & J. L. Cheng (Eds.), *Managing multinational teams: Global perspectives* (pp. 3-31). Amsterdam, Netherlands: Elsevier.

Earley, P. C., & Gibson, C. B. (2002). *Multinational work teams: A new perspective.* Mahwah, NJ: Lawrence Erlbaum.

Earley, P. C., & Mosakowski, E. (2000). Creating hybrid team cultures: An empirical test of transnational team functioning. *Academy of Management Journal. 43*(1) 26-49.

Escobar, Samuel. (2003). *The new global mission: The gospel from everywhere to everyone.* Downers Grove, IL: InterVarsity Press.

Fairfield, D. (2007). Empowered followership: Without followers, leadership is unfulfilled. *Marine Corps Gazette. 91*(11) 54-56.

Fiedler, F. E. (1967). *A theory of leadership effectiveness.* New York, NY: McGraw-Hill.

Fisher-Yoshida, B., & Geller, K. D. (2009). *Transnational leadership development: Preparing the next generation for the borderless business world.* New York, NY: Amacom.

Flick, U. (2006). *An introduction to qualitative research.* Thousand Oaks, CA: Sage.

Fusion. (n.d.). Free Merriam-Webster Dictionary Webster. Retrieved May 3, 2010, from http://www.merriam-webster.com/dictionary/fusion

Gannon, M. J. (2008). *Paradoxes of culture and globalization.* Los Angeles, CA: Sage Publications.

Gaudes, A., & Brabston, M. (2001). Virtual transactional and relational exchanges: The enabling effects of information technology. In M. Khosrowpour (Ed.), *Managing information technology in a global environment: 2001* (pp. 532-536). Information Resources Management Association International Conference. Toronto, Canada, May 20-23. Hershey, PA: Idea Group.

Gibson, C. B., & Cohen, S. C. (2003). The last word: Conclusion and implications. In C. B. Gibson & S. G. Cohen (Eds.), *Virtual teams that work: Creating conditions for virtual team effectiveness* (pp. 403-421). San Francisco, CA: Jossey-Bass.

Gibson, C. B., & Grubb, A. R. (2005). Turning the tide in multicultural teams. In D. L. Shapiro, M. A.Von Glinow, & J. L. Cheng (Eds.), *Managing multinational teams: Global perspectives* (pp. 69-95). Amsterdam, Netherlands: Elsevier.

Ginnac, F. (2004). *Building Successful Virtual teams.* Norwood, MA: Artech House.

Goldsmith, M., Greenberg, C., Robertson, A., & Hu-Chan, M. (2003). *Global leadership: The next generation.* Upper Saddle River, NJ: Financial Times Prentice Hall.

Goman, C. K. (1994). *Managing in a global organization: Keys to success in a changing world.* Menlo Park, CA: Crisp.

Graen, G. B., & Uhl-Bien, M. (1995). Relationship-based approach to leadership: Development of Leader-Member Exchange (LMX) theory of leadership over 25 years: Applying a multi-level multi-domain perspective. *Leadership Quarterly, 6*(2), 219-247.

Greenleaf. R. K. (1977). *Servant leadership: A journey into the nature of legitimate power and greatness.* Mahwah, NJ: Paulist Press.

Guerrero. L. (2007). Culture and leadership. In W. G. Rowe (Ed.), *Case in leadership* (pp. 359-393). Los Angeles, CA: Sage.

Hallowell, E. M. (1999). The human moment at work. *Harvard Business Review* 77(1) 58-66.

Hampden-Turner, C. M., & Trompenaars, F. (2000). *Building cross-cultural competence: How to create wealth from conflicting values.* New Haven, CT: Yale University Press.

Hartog, D., Deanne N., House, R. J., Hanges, P. J., Ruiz-Quintanilla, S. A., & Dorfman, P. W. (1999). Culture specific and cross-culturally generalizable implicit leadership theories: Are attributes of charismatic/transformational leadership universally endorsed? *Leadership Quarterly, 10*(2), 219-257.

Hinds, P. J., & Weisband, S. (2003). Knowledge sharing and shared understanding in virtual teams. In C. B. Gibson & S. G. Cohen (Eds.), *Virtual teams that work: Creating conditions for virtual team effectiveness* (pp. 21-36). San Francisco, CA: Jossey-Bass.

Hofstede, G. H. (2001). *Culture's consequences: Comparing values, behaviors, institutions and organizations across nations*. Thousand Oaks, CA: Sage.

Hofstede, G. H, & Hofstede, G. J. (2005). *Cultures and organizations: Software of the mind*. New York, NY: McGraw-Hill.

Hofstede, G. J. (2009). The moral circle in intercultural competence. In D. K. Deardorff (Ed.), *The Sage handbook of intercultural competence* (pp. 85-99). Thousand Oaks, CA: Sage.

House, R. J. (1971). A path-goal theory of leadership effectiveness. *Administrative Science Quarterly, 16*(3), 321-339.

Ilies, R., Judge, T., & Wagner, D. (2006). Making sense of motivational leadership: The train from transformational leaders to motivated followers. *Journal of Leadership & Organizational Studies. 13*(1), 1-21.

Janssens, M., & Brett, J. M. (2006). Cultural intelligence in global teams: A fusion model of collaboration. *Group & Organization Management, 31*(1), 124-153.

Janssens, M., & Cappellen, T. (2008). Contextualizing cultural intelligence: The case of global managers. In S. Ang & L. Van Dyne (Eds.), *Handbook of cultural intelligence: Theory, measurement, and applications* (pp. 356-371). Amonk, NY: M. E. Sharpe.

Jenkins, P. (2007). *The next Christendom: The coming of global Christianity*. Oxford, England: Oxford University Press.

Johnson, T. M, & Ross, K. R. (Eds.). (2009). *Atlas of global Christianity*. Edinburgh, UK: Edinburgh University Press.

Jung, D. I., & Avolio, B. J. (1996). Examination of transformational leadership and group process among Caucasian- and Asian-Americans: Are they different? In T. A. Scandura & M. G. Serapio (Eds.), *Research in international business and international relations* (pp. 29-66). Greenwich, CT: Jai Press.

Kellerman B. (2008). *Followership: How followers are creating change and changing leaders*. Boston, MA: Harvard Business Press.

Kelley R. (1992). *The power of followership: How to create leaders people want to fallow and followers who lead themselves*. New York, NY: Doubleday Dell.

Lau, D. C., & Murnighan, J. K. (1998). Demographic diversity and faultlines: The compositional dynamics of organizational groups. *The Academy of Management Review, 23*(2), 325-340.

Lincoln, Y. S., & Guba, E. G. (1985). *Naturalistic inquiry.* Beverly Hills, CA: Sage.

Livermore, D. A. (2009). *Cultural intelligence: Improving your CQ to engage our multicultural world.* Grand Rapids, MI: Baker Academic.

Livermore, D. A. (2010). *Leading with cultural intelligence: The new secret to success.* New York, NY: American Management Association.

Lord, R. G. (2008). Followers' cognitive and affective structures and leadership processes In R. Riggio, I. Chaleff, & Lipman-Blumen (Eds.). *The art of followership: How great followers create great leaders and organizations.* (pp. 255-266). San Francisco, CA: Jossey-Bass.

Lundy, D. J. (1999). Moving beyond internationalizing the mission force. *International Journal of Frontier Missions, 16*(3), 147-155.

Mannor, M. J. (2008). Top executives and global leadership: At the intersection of cultural intelligence and strategic leadership theory. In S. Ang & L. Van Dyne (Eds.), *Handbook of cultural intelligence: Theory, measurement, and applications* (pp. 91-106). Amonk, NY: M. E. Sharpe.

Maroosis, J. (2008). Leadership: A partnership in reciprocal following. In R. Riggio, I. Chaleff, & Lipman-Blumen (Eds.). *The art of followership: How great followers create great leaders and organizations.* (pp. 17-24). San Francisco, CA: Jossey-Bass.

Maznevski, M. L. (1994). Understanding our differences: Performance in decision-making groups with diverse members. *Human Relations, 47*(5), 531-552.

Maznevski, M. L., & Zander, L. (2001). Leading global teams: Overcoming the challenge of the power paradox. In M. E. Mendenhall, T. M. Kühlmann, & G. K. Stahl (Eds.), *Developing global business leaders: Policies, processes, and innovations* (pp. 157-174). Westport, CT: Quorum Books.

McDonough, E. F., & Cedrone, D. (2000). Meeting the challenge of global team management. *Research Technology Management, 43*(4), 12-17.

Medland, J. J. (2007). *Email's influence on perceptions of connection in a collocated work team.* (Doctoral dissertation). Lisle, IL: Benedictine University.

Mendenhall, M. E. (2001). Introduction: New perspectives on expatriate adjustment and its relationship to global leadership development. In M. E. Mendenhall, T. M. Kühlmann, & G. K. Stahl (Eds.), *Developing global business leaders: Policies, processes, and innovations* (pp. 1-16). Westport, CT: Quorum Books.

Mendenhall, M., Osland, J., Bird, A., & Oddou, G. R. (2008). *Global leadership: Research, practice, and development.* New York, NY: Routledge.

Molleman, E. (2005). Diversity in demographic characteristics, abilities and personality traits: Do faultline affect team functioning? *Group Decision and Negotiation, 14,* 173-193. doi: 13007/s10726-005-6490-7

Neher, W. W. (1997). *Organizational communication: Challenges of change, diversity, and continuity.* Boston, MA: Allyn and Bacon.

Newbigin, L. (1989). *The Gospel in a pluralist society.* Grand Rapids, MI: Wm. B. Erdmans.

Osland, J. S. (2001). The quest for transformation: The process of global leadership development. In M. E. Mendenhall, T. M. Kühlmann, & G. K. Stahl (Eds.), *Developing global business leaders: Policies, processes, and innovations* (pp. 137-156). Westport, CT: Quorum Books.

Plueddemann, J. E. (2009). *Leading across cultures: Effective ministry and mission in the global church.* Downers Grove, IL: InterVarsity Press Academic.

Pusch, M. D. (2009). The interculturally competent global leader. In D. K. Deardorff (Ed.), *The Sage handbook of intercultural competence* (pp. 66-84). Thousand Oaks, CA: Sage.

Quigley, N. R., de Luque, M. S., & House R. J. (2005). Responsible leadership and governance in a global context: Insights from the GLOBE study. In J. P. Doh & S. Stumf (Eds.), *A Handbook on responsible leadership and governance in global business* (pp. 352-379). Northampton, MA: Edward Elgar.

Ridings, C., & Gefen, D. (2001). The development of trust in virtual communities. In M. Khosrowpour (Ed.), *Managing information technology in a global environment: 2001* (pp. 374-377). Information Resources Management Association International Conference Toronto, Canada, May 20-23. Hershey, PA: Idea Group.

Riopelle, K., Gluesing J. C., Alcorde, T. C., Bada, M. L., Britt, D., McKether, W., Monplaisir, L., Ratner, H. H., & Wagner, K. H. (2003). Contest, task, and evolution of technology use in global virtual teams. In C. B. Gibson & S. G. Cohen (Eds.), *Virtual teams that work: Creating conditions for virtual team effectiveness* (pp. 239-264). San Francisco, CA: Jossey-Bass.

Rosen, R., & Digh, P. (2001). Developing globally literate leaders. *T+D, 55*(5), 71-81.

Rosen, R. H., Digh, P., Singer, M., & Phillips, C. (2000). *Global literacies: Lessons on business leadership and national cultures: A landmark study of CEOs from 28 countries.* New York, NY: Simon & Schuster.

Rubin, H. J., & Rubin, I. S. (2005). *Qualitative interviewing: The art of hearing data.* Thousand Oaks, CA: Sage.

Scheuerman, E. A. (2007). *E-Care: Using email as a tool for effective member care.* (Doctoral dissertation). La Mirada, CA: Biola University.

Schmidt, W. V., Conaway, R. N., Easton, S. S., & Wardrope, W. J. (2007). *Communicating globally: Intercultural communication and international business.* Los Angeles, CA: Sage.

Shaw, J. B. (2004). The development and analysis of a measure of group faultlines. *Organizational Research Methods, 7,* 66-100. doi: 13177/1094428103259562

Shokef, E., & Erez, M. (2006). Global work culture and global identity, as a platform for a shared understanding in multicultural teams. In Y. Chen (Ed.), *National culture and groups* (pp. 325-352). Amsterdam, Netherlands: JAI Press.

SIL International. (2014a,). About SIL/SIL International. Retrieved from http://www.sil.org/about

SIL International. (2014b). Discover SIL/SIL International. Retrieved from http://www.sil.org/about/discover

Simons, G. F., Vázquez, C., & Harris, P. R. (1993). *Transcultural leadership: Empowering the diverse workforce.* Houston, TX: Gulf.

Stanko, T. & Gibson, C. B. (2009). The role of cultural elements in virtual teams. In R. S. Bhagat & R. M. Steers (Eds.), *Cambridge handbook of culture, organizations, and work* (pp. 272-304). Cambridge, UK: Cambridge University Press.

Stogdill, R. M. (1974). *Handbook of leadership: A survey of theory and research.* New York, NY: The Free Press.

Strauss, A., & Corbin, J. (1990). *Basics of qualitative research: Grounded procedures and techniques.* Newbury Park, CA: Sage.

Tan, J. (2004). Cultural intelligence and the global economy. *Leadership in Action, 24*(5), 19-21.

Teagarden, M. B. (2007). Best practices in cross-cultural leadership. In J. A. Conger & R. E. Riggio (Eds.). *The practice of leadership: Developing the next generation of leaders* (pp. 300-330). San Francisco, CA: Jossey-Bass.

Thatcher, M. B., Jean, K. A., & Zanutto, E. (2001). Cracks in diversity research: The effects of diversity faultlines on conflict and performance. *Group Decision and Negotiation, 12*(5), 217-241.

Thomas, D. C., & Inkson, K. (2009). *Cultural intelligence: Living and working globally.* San Francisco, CA: Berrett-Koehler.

Tichy, N. (1992). Leadership development as a lever for global transformation. In V. Pucik, N. Tichy, & C. K. Barnett (Eds.), *Globalizing management creating and leading the competitive organization* (pp. 47-60). New York, NY: John Wiley.

Trezzini, B. (2008). Probing the group faultline concept: An evaluating of measures of patterned multi-dimensional group diversity. *Quality & Quantity, 42*, 339-368. doi: 13007/z11135-006-9049-z

Trompenaars, F., & Hampden-Turner, C. H. (1998). *Riding the waves of culture: Understanding cultural diversity in global business.* New York, NY: McGraw Hill.

Tyran, K. L., Tyran, C. K., & Shepherd, M. (2003). Exploring emerging leadership in virtual teams. In C. B. Gibson & S. G. Cohen (Eds.), *Virtual teams that work: Creating conditions for virtual team effectiveness* (pp. 183-195). San Francisco, CA: Jossey-Bass.

Van Dyne, L., Ang, S., & Koh, C. (2008). Development and validation of the CQs: The cultural intelligence scale. In S. Ang & L. Van Dyne (Eds.), *Handbook of cultural intelligence: Theory, measurement, and applications* (pp. 16-38). Amonk, NY: M. E. Sharpe.

Wankel, C. (Ed.). (2008). *21st century management: A reference handbook.* Los Angeles, CA: Sage.

Zayani, F. A. (2008). *The impact of transformational leadership on the success of global virtual teams: An investigation based on the multifactor leadership questionnaire.* (Doctoral dissertation). Minneapolis, MN: Capella University.

Ziegler, B. (1995, June 28). Virtual power lunches will make passing the salt an impossibility. *Wall Street Journal*, p. B1.

APPENDIXES

APPENDIX A

LIST OF INTERVIEW PARTICIPANTS

Table A1

Demographic Information for Interview Participants

Code	Gender	Age	Service Years	Country of Origin	Comm. Method*	Role	Location	Interpreter Needed
A1	M	30s	6-10	Singapore	F-to-F	L	Thailand	No
A2	M	30s	0-5	Thailand	F-to-F	Fol	Thailand	No
A3	M	30s	0-5	Thailand	F-to-F	Fol	Thailand	No
A4	F	30s	0-5	Thailand	F-to-F	Fol	Thailand	No
A5	F	30s	6-10	Myanmar	F-to-F	Fol	Thailand	No
A6	F	30s	0-5	Thailand	F-to-F	Fol	Thailand	Yes
A7	M	30s	0-5	Thailand	F-to-F	Fol	Thailand	No
A8	F	20s	0-5	Philippines	F-to-F	Fol	Thailand	No
B1	F	50s	21-30	USA	F-to-F	L	Philippines	No
B2	M	50s	21-30	USA	F-to-F	L	Philippines	No
B3	F	50s	21-30	USA	F-to-F	Fol	Philippines	No
B4	F	60s	21-30	USA	Skype	Fol	Philippines	No
B5	M	60s	21-30	USA	Skype	Fol	Philippines	No

--continued on next page--

--continued from previous page--

Code	Gender	Age	Service Years	Country of Origin	Comm. Method*	Role	Location	Interpreter Needed
B6	M	30s	11-20	Philippines	F-to-F	Fol	Philippines	No
B7	M	50s	21-30	New Zealand	Skype	Fol	New Zealand	No
B8	M	50s	21-30	USA	F-to-F	Fol	Philippines	No
B9	F	50s	21-30	Malaysia	Skype	Fol	Malaysia	No
C1	M	40s	11-20	Hong Kong	Skype	L	Nepal	No
C2	M	40s	6-10	Nepal	F-to-F	Fol	Nepal	No
C3	M	40s	11-20	New Zealand	F-to-F	Fol	Nepal	No
C4	F	50s	0-5	Hong Kong	Skype	Fol	Hong Kong	No
C5	F	40s	11-20	United Kingdom	F-to-F	Fol	Nepal	No
C6	M	40s	21-30	USA	Skype	Fol	USA	No
C7	M	30s	11-20	USA	F-to-F	Fol	Nepal	No
C8	M	40s	11-20	United Kingdom	F-to-F	Fol	Nepal	No
C9	F	40s	11-20	Korea	F-to-F	Fol	Nepal	No
D1	M	40s	11-20	USA	F-to-F	L	Philippines	No
D2	F	50s	31-40	USA	F-to-F	Fol	Philippines	No
D3	F	50s	21-30	USA	F-to-F	Fol	Philippines	No
D4	F	40s	6-10	Korea	Skype	Fol	Korea	No
D5	F	40s	11-20	USA	F-to-F	Fol	Philippines	No
D6	F	50s	21-30	New Zealand	F-to-F	Fol	Philippines	No

--continued on next page--

--continued from previous page--

Code	Gender	Age	Service Years	Country of Origin	Comm. Method*	Role	Location	Interpreter Needed
D7	F	60s	31-40	Japan	F-to-F	Fol	Philippines	No
D8	M	60s	21-30	USA	F-to-F	Fol	Philippines	No
D9	M	60s	31-40	Japan	F-to-F	Fol	Philippines	No
E1	F	50s	21-30	USA	F-to-F	L	Philippines	No
E2	F	30s	6-10	Philippines	F-to-F	Fol	Philippines	No
E3	F	30s	6-10	Philippines	F-to-F	Fol	Philippines	No
E4	F	20s	0-5	USA	F-to-F	Fol	Philippines	No
E5	M	30s	0-5	USA	F-to-F	Fol	Philippines	No
E6	F	20s	0-5	Philippines	F-to-F	Fol	Philippines	No
E7	M	30s	11-20	Canada	Skype	Fol	Canada	No
E8	F	40s	6-10	Hong Kong	Skype	Fol	Hong Kong	No
E9	M	30s	6-10	Philippines	F-to-F	Fol	Philippines	No
E10	F	40s	11-20	Korea	F-to-F	Fol	Philippines	No
E11	M	40s	11-20	Korea	F-to-F	Fol	Philippines	No
E12	M	40s	6-10	Korea	F-to-F	Fol	Philippines	No
F1	M	50s	21-30	Indonesia	F-to-F	L	Indonesia	No
F2	F	20s	0-5	Indonesia	F-to-F	Fol	Indonesia	Yes
F3	F	20s	0-5	Australia	F-to-F	Fol	Indonesia	No
F4	F	40s	11-20	Korea	F-to-F	Fol	Indonesia	No

--continued on next page--

--continued from previous page--

Code	Gender	Age	Service Years	Country of Origin	Comm. Method*	Role	Location	Interpreter Needed
F5	F	60s	31-40	USA	F-to-F	Fol	Indonesia	No
F6	M	50s	31-40	USA	F-to-F	Fol	Indonesia	No
F7	M	60s	31-40	Korea	F-to-F	Fol	Indonesia	No
F8	F	20s	0-5	Indonesia	F-to-F	Fol	Indonesia	Yes
F9	F	30s	0-5	Indonesia	F-to-F	Fol	Indonesia	No
F10	M	40s	6-10	Korea	F-to-F	Fol	Indonesia	No
F11	F	30s	6-10	Korea	F-to-F	Fol	Indonesia	No
G1	M	30s	11-20	India	F-to-F	L	Kenya	No
G2	M	30s	0-5	India	F-to-F	Fol	Kenya	No
G3	M	30s	6-10	Kenya	F-to-F	Fol	Kenya	No
G4	M	30s	6-10	India	F-to-F	Fol	Kenya	No
G5	M	30s	0-5	Ghana	F-to-F	Fol	Kenya	Yes
G6	M	30s	0-5	Kenya	F-to-F	Fol	Kenya	No
G7	M	30s	6-10	India	F-to-F	Fol	Kenya	Yes
G8	M	30s	0-5	Ethiopia	F-to-F	Fol	Kenya	Yes
H1	F	60s	41-40	USA	F-to-F	L	Philippines	No
H2	M	60s	41-40	USA	F-to-F	L	Philippines	No
H3	F	40s	21-30	Germany	F-to-F	Fol	Philippines	No
H4	M	50s	11-20	USA	F-to-F	Fol	Philippines	No

--continued on next page--

--continued from previous page--

Code	Gender	Age	Service Years	Country of Origin	Comm. Method*	Role	Location	Interpreter Needed
H5	M	20s	0-5	USA	Skype	Fol	Philippines	No
H6	F	50s	11-20	USA	F-to-F	Fol	Philippines	No
H7	F	30s	11-20	Philippines	F-to-F	Fol	Philippines	No
H8	M	40s	0-5	Philippines	F-to-F	Fol	Philippines	No
H9	F	40s	11-20	Costa Rica	F-to-F	Fol	Philippines	No

Note. *Communication method used for interview.

M = Male. F = Female. F-to-F = Face-to-face. L = Leader. Fol = Follower

APPENDIX B

SEMI-STRUCTURED INTERVIEW QUESTIONS

Questions about the background information of the participants:

1. How did you become involved with SIL (or partner organization)?
2. How long have you worked for SIL (or partner organization)?
3. What kinds of work have you done with SIL (or partner organization)?
4. What is your current role with SIL (or partner organization)?

Questions to the leaders:

1. Can you describe a desirable leader in SIL (or partner organization)? (You may talk about a specific person without mentioning a name.)
2. What qualities do you expect from the followers? (Or what words come to mind when you think of *followership*?)
3. Describe an ideal follower in SIL (or partner organization). (You may talk about a specific person without mentioning a name.)
4. Please relate one or more incidents in which you could not understand the behavior of one of your team members (followers) because of the different cultural understanding of leadership and followership issues?
5. How would you address issues with your team members (followers) if you had to tell them they were not doing good work and needed improvement?

6. What are the joys and challenges of being a leader?

Questions to the followers:

1. What qualities do you expect in your leader at SIL (or partner organization)? Describe a desirable leader in SIL (or partner organization)? You may talk about a specific person without mentioning a name.

2. Describe an ideal follower in SIL (or partner organization)? You may talk about a specific person without mentioning a name.

3. Describe any incidents when you could not understand your leader's behavior because of a different cultural understanding on the leadership and followership issues?

4. How would you address your leader if you don't agree with him or her?

Questions about communication methods:

1. How do you normally communicate with your leader (or follower)? (face-to-face, email, Skype, or any other methods)

2. If you communicate with your supervisor through computer most of the time, how often do you see your supervisor face-to-face?

3. What have been the benefits and difficulties of different communication methods?

APPENDIX C

PEER REVIEW

This section provides feedback from eight SIL people who did not participate in the interview part of this study. I selected eight people who were based in the same country, and who were a mixture of leaders and followers. Eight reviewers made more than 10% of the 75 interviewees. I tried my best to approximate the cross-cultural mix of the interviewees of this research by having four different nationalities. One person participated in the peer review session via Skype. The peer-review was done on February 20, 2014, as one group. Table D1 itemizes their gender, age, nationality, service years, and job title.

In the beginning of the peer review session, I explained the purpose of this research, the grand tour and subquestions that guided this dissertation, the demographic information of the interviewees, and the criteria for selecting teams for interviews. Before I gave my findings, I asked them the same questions that I asked the interviewees so that these reviewers would have time to think about their own opinions about leadership and followership. Here are the two questions that I asked them.

1. How do you describe qualities of effective leaders in SIL?
2. How do you describe qualities of effective followers in SIL?

The following reports feedback of the peer review group.

Table C1

Demographic Information of the Reviewers.

Name	Gender	Age	Country of Origin	Service Years	Job Title
Reviewer 1	F	60s	USA	30	Public history archive specialist
Reviewer 2	M	60s	USA	30	Professional development consultant
Reviewer 3	F	60s	USA	30	Translator
Reviewer 4	F	40s	USA	21	Assistant director
Reviewer 5	F	40s	Australia	7	Executive assistant
Reviewer 6	M	40s	Australia	7	Director
Reviewer 7	F	50s	Singapore	20	Translator
Reviewer 8	F	40s	Korea	12	Media specialist

Leadership and Followership

Everybody agreed that expectations of leadership were more than the followers:

"When I was trying to jot down followership qualities, hmm, I have never thought about that" (Reviewer 3).

"Yes" (Reviewer 8).

"What is that?" (Reviewer 1)

One question that arose was whether this dissertation categorized data by the gender differences. My answer was that the gender issue was not the scope of this dissertation.

One person commented that a leader was different from a manager and asked me if I differentiated a leader from a manager for this research, because she had a hard time of agreeing or disagreeing with the findings. My answer was that the interviewees defined either a leader of an organizational unit or leaders in SIL or in its partner organizations in general. I did not make a decision on who the leader was but the interviewees did.

Several reviewers stated that SIL people may look for a visionary type of leader for the country level and above but a supportive and administrative type of person for the middle management level and down: "I think that it's very dependent on the roles. If you are looking for a leader working with the translation teams, the quality I might be looking for is quite different from a leader like a director of the Asia Area" (Reviewer 6).

There were very different responses about the leaders valuing task-oriented competencies more than the relational qualities. One person disagreed with the findings and stated that leaders and followers valued the relational qualities in SIL. But other people agreed with the findings:

> I think it's not a surprise in a sense that most of the leaders are homegrown leaders. Most of them start here (his hand pointed low position) and work their way up. So the followers are very much task-oriented. And you take that value with you as you move up. So that's not surprising. (Reviewer 6)

> "We recruit task-oriented people" (Reviewer 1).

> "Of course, very task-oriented… what's interesting to me is that followers are expecting that to change as the person moves into a leadership. That's probably not realistic" (Reviewer 6).

> "It might be a safe way to say that they want to be listened to" (Reviewer 1).

> "Yes, that's right" (Reviewer 6).

Relational Qualities

The majority of people agreed on the fact that communication was the most desirable quality:

> I'm not surprised about that [communication became the most desirable quality]. Last January conference, that was very high value that came out of the discussions that we had. One of the value came out was that we needed to find a better way to communicate with each other. So I'm not surprised to hear that. From leadership, we are very much interested in communication from grassroots to global. To make that work, communication has to go in both directions… We are trying to be an organization that goes from grassroots to the global meaning that globally decisions are not made without input from grassroots level. (Reviewer 6)

Another person added the importance of having good communication between leaders and followers: "We have to really work at communication, because those [email and text] are not easy ways to communicate well. So we have to overcome those ways and work even harder" (Reviewer 2).

He continued talking about the fact that leaders were not necessarily co-located with the followers and so communication became more of issue in SIL than in other organizations:

> You made a good point about those ways, because we are doing more and more that supervisors are not right maybe where the people are so they want more face-to-face and they want more communication. So I think your research is pointing out very healthy, good things. It's not the answer but it tells us we need to remember to work even harder. When I wrote down the leadership qualities, three out of the four things I wrote down had to do with communication. (Reviewer 2)

Another person said that because of the financial difficulties SIL was having, having face-to-face meetings would be even harder:

> I think one of the factors jumping out is that leader might not be where the followers are. The followers are not in one place. And the recent budget cuts will have an effect... But with budget cuts happening last year, leaders were not able to travel and not able to gather their followers together so often to do face-to-face as much as they want to. (Reviewer 6)

One person asked if the qualities the interviewees wanted to see were deficiencies or desired qualities: "The things we wrote down, are we thinking of deficiencies? Like the things we like to see not really seeing or we are thinking more positive side" (Reviewer 6).

> "I was just thinking of the positive side. Sometimes you compare the leaders that you had previously" (Reviewer 4).
>
> "So it is experience reflective" (Reviewer 1).
>
> "So it doesn't mean that you are upset with a leader now" (Reviewer 4).
>
> "I put some leadership qualities that I appreciate" (Reviewer 6).

One person asked how language affected the issue of communication: "Was there any input about medium of language? Like English as the medium of language…Was there any that kind of opinion revealed in your research?" (Reviewer 8). I answered that there were a lot of comments about the language issue. Because of the language deficiency, they wanted to have face-to-face meetings with a leader so that they could communicate through the facial expressions and body language.

Task-Oriented Competencies

One person expressed her surprise that "hardworking" was the most important quality in task-oriented competencies on followership: "I am surprised that hard-working came up as the most important issue from the followers" (Reviewer 3).

One person doubted that leaders being supportive of followers was the highest quality that leader saw in themselves. She said that followers usually developed themselves. I explained that the leaders were trying to find resources for the followers like being a middleman. After the explanation the person who disagreed was able to understand.

Another person said that a leader from a small organization (or a team) may have different leadership ideas versus a leader from a big organization (or a team):

> A leader from a small organization or a team…, the role may be the ones to be supportive of followers. I am thinking more of a leader of an Asia Area or a global level. I would consider the high priority is setting directions and vision and leading the organization forward… I think it would be depending on the context of a leader, what is a leader's oversight. (Reviewer 6)

One person agreed, reflected and shared her experiences about the findings that a leader wanted followers to take initiatives and be responsible. Several years ago, she worked with a media project that involved with various ethnic groups. She trained them and at the end they shared their responsibilities, caught the vision, and continued with their project without supervision from outside. She could well relate with the research findings about follower's taking initiative and being responsible as good qualities in followership.

Character-Related Qualities

Everybody agreed with the research findings about the character related qualities and did not provide much feedback on this topic: "I like that the followers demanded her leader with character. Personal character is valued as a leader" (Reviewer 1). One question came up about character related qualities in leadership: "Is he willing to accept that he is not perfect? Some leaders have weaknesses" (Reviewer 7). I explained that that quality came out from the research.

Spiritual Qualities

This research pointed out that spiritual qualities were not mentioned a lot. There was a lot of discussion about why this was so. Several people said that spiritual qualities were assumed if one was a member of SIL. One person wondered why people assumed spiritual qualities while they did not assume other character-related qualities. Another person replied to that comment that everybody had different character traits but spiritual qualities were the same, and that was why it was assumed.

One person suggested that another possibility for the low rank of spiritual qualities could be that some SIL respondents, especially Westerners, considered a person's spiritual life to be a very personal and private matter between the leader/follower and God. Therefore, they did not feel at liberty even to discuss this or have too many expectations in this area, feeling like it was none of their business.

One person stated that the reason SIL people did not mention spiritual qualities as much in leadership was that spiritual qualities were reflected in character: "Spiritual quality is reflected in character. I think that was probably why people didn't say spiritual qualities because the character qualities are the fruit of spiritual qualities" (Reviewer 4). Everybody agreed with her on this: "You can observe the characters to know how spiritual they are" (Reviewer 2).

Another person said that spiritual qualities were very important for both leader and follower and she was very surprised: "I listed the spiritual quality as a very important quality to be expected. I wrote down spiritual quality as the key element in the leadership" (Reviewer 8).

One person asked a Korean reviewer about how much emphasis was put on the spiritual qualities of the leaders of the Global Bible Translators, a Korean organization. The answer was that Global Bible Translators put a lot of emphasis on prayer and spiritual qualities not only with leaders but also with followers and supporters. After listening to that comment, the person who asked the question stated the necessity to learn from other cultures.

One person mentioned that maybe the task orientation of organizational culture might be a hindering factor of having spiritual qualities:

> Maybe it's the nature of the work of SIL. Very technical organization which focuses on linguistics and translation... So spiritual qualities don't rank very high. When I'm with the review committee in R language, I'm supposed to checking the work... [not worshipping together with people] because that eating into the time when I'm supposed be training them. (Reviewer 7)

Cultural Intelligence (CQ)

Everybody was in agreement with the importance of CQ for both leaders and followers. There weren't many discussions or comments about CQ:

> I think I would agree with what's there... Obviously the leaders' cultural background is a necessary felt need for the followers. They are identifying something was missing. Maybe the leaders being too monocultural, not making allowances for the diversity in the teams, perhaps?" (Reviewer 6)

I answered that not all leaders experienced cross-cultural leaders but most of the followers experienced cross-cultural leaders as their leader.

Communication Methods

Everybody was in agreement with the findings on communication methods. Several comments added to my information pool:

> I agree very strongly with some of the comments that face-to-face is so important. People do want more of that. Like Reviewer 6 mentioned that face-to-face is harder to do because of lack of funds apparently. But it's so important. (Reviewer 4)

Another person made a comment on email communication:

> I like this part. It said about email communication rise to a lack of relationship and misunderstandings. What I wrote down was if you had the relationship first, if

> you had face-to-face, if you know the person, then when you email, it's easier to get the true meaning, if you know how the person is. If you had a relationship, you don't get the misunderstanding quite so much." (Reviewer 2)

I reported him that my interview data covered what he said.

Another person made a comment about the use of phone calls:

> Your findings said that they use phone call significantly less. I wonder if it would be more effective to use them more, if we can't meet face-to-face. I find those to be more effective a lot of times more than email. At least you can hear the person's voice. You can chit chat a little bit. It's not so blunt. It seems like written communication really misunderstands so easily. (Reviewer 4)

I also said that my interview data covered what she shared.

APPENDIX D

THE TABLES OF THE LEADERSHIP AND FOLLOWERSHIP QUALITIES

Table D1

Summary of Relational Leadership Qualities Desired by Leaders

Terms Chosen by Axial Coding	Terms Used by Open Coding
Communicate (6)	Communicate with the followers (5)
	Listen to the followers (1)
Care about followers (6)	Care (3)
	Visit the followers (2)
	Encourage (1)
Build teamwork (2)	Build a team (1)
	Team bonding (1)
(Dropped concept)	Being relational (1)

Note. The numbers in the parentheses indicate the number of occurrences.

Table D2

Summary of Relational Leadership Qualities Desired by Followers

Terms Chosen by Axial Coding	Terms Used by Open Coding

Communicate with the followers (68)	Listen to the followers (33)
	    Listen
	    Did not listen
	Communicate (27)
	    Regular communication
	    Communicate prior to make a decision
	    Miscommunication
	    Organizational changes in communication
	    Cultural issues in communication
	Communicate disagreement (8)

Care about followers (31)	Care (17) Encourage (10) Help personal issues (4)
Be relational (29)	Friendship (11) Relational (7) Approachable (5) Mentoring relationship (3) Spend time together (2) Hierarchical relationship (1)
Appreciate follower (13)	Trust followers (6) Value followers (5) Respect followers (2)
Understand followers (9)	Understand (9)
Promote teamwork (8)	Promote teamwork (5) Promote unity (3)
(Dropped concepts)	Serve others Work with other leaders

Note. The numbers in the parentheses indicate the number of occurrences.

Table D3

Summary of Relational Followership Qualities Desired by Leaders

Terms Chosen by Axial Coding	Terms Used by Open Coding
Communicate (10)	Communicate (6)
	Contribute input (3)
	Listen (1)
Respect (6)	Respect (3)
	Trust (2)
	Obey (1)
Encourage (4)	Encourage (2)
	Support (1)
	Help (1)

Note. The numbers in the parentheses indicate the number of occurrences.

Table D4

Summary of Relational Followership Qualities Desired by Followers

Terms Chosen by Axial Coding	Terms Used by Open Coding

Communicate (52)	With the leader (49):
	     Provide input (20)
	     Listen (7)
	     Ask questions (4)
	     Cultural aspect of communication (4)
	     Communicate disagreement (4)
	     Initiate communication (3)
	     Express needs (3)
	     Report properly (2)
	     Report regularly (2)
	 With team members (3)

Care and encourage (10)	Care for team members (3) Care for leaders (2) Encourage (2) No gossiping (1) No complaining (1) Build up each other (1)
Trust (9)	Trust (9)
Unity (7)	Unity (4) Team player (2) No agreement (1)
Serve and respect (7)	Serve (3) Recognize leader's authority (3) Respect leader (1)
Understand people (6)	Understand team members (4) Understand leader (2)
(Dropped concept)	Knows position (1)

Note. The numbers in the parentheses indicate the number of occurrences.

Table D5

Summary of Task-Oriented Leadership Competencies Desired by Leaders

Terms Chosen by Axial Coding	Terms Used by Open Coding
Develop followers (16)	Support the followers (7) Build up the followers (6) Know and use follower's gifts (3)
Have a vision (6)	Vision (4) Directions (2)
Handle conflict (4)	Handle conflict (4)
Be a decision maker (3)	Decision maker (3)
Motivate (3)	Motivate (3)
Have holistic understanding of the work (2)	Holistic understanding of the work (2)
(Dropped concepts)	Prioritize Handle many works Give freedom Passion Bringing results

Note. The numbers in the parentheses indicate the number of occurrences.

Table D6

Summary of Task-Oriented Leadership Competencies Desired by Followers

Terms Chosen by Axial Coding	Terms Used by Open Coding
Have vision and provide directions (31)	Have vision and goals (20) Provide directions (11)
Develop followers (25)	Build up followers (12) Support followers (8) Know follower's strengths (3) Use follower's gifts (2)
Do not micromanage (19)	Do not micromanager (8) Give follower freedom or autonomy (7) Admin type of leader (4)
Attitudes toward work (10)	Committed (3) Passionate (3) Initiative (2) Work hard (2)
Delegate (10)	Delegate (7) Give follower opportunity (3)
Have administrative skills (9)	Prioritize (4) Coordinate (2) Organize (1) Plan (1) Oversee (1)
Solve problem (8)	Solve problem (5) Mediate (3)
Direct (7)	Lead (5) Motivate (2)
Make decisions (5)	Make decisions (5)
(Dropped concept)	Understand work

Note. The numbers in the parentheses indicate the number of occurrences.

Table D7

Summary of Task-Oriented Followership Competencies Desired by Leaders

Terms Chosen by Axial Coding	Terms Used by Open Coding
Take initiative (6)	Take initiative (6)
Be responsible (5)	Have ownership (2) Be Responsible (2) Work hard (1)
Follow a leader (4)	Follow a leader (4)
Have leadership mindset (2)	Have leadership mindset (2)
(Dropped concept)	Have passion (1)

Note. The numbers in the parentheses indicate the number of occurrences.

Table D8

Summary of Task-Oriented Followership Competencies Desired by Follower

Terms Chosen by Axial Coding	Terms Used by Open Coding
Work hard (14)	Work hard (7) Capable (2) Different understanding of working hard (2) Be responsible for their work (1) Produce result (1) Do their duty (1)
Follow (13)	Follow (12) Follow with critical mind (1)
Goal oriented (8)	Have same goal (5) Commit to the goal (2) Understand directions (1)
Work together (4)	Work together (4)
Understand work (4)	Understand work (4)
Make decisions (4)	Make decisions (4)

Note. The numbers in the parentheses indicate the number of occurrences.

Table D9

Summary of Character-Related Leadership Qualities Desired by Followers

Terms Chosen by Axial Coding	Terms Used by Open Coding
Personal characteristics (38)	Wisdom (9) Humility (9) Honesty (6) Patience (4) Integrity (4) Positive attitude (2)

--continued on next page--

--continued from previous page--

Terms Chosen by Axial Coding	Terms Used by Open Coding
Personal characteristics (38) (continued)	Faithful (1) Moral (1) Has common sense (1) Not easily angered (1)
Interpersonal skills (27)	Fair (8) Trustworthy (4) Accountable (2) Selfless (2) Respectful (2) Loving (1) Forgiving (1) Independent (1) Gentle (1) Transparent (1) Loyal (1) Polite (1) Has sense of humor (1) Has realistic expectations of followers (1)
Work-related competencies (17)	Leads by example (8) Flexible (2) Accepts criticism (2) Has Authority (2) Charismatic (1) Confident (1) Be a learner (1)
Background and ability (11)	Experienced (6) Has Linguistic ability (3) Intelligent (1) Age (1)

Note. The numbers in the parentheses indicate the number of occurrences.

Table D10

Summary of Character-Related Followership Qualities Desired by Followers

Terms Chosen by Axial Coding	Terms Used by Open Coding
Independency (11)	Independency (9) Strongly willed (1) Self sufficient (1)
Obedience (6)	Submissive (3) Obedient (2) Complying (1)
Integrity (5)	Integrity (2) Honesty (2) Accountable (1)
Loyal (3)	Loyal (2) Faithful (1)
Humility (2)	Humble (1) Putting aside ones desire (1)
(Dropped concepts)	People oriented Flexible Not taking things personally Patient

Note. The numbers in the parentheses indicate the number of occurrences.